"Bash Dibra leads us through various and very often complex parts of the human–canine relationship and shows us not only how it can work but how we can make it work."

—Roger A. Caras, President, ASPCA

"Good professional advice on specific problems . . . recommended."

—*Booklist*

"A handy, readable problem-solving guide for dog owners."

—*Library Journal*

"Bash Dibra is recognized as an authority and deservedly so. His lucid writing and great experience as a trainer and behaviorist are reflected in this fine book. I recommend it highly."

—William J. Kay,
Chief of Staff, The Animal Medical Center

"Bash's book teaches dog owners how to solve their pet problems, making their dogs ideal candidates to earn certificates proclaiming them Canine Good Citizens."

—Jim Dearinger, administrator of the American Kennel Club's Canine Good Citizen Program

---

Bashkim Dibra has trained dogs for celebrities from Kim Basinger to Henry Kissinger, as well as for countless canine roles in film, TV, and advertising. He lives in New York City. **Elizabeth Randolph,** the author of numerous books and articles on pet care, also collaborated on *Dog Training by Bash* (Dutton/Signet). She lives in Mamaroneck, New York, and Longboat Key, Florida.

BASHKIM DIBRA
WITH ELIZABETH RANDOLPH

TEACH

YOUR DOG

TO

BEHAVE

SIMPLE SOLUTIONS TO OVER
300 COMMON DOG BEHAVIOR
PROBLEMS FROM A TO Z

FOREWORD BY ROGER A. CARAS,
PRESIDENT, ASPCA

A SIGNET BOOK

SIGNET
Published by New American Library, a division of
Penguin Putnam Inc., 375 Hudson Street,
New York, New York 10014, U.S.A.
Penguin Books Ltd, 27 Wrights Lane,
London W8 5TZ, England
Penguin Books Australia Ltd, Ringwood,
Victoria, Australia
Penguin Books Canada Ltd, 10 Alcorn Avenue,
Toronto, Ontario, Canada M4V 3B2
Penguin Books (N.Z.) Ltd, 182–190 Wairau Road,
Auckland 10, New Zealand

Penguin Books Ltd, Registered Offices:
Harmondsworth, Middlesex, England

Published by Signet, an imprint of New American Library, a division of
Penguin Putnam Inc. Previously published in a Dutton edition.

First Signet Printing, March 1994
20   19   18   17   16   15   14   13   12   11   10

REGISTERED TRADEMARK—MARCA REGISTRADA

Printed in the United States of America

ACKNOWLEDGMENTS

Many thanks to our families and friends for their continuing help and support during the time we were working on this book. Special thanks to our editor, Michaela Hamilton, for all of her help and encouragement.

FOREWORD

The relationship between human beings and dogs has the potential for being one of the most rewarding experiences we can have. It does fall short of our relationships with immediate family and close friends, but it has the potential to exceed just about all others. The man-dog relationship can also be a nightmare, if it is ill-conceived, ill-planned, or ill-managed. Generally, man is the more intelligent of the two species and can be expected to make the choice of which it is to be—heaven or hell on earth.

Once the right dog is chosen, and it can be many of the literally hundreds of pure-bred breeds known in the world, or it can be a perfectly wonderful random-bred dog, it is up to man or woman (and child, of course) to design the relationship through the exercise of his intelligence and inherent sensitivity. This is what Bash Dibra's book is all about.

Far too many bonding attempts fail because the person is unwilling to assume the role of alpha dog. Dogs are directly descended from wolves, and wolves have a unique hierarchical system of unit management, be the unit a female with her cubs, a mating pair, a family unit, or a much larger pack. There must be one creature in charge and, clearly, if it's to be in a human home, in a human environment, in society, that "person" in charge must be the human member of the team, i.e., man is the alpha wolf.

Once man does assert his dominance, then it behooves

the person in charge to be benevolent, be understanding, and not take advantage of the position to abuse or to take out frustrations or anger. Anger, when dealing with a dog, is about as useful as a sledge hammer in fixing an automobile engine.

Bash Dibra leads us through various and very often complex parts of the human-canine relationship and shows us not only how it can work but how we can make it work.

If you have a dog, and the dog is well behaved and is a good, solid friend to you, and you to it, you are probably at lower risk for a heart attack, high blood pressure, and many other ailments than you otherwise might be. The medical literature is full of this now-accepted fact. If the dog is not well behaved, however, you are probably going to spend most of your life perched on the edge of a nervous breakdown. The choice is yours, and Bash Dibra shows you how to make that all-important choice. He is to be listened to, for he is a man of enormous experience, and very good will.

ROGER A. CARAS,
PRESIDENT, ASPCA

HOW CAN THIS BOOK HELP YOU SOLVE YOUR DOG'S BEHAVIOR PROBLEMS?

Bashkim (Bash) Dibra has solved the dog behavior problems of literally thousands of people over the years. His unique approach to correcting doggy misdeeds for socialites, celebrities, and CEOs has earned him the title "Dog Trainer to the Stars." Recently, talk-show hostess Joan Rivers dubbed him Saint Bash after he successfully worked with her Yorkie, Spike.

In his first book, *Dog Training by Bash,* Bash explained his theory and philosophy of dog training. Now he goes on to more practical applications. In this book Bash shares his problem solving secrets with you and gives clear, simple solutions to all of your dog behavior problems. With more than 300 topics covered in easy-to-follow A-to-Z format, there's an answer to every possible problem a dog owner might have.

In addition to entries on problems, there are many boxes containing tips, facts, and definitions relating to dog behavior. Information on behavior modification aids, from nasty-tasting Liquids to Noisemakers to Water Balloons, is included. A section in the beginning of the book will help you interpret your dog's body language so you can understand how your pet feels in a given situation and what it's trying to tell you by its actions.

The gamut of topics includes common problems never discussed in a dog behavior book before and touches all stages of a dog's life, from puppyhood to old age. Topics range from serious problems such as Aggressive Behavior and Destructive Behavior to less serious but nevertheless annoying habits like Jumping and Toilet-Paper Unrolling. Medical and physical conditions that may seem to an owner to be behavior problems, such as Drooling and Snoring, are also discussed.

For each problem Bash provides a number of solutions, or treatment steps, from which to choose the ones that best suit you and your pet. There are quick fixes designed for immediate relief, along with more complicated treatments needed for long-term behavior modification and maintenance. Bash likens these different approaches to weight-loss programs. A quick fix will allow you to lose weight in ten days, but the pounds will come back as soon as you stop. If you really want to lose weight permanently you have to take the longer route of understanding, behavior modification, and maintenance.

Throughout this book, Bash's unique approach to dogs and inimitable style of presentation shine through. Just as he did in *Dog Training by Bash,* Bash continues to explain *why* a dog may be misbehaving, based on his deep understanding of wolf pack behavior and its influence on all dogs. These insights can help *you* deal with your dog's behavior problems in a more understanding and effective way.

You'll find there are a great many cross-references in this book. That's because so many dog behavior problems are interconnected and one thing very often leads to another. The cross-references will enable you to gain a clearer picture of your dog's behavior problems and will provide additional suggestions for solving them.

Teach Your Dog to Behave is destined to become *the* dog owner's Bible. It's a book you will refer to time and again, year after year, for as long as you own a dog.

ELIZABETH RANDOLPH

HOW TO INTERPRET YOUR DOG'S BODY LANGUAGE, FACIAL EXPRESSIONS, AND VOCALIZATIONS

Over the centuries wolves evolved an elaborate system of body language, facial expressions, and vocalizations to communicate with each other. Domestic dogs also use this means of communication, and all of these signals are easily understood by other dogs. If you can learn to interpret how your dog is feeling by observing its posture and expression and listening to it, you'll be well on the way to successful communication with your pet and better equipped to solve any behavior problems that arise.

Following are some major canine attitudes and their typical outward manifestations.

AGGRESSIVE

Ears   Back, close to head.
Eyes   Narrow or staring challengingly.
Mouth/teeth   Lips open, drawn back to expose teeth bared in a snarl. Possible jaw snapping.
Body   Tense. Upright. Hackles on neck up. Completely Dominant position.
Tail   Straight out from body. Fluffed up.
Vocalization   Snarl. Growl. Loud bark.

ALERT

Ears   Perked-up. Turning to catch sounds.
Eyes   Open normally or wide.

Mouth/teeth Mouth closed or slightly open with teeth covered.
Body Normal. Possibly standing on tiptoe. Slightly Dominant position.
Tail Up. Possibly wagging.
Vocalization None. Low whine or alarm bark.

ANXIOUS

Ears Partially back.
Eyes Slightly narrowed.
Mouth/teeth Mouth closed, or slightly open in a "grin."
Body Tense. Slightly lowered in a Submissive position.
Tail Partially lowered.
Vocalization Low whine or moaning-type bark.

CHASE, BEGINNING STAGE

Ears Perked-up, forward-pointing.
Eyes Wide open. Very alert.
Mouth/teeth Mouth slightly open. Excited panting.
Body Tense. Crouched low in predatory position. Legs bent, poised to run.
Tail Extended straight out from body.
Vocalization None.

CURIOUS/EAGER/EXCITED

Ears Perked-up, forward-pointing.
Eyes Wide open.
Mouth/teeth Mouth open, teeth covered. Possible panting.
Body Normal stance. Possible wiggling, standing on tiptoe, or pacing.
Tail Up. Wagging.
Vocalization Excited short barking, whining.

DOMINANT

Ears Up straight or forward.

Eyes Wide open, staring.
Mouth/teeth Mouth closed or slightly open.
Body Very tall posture. Hackles may be up.
Tail Stiffened and fluffed. Up or straight out from body.
Vocalization Low, assertive growl or grunt.

FEARFUL

Ears Laid back flat and low on head.
Eyes Narrowed, averted. Possibly rolled back in head, whites showing.
Mouth/teeth Lips drawn back to expose teeth.
Body Tense. Crouched low in submissive position. Shivering, trembling. Possible secretion from anal scent glands.
Tail Down between legs.
Vocalization Low, worried yelp, whine, or growl.

FLIGHT, BEGINNING STAGE

Ears Back.
Eyes Wide open. Possibly rolled back with whites showing.
Mouth/teeth Slightly opened mouth. Possible drooling.
Body Tense. Shivering. Low, poised to run.
Tail Low or between legs.
Vocalization None. Possible yelp or whine.

FRIENDLY

Ears Perked-up.
Eyes Wide open. Alert look.
Mouth/teeth Relaxed, possibly slightly open, "smiling" mouth.
Body Normal posture. Still, or possible wiggling of whole rear end.
Tail Up or out from body. Wagging.
Vocalization Whimpering, yapping, or short, high bark.

GUARDING

Ears Perked-up. Forward.
Eyes Wide open, alert.
Mouth/teeth Mouth slightly open, teeth bared. Snapping or gnashing of teeth.
Body Tense. Rigid. Hackles up. Standing very tall in an aggressive or dominant stance.
Tail Rigid. Held straight out from body. Sometimes fluffed.
Vocalization Loud alert bark. Growl. Snarl.

PLAYFUL/HAPPY

Ears Perked-up and forward, or relaxed.
Eyes Wide open. Sparkly/merry-looking.
Mouth/teeth Mouth relaxed and slightly open, teeth covered. Excited panting.
Body Relaxed, or front end lowered, rear end up in the air, wiggling in a play-bow. Excited bouncing and jumping up and down. Circling around and running forward and back in an invitation to play.
Tail Wagging vigorously.
Vocalization Excited barking. Soft play-growling.

PREDATORY

Ears Alert. Held forward or backward to catch sounds.
Eyes Wide open, staring, focusing.
Mouth/teeth Mouth closed.
Body Rigid. Low to ground, ready to spring forward. Quietly sniffing the air.
Tail Straight and low.
Vocalization None (so the prey won't be alerted).

SUBORDINATE (SUBMISSIVE)

Ears Down, flattened against head.
Eyes Narrowed to slits or wide open, whites showing.
Mouth/teeth Lips pulled way back from teeth in a

"grin." Nuzzling or licking other animal or person on face.

Body Lowered to ground, front paw raised. Lying on back, belly up. Possible urine leaking/dribbling. Possible emptying of anal scent glands.

Tail Down, between legs.

Vocalization None, or low, worried whining. Possible yelping/whimpering in fear.

NOTE TO THE READER

Cross-references are indicated by *see* or *see also* followed by the entry heading, and in some cases a subheading. In addition, when a word or phrase is capitalized in the text, the reader can expect to find an entry for that subject in the book. For example, the sentence "It's particularly important for a hyperactive puppy to have a well-structured Schedule" alerts the reader to the boxed entry SCHEDULES FOR PUPPIES AND OLDER DOGS.

ABNORMAL ACTIVITY LEVELS

HYPERACTIVITY

Problem 1: (See also PLAY, EXCESSIVE.) When the Rollinses start to play with their nine-month-old shepherd, the puppy gets so excited that she runs around mindlessly, bumping into things and paying no attention at all to her owners. Finally she becomes so exhausted she falls in a heap. The Rollinses fear that she's going to hurt herself as she hurtles around and wonder what to do so she won't become so hyperactive.

Problem 2: Alice bought an adorable spaniel puppy for her recently widowed mother. Her mother was delighted, but the very next day Alice got a worried call. "There's something wrong with the puppy," her mother said. "I can't get her to lie down, or even sit in my lap for a minute. All she does is walk around and around the apartment without stopping. I even heard her moving around in the middle of the night. She doesn't seem to get tired, but she's exhausting me with all this activity. What's more, she tried to nip me when I went to pick her up."

DIAGNOSIS
These problems represent two different types of hyperactivity.

Problem 1: This is a behavior problem. Overexcitable

dogs may overreact to outside stimulation. Normal play activity causes them to become hysterical and act in an out-of-control way. This can be compared to the way children lapse into "silly fits" when they're overtired and overstimulated.

Problem 2: This is a special physical problem called *hyperkineticism.* Puppies with this problem require no outside stimulation to become overactive and tense. They are overexcited and hyperactive all of the time and literally cannot stay still. They may even react with a nip when someone attempts to stop them from moving.

TREATMENT

Problem 1: The treatment for a hyperactive dog is to work quietly and calmly to modify its extreme reactions.

- It's particularly important for a hyperactive puppy to have a well-structured Schedule. Puppies such as this need to know what to expect, when, so there are no surprises to startle or upset them.
- Avoid play activity with a hyperactive pup, but confine your interaction, indoors and out, to sitting quietly, talking to the dog, and stroking it gently from time to time. Keep your actions calm and low-key.
- The minute the puppy begins to show signs of hysteria or hyperactivity, snap on its leash and begin to walk calmly with it if you're outdoors. If you're inside, take it quietly to its Crate.

Problem 2: Fortunately, many pups outgrow hyperkineticism, but in the meantime it's important to get veterinary help right away. Sometimes a change in diet can modify this problem, and there are effective medications to help calm a hyperkinetic dog.

LOW ACTIVITY LEVEL *(See also* OBESITY.*)*

Problem: A couple fell in love with a bulldog pup, Jake. He was just three months old when they got him, and loved to play ball in the house and romp in the yard with them. Now Jake is almost two and, although he seems to be perfectly happy, he's lost all of his energy. It seems as if he hardly wants to move. He goes on short walks with his owners, but as soon as he finishes his "business" he turns around and heads for home. If they try to play ball with him, Jake simply looks at his owners with a "Leave me alone" expression.

DIAGNOSIS

Many dog breeds, bulldogs among them, are not particularly active by nature. When there is no compelling reason to move, they prefer to remain still. This is not a problem for a dog unless it leads to Obesity. Excess fat will further reduce activity, because a dog that's too heavy will be uncomfortable when it moves around. There can be other medical reasons for a dog's inactivity, such as a thyroid imbalance, a joint problem, or a poor diet that doesn't provide the animal with sufficient usable energy.

TREATMENT

- The first thing to do when a dog seems to be unusually inactive is to take it to a veterinarian for a complete physical examination and advice as to the proper balanced diet.
- If the dog is well, encourage it to be more active. Remember, however, some dog breeds will never become really active no matter how hard you work with them.
- Develop an exercise plan for the dog that you will be able to stick to. Gradually increase the length of your walks outdoors. Many formerly lethargic dogs will begin to enjoy walking once they're in better shape.
- If you have two dogs, walk them together using a Coupler—a leash that ends with two short sections to attach to two dogs' collars. The slower dog will be forced to move more quickly to keep pace with the faster one and will benefit more from its walks.
- Indoors, you can encourage a dog to move if it has a favorite toy or chewbone by tossing the object across

the room from time to time. If the dog isn't overweight, tempt it to move by dangling a food treat or dog biscuit.

- If you have access to a Treadmill, this is an excellent way to provide a dog with extra exercise.

ACRAL LICK DERMATITIS/GRANULOMA

When a dog constantly licks itself, it can seem to an owner to be an annoying behavior problem, but it may be something the dog cannot control. Acral lick dermatitis is the name given to an obsessive-compulsive canine disorder in which the dog continuously licks and bites itself, usually on one spot—most commonly the "wrist" joint of one leg. Eventually, the skin in the licked area becomes hairless, darkened, smooth, and hard. All dogs can develop this condition, but breeds that are large and active are affected most often—Great Danes, Dobermans, retrievers, and shepherds among them.

No one knows for sure what causes the behavior. Joint pain and local irritation are possible initiating factors, and boredom and other psychological conditions such as anxiety have also been cited. Onset is usually at five years of age.

Recently, there has been a lot of research into ways to treat this disorder. Acupuncture has proved useful, as have antidepressant drugs that are used for human patients. Check with your veterinarian for the most recent developments on the treatment of acral lick dermatitis.

See also box, FLANK SUCKING, p. 125; *box,* OBSESSIVE-COMPULSIVE BEHAVIOR IN DOGS, p. 222.

ACTING "FUNNY" *See box,* BEHAVIOR CHANGES, p. 33.

AFFECTION, EXCESSIVE/DEMANDING *(See also*
BARKING PROBLEMS: EXCESSIVE BARKING; LEANING ON PEOPLE;
LICKING PROBLEMS: LICKING PEOPLE/OBJECTS; MOUTHING;
WHINING.)

Problem: Bill loves his corgi, Missy, but this is too much! He works at home and every time he sits down at his desk the dog sits on the floor by his side and nudges and nudges at his ankles. If he doesn't respond right away, she whines, pulls at his pants leg, and eventually begins to bark for attention. When he does cave in, stops working, and leans down to pet her, she licks his hand and arm continuously, and then begins the entire process again as soon as he stops. He's beginning to think he'll have to close Missy up in another room if he's ever going to get any work done.

DIAGNOSIS
This kind of overdemanding behavior is the sign of an unruly, bad-mannered dog that has never been taught how to control itself.

TREATMENT
The dog must be taught the limits of proper behavior.

- To stop the dog's annoying actions immediately, leash it. Attach the leash to a doorknob or the leg of a piece of furniture in the room, far enough away so that the animal can't reach you. Tell the dog to sit, and don't give in to its entreaties to be let free.
- If the dog has been taught basic obedience *(see box,* OBEDIENCE TRAINING, p. 218), go through all of the steps and reteach them until you reach the point where you can control the dog with "NO" when it becomes too demanding. If it has not been obedience-trained, now is the time to do so.
- Ideally, you can teach your dog to Go to Your Place, where it will stay quietly in the room with you in its bed or on its mat until you are ready to give it some attention.

- Alternately, if you crate-train your dog it will sleep happily in its crate in the room with you while you work.

AFRAID See FEARFULNESS.

AGGRESSION (See *also* box, AGGRESSIVE BEHAVIOR IN DOGS, p. 7; BITING PEOPLE; GROWLING; *box*, RAGE SYNDROME, p. 252.)

NOTE: *You are dealing with a potentially dangerous situation when a dog shows any signs of aggression. Be extremely careful. Before you do anything else have the dog checked over by a veterinarian to be sure there is no medical cause for the problem. If you have any difficulty following the treatment steps I've outlined, or if the dog doesn't respond to the treatment, seek help from a professional trainer immediately. This is especially important if the dog's aggressions are directed at humans.*

AGGRESSION TOWARD PEOPLE See DOMINANCE-RELATED AGGRESSION; FEAR-INDUCED AGGRESSION; FOOD-GUARDING AGGRESSION; IDIOPATHIC AGGRESSION; LEARNED AGGRESSION; MATERNAL AGGRESSION; OBJECT-GUARDING AGGRESSION; TERRITORIAL AGGRESSION.

AGGRESSION TOWARD OTHER ANIMALS See FOOD-GUARDING AGGRESSION; INTER-DOG AGGRESSION; INTERMALE AGGRESSION; MATERNAL AGGRESSION; PREDATORY AGGRESSION; TERRITORIAL AGGRESSION.

AGGRESSIVE BEHAVIOR IN DOGS

When a dog displays aggressive behavior it is acting "in a hostile fashion that may lead to attack." Aggression is a natural, reflexive reaction of all dogs, part of their pack orientation. In normal pack interaction it's often necessary for an animal to be aggressive, either to retain its position in the pack hierarchy or to protect its territory, its food, its young, or itself. Individual dogs may be more aggressive than others, and some breeds have naturally high territorial instincts that may lead to aggression: herding dogs, working dogs, and terriers, for example. A dog can also be made aggressive if it's trained incorrectly or overharshly.

Whether it's directed toward humans or other animals, a dog's aggressive behavior can't be tolerated in our society. As a responsible dog owner, you must learn to recognize signs of aggressive behavior in your pet and deal with them immediately.

For how to do this, see HOW TO INTERPRET YOUR DOG'S BODY LANGUAGE, FACIAL EXPRESSIONS, AND VOCALIZATIONS, p. xi. *See also box*, DOMINANT BEHAVIOR, p. 98; *box*, FOOD-GUARDING BEHAVIOR, p. 131; HERDING BEHAVIOR PROBLEMS; LEARNED AGGRESSION; MATERNAL AGGRESSION; *box*, PACK BEHAVIOR, p. 230; *box*, TERRITORIAL BEHAVIOR, p. 289.

When prior arrangements are made, a small dog such as Kimberly, a Yorkshire terrier, can often accompany its owner in the cabin of a plane in an airplane-approved carrier. (Bruce Plotkin)

AIRPLANE TRAVEL

Problem: Rob and Jane live in New York, and a special work assignment means that in two months they'll leave for Denver, where they'll live for six months or so. Naturally, they want to take their five-year-old standard poodle, Beau, with them. They have made all of the proper arrangements with the airline, have purchased the necessary crate, and have had Beau checked out by their veterinarian, but are very concerned about how the dog will react to the trip. Whenever they go away they leave Beau with Jane's mother, who lives nearby, so he's never traveled before or been in a crate or cage.

DIAGNOSIS
Owners are wise to recognize that an older dog is quite set in its ways and will need some conditioning in order to withstand an airline trip with no major upset. Not only does it need to become used to staying quietly in a crate, but it will also have to learn to tolerate loud noises and strange people all around. *See also box,* SOCIALIZATION, THE KEY TO A WELL-ADJUSTED DOG, p. 271.

TREATMENT
Some dogs will have no trouble adjusting to air travel, but if your dog is nervous or easily upset you'll have to go very slowly to keep the entire experience on a positive note. If the steps below don't seem to be working, or you are particularly concerned about your dog for some reason, be sure to consult with your veterinarian, who may feel it would be wise to tranquilize your pet.

- Place the carrying case somewhere in the house and leave it, door open, in a spot where the dog can get into it and explore it.
- If the dog shows no interest in exploring the inside of the case, put a favorite toy or food treat way in the back.
- Once the dog has become used to going into the case and backing right out, close it in the case for a few minutes while you stay in the room.
- If the dog becomes upset with the door closed, sit on the floor next to the case and pet the dog, talking soothingly. Let it out before it becomes panicky—you don't want the dog to associate an unpleasant experience with the carrying case.
- After a time, depending on how the dog reacts, put a favorite toy, chewy, or food treat in the case and leave the room while the dog is in the case. At this point many dogs will go to sleep, but if your dog begins to

protest, go back, talk soothingly, and try to persuade it to stay in the case a while longer. Remember to keep everything pleasant. Don't scold the dog or yell at it— you want it to get to the point when it will accept the case calmly.

- If you have a station wagon or have access to one, it is very helpful if you can take the dog for a drive in the case so it can become accustomed to motion.
- It's also important for a dog to become used to crowds and noise, especially if it's led a fairly sheltered life. Take the dog on a short leash into malls, crowded streets, railroad stations—wherever there's loud noise, confusion, and lots of people coming and going. Stop, make the dog Focus on you, and talk soothingly to it the minute you sense it's becoming frightened or nervous.
- Ideally, if you live near enough to an airport and your pet seems to require more conditioning, take the dog to the airport in the travel case for a trial run or two. If you can get permission, put the case on the baggage belt and let it go around a few times. The dog will learn that nothing bad is going to happen to it and that you will be there to greet it after the trip.
- On the day of the trip keep things calm and matter-of-fact. Allow ample time to get to the airport so you're not breathless and rushed. If you're at all anxious, your dog will sense it and become anxious too. Give your dog a favorite toy or something to chew on during the trip.

ALOOFNESS

Problem 1: Georgianne's mother and father are coming to visit for the first time since she and her husband, David, moved to another city. She's all excited and especially wants her parents to meet Timmy, a beautiful shepherd she and David adore. Georgianne knows her father in particular will like him; he's always taken to dogs and they to him.

But when her parents settle down in the living room af-

ter their arrival, Timmy lies on the other side of the room
and just looks at them. He isn't exactly unfriendly, but he
certainly doesn't warm up the way Georgianne had expected him to. "I guess he just doesn't like me," her father says. "First time that's ever happened." Georgianne
feels awful and wonders what's the matter with Timmy.

Problem 2: Amy was really happy when she moved
and was within a couple of blocks of the park. "This will
be great for Leo," she told her sister. "There's a doggy
'playground' right near me. Now Leo will be able to
make a lot of new friends." Leo was her eight-month-old
chow chow puppy. The next day Amy took Leo to the
area where a lot of dogs were running around chasing
each other and playing together. She took his leash off
and gave him a little shove toward the other dogs. Leo
stood his ground and turned around to look at her as if to
say, "What do you want me to do? I have no interest in
these other dogs." Amy was amazed and troubled. She
wondered why Leo didn't want to play like all the other
"normal" young dogs.

DIAGNOSIS

Some individual dogs and certain dog breeds, shepherds
and chow chows among them, are naturally wary of and
aloof with strangers—people and dogs that they don't
know. This is a natural reaction of dogs that have been
bred to develop strong guarding instincts. They hold back
intentionally until they have an opportunity to assess the
situation very carefully.

TREATMENT

When there is no hostility involved and the dog simply
remains aloof, there is no need to do anything. Explain to
friends and family that there's nothing personal about it—
the dog acts the same way with everyone outside the
immediate family.

Problem 1: Don't force a dog to be friendly with people it doesn't know or it may simply go farther into its
shell. Allow the dog to remain in the room with visitors.

After several visits the dog will probably warm up to the visitors a bit.

Problem 2: If you really think it's important for your dog to play with other dogs, you'll have to socialize it to one dog at a time. Find someone with a particularly friendly puppy and both of you take the dogs off somewhere alone and introduce them, keeping them leashed. If your dog acts upset, or tries to get away from the other dog's advances, slow down and start over. With a lot of patient work you may be able to get your pet to accept one or two other dogs as "playmates."

ALPHA POSITION

I often talk about establishing the "Alpha position" with your dog. To understand what I mean, you need to consider Pack Behavior. In the pack, the most dominant animal is the Alpha animal, or leader. When you take a dog into your home, your family becomes its pack. Every pack must have an Alpha animal, or leader. If you don't want your dog to take over that role you must assume it yourself. Establish your leadership in your pet's eyes by acting in a firm, consistent, considerate, and loving manner. Only then will your dog look up to you and aim to please you.

See also box, DOMINANT BEHAVIOR, p. 98.

ANTHROPOMORPHISM

By dictionary definition, anthropomorphism is "the attribution of human motivation, characteristics, or behavior to animals." It's very natural for dog owners to sometimes think of their pets in human terms—we often call our animals by human names and they in turn often become, literally, family members. They eat with us, sleep with us, play with us, and keep us company.

Problems can arise when we take this too far, however, and expect a dog to understand human speech and reasoning—"I'm going out now, but I'll be back at two and I want you to be good"; "Don't run in the street or you'll be hit by a car"; "I'll spank you if you knock over the garbage again." Or when we assign human emotions to a pet to explain its actions—"He must love you more, that's why he growls at me"; "Susie's wetting on the rug to get back at us because she's jealous of the new puppy."

If your dog is going to be able to function safely, contentedly, and in a well-behaved manner in your world you must learn to understand its actions in canine, not human, terms and communicate with it in a way it can understand.

See box, EMOTIONS—DO DOGS HAVE THEM?, p. 110; HOW TO INTERPRET YOUR DOG'S BODY LANGUAGE, FACIAL EXPRESSIONS, AND VOCALIZATIONS, p. xi.

ANXIETY IN DOGS

Anxiety is a state of uneasiness, apprehension, and distress. The most common form of anxiety in pets is called Separation Anxiety, brought about by worry when owners are absent. I will deal with this elsewhere.

Any change in the normal routine can also make a dog anxious. Travel or a move, a new family member, pet, or neighbor, even new furniture may make a dog feel upset, anxious, worried. When a dog feels this way it doesn't know how to deal with it except by "acting up" in some way. It may bark, house-soil, chew, be destructive, or indulge in some other undesirable action. You can help offset this kind of behavior if you anticipate your dog's worry and prepare it for a change. Most dogs are very sensitive to their owners' moods, so try not to contribute to your pet's anxiety by acting worried yourself.

See also FEARFULNESS; OLDER DOG PROBLEMS: BEHAVIOR CHANGES; PANTING, EXCESSIVE; SEPARATION ANXIETY.

APPETITE PROBLEMS

EXCESSIVE APPETITE *(See also box,* FOOD REWARDS AS TRAINING TOOLS, p. 132; GARBAGE STEALING/DUMPING; GULPING FOOD; OBESITY.)

Problem: Adele is becoming quite literally fed up with her American foxhound, Lad. The four-year-old dog used to amuse her with his "bottomless pit" imitation, but now the dog's constant demands for food are getting her down. As soon as she gets up to go to the door, for instance, or put laundry in the dryer, Lad runs back and forth between her and the kitchen, panting and whining as if he's starving to death. She knows he can't really be hungry, but if she doesn't give in and feed him one or two dog biscuits, he keeps up the running, whining routine until she can stand it no more. Not only is this constant feeding a nuisance, but Lad is beginning to look quite plump.

DIAGNOSIS

As long as you've had a veterinarian make sure there's nothing wrong with your dog, the old saying "Food is love" can be applied here. The dog is probably bored. It's found that one way to break the monotony and get some attention is to feign starvation. Each time you give in to its act it serves to reinforce the dog's belief that this is a very good idea.

TREATMENT

There are several things you can do to get a dog's mind off food.

- Boredom is usually a factor in canine gluttony, so try to spend some additional daily time with your dog. Play with it, walk it, groom it, or just talk to it. If you give your dog some extra love it won't feel the need to ask for food in order to get attention.
- Redirect your dog's desire to eat by giving it something good to chew on. A Bone or Chew Toy will provide excellent oral satisfaction and entertainment at the same time.
- Talk to your veterinarian about your dog's diet. Perhaps your pet needs food that's more filling and satisfying.
- Some dogs may actually feel hungry during a twenty-four-hour period when they're fed only one meal a day. In this case it may help if you divide your pet's usual "dinner" into smaller portions that are fed several times during the day. If you're at home, four small meals a day are excellent; when you're out all day, two meals, or two meals and a bedtime snack, may be better than one large meal for your dog and may end its asking for between-meal snacks.

LOSS OF APPETITE/ACTING FINICKY(See *also* TOOTH CARE PROBLEMS.)

Problem 1: Jack, a tiny, feisty Yorkshire terrier, is worrying his owner, Anne. He always used to eat the nice-looking, nice-smelling canned dog food the veterinarian recommended. But ever since he stayed for a week with Anne's mother, who spoiled him, Jack takes one sniff of his food and walks away from the bowl. For a day Anne threw out his food, but then, fearful that he'd starve, she added a bit of leftover chicken breast to Jack's meal. Now Jack won't touch his food unless something's added—a spoonful of cottage cheese, a bite of hamburger, a bit of gravy, etc. Unless the added treat is well mixed into his regular dog food, Jack eats the special food off the top of the bowl and walks away, scorning the dog food. Anne knows that it's bad for Jack to eat rich food, but what can she do?

Problem 2: Molly, a ten-year-old cocker, has to lose weight. The veterinarian says her heart will give out soon if she doesn't shed at least five pounds. The problem is that Molly absolutely refuses to eat her special diet food. Her owner doesn't blame the dog—the food doesn't look very good to him. He's thinking of adding a bit of gravy to make the food more appealing.

DIAGNOSIS

Loss of appetite or refusal to eat can have a medical cause. But if a dog is otherwise healthy and has been recently checked over by a veterinarian, you can be sure this is an attention-getting device—a kind of game for the dog. An overly anthropomorphic owner often assumes the reason for a dog's refusal to eat is that the food doesn't look good by human standards *(see box,* ANTHROPOMORPHISM, p. 13). Sometimes the owner will switch from brand to brand and flavor to flavor in an effort to find just the "right" food. (That's why commercial dog foods are made to appeal to human, not canine, eyes and noses.) Dogs are omnivorous animals and, if they are really hungry, will eat any food they are given. Often the "Do you really expect me to eat *that*?" act is a direct result of an oversolicitous owner who immediately jumps to the conclusion a dog "doesn't like" some food just because the animal doesn't bolt it down immediately. Most domestic dogs are so well fed that it's rare for them to actually bolt down their food like their wild cousins.

TREATMENT
In both cases, you have to convince yourself that it's best for your dog to eat a proper diet of dog food. If you're not on firm ground yourself you'll probably cave in again as soon as the dog refuses to eat.

- If you're sure your dog is healthy, withhold *all* food for twenty-four hours. Give the dog free access to water, and walk or exercise it in the usual way. At the end of twenty-four hours, offer a small portion of the food you want the dog to eat. If it is not eaten in fifteen minutes, take it away. Wait a few hours and offer the food again. Continue to do this until the dog eats. At this point, give the animal enough to make up a normal portion of food. Don't make a big fuss over the dog; act as if it's a perfectly normal event for it to eat its food.
- Be sure the food you're offering your dog is palatable. Throw uneaten food away and offer fresh the next time; or cover it tightly and refrigerate it. Before offering the food to your dog again, warm it to room temperature.
- Never allow a small-breed puppy under nine months to go without nourishment for more than twelve hours or it may develop hypoglycemia.

ATTACHMENTS, EXCESSIVE

TO AN OBJECT See OBJECT-GUARDING AGGRESSION; TERRITORIAL AGGRESSION.

TO A PERSON See AFFECTION, EXCESSIVE/DEMANDING; ONE-MAN DOGS.

ATTACKING See AGGRESSION; *box*, RAGE SYNDROME, p. 239.

ATTENTION PROBLEMS

ATTENTION-GETTING ACTIONS See AFFECTION, EXCESSIVE/DEMANDING; APPETITE PROBLEMS: LOSS OF APPETITE/ACTING FINICKY; BARKING PROBLEMS: EXCESSIVE BARKING; CHEWING PROBLEMS; HOWLING; LAMENESS, SYMPATHY; LICKING PROBLEMS; MOUTHING; NIPPING; TAIL-CHASING/BITING; TOILET-PAPER UNROLLING; WHINING; YAPPING/YIPPING BEHAVIOR.

PAYING MORE ATTENTION TO ONE PERSON THAN ANOTHER

Problem 1: When Ginny and Don were married, Ginny wasn't working and decided to get a puppy as company for her. The little mixed breed terrier, Phil, was a delightful companion for Ginny. But every evening when Don arrived home from work, Phil paid absolutely no attention to her at all. He followed Don around as if he was afraid he'd lose him. Ginny was puzzled and hurt by Phil's apparent "disloyalty" to her.

Problem 2: Andrea and Arthur have a mixed-breed hunting-type dog named Homer, whom they both adore. Arthur's new job takes him out of town for a week or more every month, so Andrea has become Homer's primary caretaker by default. When she gets home from work she feeds him and often takes long walks with him, especially when Arthur's away. One day Arthur came home from a trip in the middle of the afternoon. When he walked in the house he was greatly surprised at Homer's lukewarm greeting, especially as the dog went crazy with delight when Andrea came home later. Arthur's feelings were hurt. "I guess he doesn't like me anymore," he told his wife.

Problem 3: The Jenkinses live in a large apartment in New York and have two Westies, Ike and Mike. Mrs. Jenkins is on the boards of several charitable organizations and usually is out all day. Mr. Jenkins leaves home before seven in the morning and rarely gets back until eight at night. The children are in school during the day and are involved in a number of after-school activities, and the housekeeper is busy attending to the apartment. So the Jenkinses hired a dog walker for Ike and Mike. She comes three times a day—first thing in the morning, about three in the afternoon, and after the dogs have had their supper, at seven. Mr. Jenkins walks them at night before bed.

One afternoon Mrs. Jenkins was at home because a meeting had been canceled when Kathy, the dog walker, arrived. Ike and Mike dashed to the door before Kathy even came in, and when she squatted down in the doorway they covered her face with doggy kisses and bounced around her gleefully, all the while letting out little squeals of joy. As she watched this from the living room, Mrs. Jenkins thought, "My goodness, those dogs make more fuss over that girl than they do over me or even the children! I wonder why."

DIAGNOSIS

Problem 1: A dog is naturally happy to see its owner when the owner comes home after being out all day.

Problem 2: When one owner's frequent long absences result in another owner's becoming its principal caretaker, it shouldn't be a big surprise if a dog reacts with disinterest when the frequently absent owner arrives at the house. After all, the frequently absent owner is not the one who's going to feed or walk the dog.

Problem 3: Dogs will always be very happy to see a dog walker who meets their needs on a regular basis and gives them love and affection three times a day—more often than any family member does.

TREATMENT

These are really not "problems," except in the eyes of the slighted owners. It's foolish to attribute complicated motivations to a dog's perfectly natural actions. After a period of time, when one person meets a dog's needs more than another does, the dog will react to the caretaker's arrival with delight. It's easy to fall into the trap of anthropomorphizing and thinking, "He likes you more," but if you took over the caretaking the dog would soon like *you* more. If a dog's behavior causes friction between people, there are a couple of things that may help.

Problems 1 & 2:

- When a dog seems to respond to one owner over another, if you are the "preferred" owner, limit your greeting of the dog to a hearty pat and "hello," and then go about your business.
- If you want to walk the dog or play with it, include your partner in the activities. Walk the dog together, go outside and play three-way-catch, and be sure you both are present when the dog is fed.

Problem 3:

- When a dog seems to prefer its regular walker to you, you can quickly win its affections back if you begin to walk it yourself instead of hiring someone else to do so.
- Don't make the mistake of allowing a dog's obvious delight in one individual or another to become a bone of contention or undermine your own good relationship with your dog.

AUTOMATIC BEHAVIOR

Problem 1: Alfie is a large Newfoundland who was adopted by his present owners when he was about a year old. He is usually very obedient and well behaved, but has a very peculiar reaction every time his owner picks up the leash to take him for a walk. He plops down on the floor automatically, as if a switch has been thrown, and won't budge. Given his size, it's impossible for his owner to move him bodily, and no amount of inducement can get him up on his feet.

Problem 2: Jane's Afghan hound, Ned, acts in the most peculiar way. He is well trained and walks right along with her when they go out. That is, until he sees another dog on a leash approaching them on the street. As the other dog nears, Ned plops down right on the sidewalk by Jane's side and refuses to get up. As soon as the other dog has passed, Ned begins to walk again as if nothing's happened.

Problem 3: Josephine has a new puppy, Rover. He's just beginning to be properly housebroken. First thing in the morning, before she's even had her coffee, Josephine puts Rover's leash on and takes him out for a walk. But instead of walking, Rover simply lies down when they get out on the road. Josephine has tried everything. She goes to the end of the leash and calls him, to no avail; then she attempts to make him walk by pulling on the leash, but he just stubbornly stiffens his legs and stays in place. Finally she loses patience—she wants to go back indoors and have her coffee—so she picks the pup up, puts him down by the side of the road in some grass, waits until he finally goes to the bathroom, and carries him back indoors. "This is some way to walk a dog!" she says to herself, and wonders what's the matter with Rover.

DIAGNOSIS

Each of these dogs is practicing avoidance by its automatic behavior. A dog that lies down at the sight of its leash is being stubbornly defiant because it doesn't want to take a walk. The dog figures if it lies down and stays put it may be able to avoid the exercise it detests.

The dog that plops down in the middle of its walk has more complicated reasons for its actions. It knows perfectly well how to heel and stay along with its mistress, but when the dog spots another dog coming along it wants to avoid a confrontation with that dog, so it simply lies down until the other animal passes. It's acting Submissive to the other dog by lowering itself (see HOW TO INTERPRET YOUR DOG'S BODY LANGUAGE, FACIAL EXPRESSIONS, AND VOCALIZATIONS, p. xi).

A puppy will often lie down when a leash is put on it because it has no idea what it's supposed to do. When a puppy's unsure what's expected of it, it often reacts by simply avoiding the whole thing and lying down.

TREATMENT
The treatment for each problem is slightly different.

Problem 1: If a dog doesn't want to walk, you have to get it used to wearing a leash.

- Take the dog's collar off. Attach the leash to the collar and put the collar back on the dog. Allow the dog to walk around the house dragging the leash for a while. Then pick the leash up and lead the dog outside.
- Another method to use with a well-behaved dog is to lead the dog outside while you hold on to its collar. Once outside, snap the leash onto the dog's collar and proceed to walk.

Problem 2: When a dog balks at the sight of an approaching dog, its behavior must be modified so it will keep right on walking with you and pay no attention to the other animal.

- High Collar the dog immediately as soon as you see another dog on the horizon. This will make it Focus on you instead of the other dog, and you can keep right on walking past the other dog. After a few times a dog will usually realize that everything will be all right if it walks past another dog on the street.

Problem 3: A puppy needs to be taught proper leash-walking techniques so it will know what's expected of it when you take it out.

- Follow a standard training manual to teach a puppy to walk on a leash.

AUTOMOBILE CHASING/MANNERS/TRAVEL:
See CAR PROBLEMS.

B

BABY, RELATIONSHIP WITH See CHILDREN AND DOGS: TODDLERS AND DOGS; JEALOUSY: JEALOUSY OF A NEW BABY.

BALKINESS See STUBBORNNESS.

BALLOONS See *box*, WATER BALLOONS AS TRAINING TOOLS, p. 320.

BALL-PLAYING FETISH (See *also* PLAY PROBLEMS: EXCESSIVE PLAY.)

Problem: Otis, a big five-year-old Chesapeake Bay retriever, is becoming a real problem. He loves to play ball and would spend every waking minute chasing and fetching a tennis ball if his owners cooperated. He nags and nags his owners to toss the ball, picks the ball up and throws it at them, and when they don't respond, barks and barks. When they do toss the ball, he retrieves it immediately and commences to beg to have it thrown again, and again, and again. Sometimes he even paws at them in an effort to get their attention to throw the ball. They like to play ball with him, but this is becoming ridiculous! It's getting so they can't spend a peaceful moment when he's around.

DIAGNOSIS

This is an example of play behavior that's escalated into a nuisance. Many dogs like to play ball, but with some, retrievers in particular, the game can become an obsession. This kind of extreme ball fetishism may lead to excessive barking and can even develop into Circling Behavior.

TREATMENT

When an animal becomes fixated on a certain play object such as a ball, it's almost impossible to break it of the fetish altogether. What's more, ball playing is probably an enjoyable experience for both of you. However, if you realize your dog is becoming obsessive about ball playing you'll have to bring it under control.

- First, collect all of the loose balls that have accumulated in the house and yard and put them away in a spot where the dog can't get them.
- Make it a rule never to play ball inside. Instead, provide your dog with several sturdy Bones and Chew Toys.
- When *you* want to play ball, take the dog outside. Toss the ball as many times as you want, and when you want to stop, pick up the ball and put it away and say, "That's all." After you've given a verbal sign to the dog that the ball-playing session is over, don't give in to any pleas to toss it just once more. Instead, give your dog another toy.
- If your dog is very insistent and continues to beg you to play some more, snap its leash on at the end of the ball playing and take it for a short, brisk walk before you go indoors.

BARKING PROBLEMS

EXCESSIVE BARKING (See also HOWLING; SEPARATION ANXIETY; *box*, TERRITORIAL BEHAVIOR, p. 289; *box*, VOCALIZING BEHAVIOR, p. 318; YAPPING/YIPPING BEHAVIOR.)

Problem 1: Jennie, a bichon frisé, is really bothering her owners with her constant barking. Every time they sit down to eat she barks to be let out, and a few minutes later she barks to come in. If they're quietly reading or watching TV in the evening, she stands in the middle of the room and barks until someone plays with her or gives her a biscuit. She even wakes them up in the middle of the night barking to go out in the yard.

Problem 2: When Sue went back to work it meant she had to leave her five-year-old Sealyham terrier alone all day. She'd often left the dog alone in a fenced-in yard for a few hours with no problem, so she wasn't too worried. The first day, everything seemed fine when Sue got home. But two days later, her next-door neighbor came over to complain as soon as Sue walked in the door. "You're going to have to do something about that dog," she said. "Her hysterical barking all day long is keeping my baby awake."

Problem 3: The Slones' Dandie Dinmont terrier was a wonderful watchdog. In fact, he was too wonderful. His never-ending barking had become a pain. He barked at every person or dog that walked by on the sidewalk, and his barking became hysterical if someone like the mailman came up the front walk. Worst of all, when a visitor arrived the dog wouldn't stop barking even after the person was in the house, but stood in the middle of the living room and kept right on barking until one of his owners picked him up and put him outdoors.

DIAGNOSIS

Barking is one form of vocal communication for a dog. It is a way to tell its pack (family) that someone is approaching at the same time it warns the stranger away from the dog's territory. Most dog owners like their pets to bark in a reasonable way to alert them when a stranger approaches. But when the barking is excessive it becomes a problem.

The habit of excessive barking can have a number of causes, or a combination of several. It may be learned by a small puppy in the litter if its mother and littermates bark continuously. Owners who praise a puppy each time it barks can create an adult dog with a barking problem, and spoiled, badly trained dogs may use barking as an attention-getting device. An owner who picks up a dog each time it barks simply confirms the animal's belief that this is an excellent way to get attention. A dog may also bark excessively when it's lonely or anxious and wants someone to come and get it—in this case it's one symptom of Separation Anxiety. Highly territorial dogs often indulge in excessive barking as a warning signal.

TREATMENT
Excessive barking can be a very difficult habit to break, especially if you aren't home all of the time. Before you attempt to treat excessive barking you should try to determine what the cause, or causes, of the problem are. In each instance your aim is to let the dog know you are pleased with it when it stays quiet and doesn't bark, but you must be careful not to give Mixed Messages. Don't praise a dog the minute it stops barking—it won't know if you are praising it for barking or for stopping. Reserve your praise for times when the dog remains quiet for long periods of time.

On the other hand, you probably don't want your dog to stop barking altogether. If the dog is trained to focus on you it will probably learn to look at you after it's barked once or twice at an appropriate time. Then you can praise your pet and let it know that *this time* you're pleased that it barked.

Problem 1: When a spoiled dog wants constant attention from you, it's probably because you've responded to the dog's demands every time it barked and now it feels it can run you.

- The treatment in this case should be the same as that prescribed for a dog that demands affection; *see* AFFECTION, EXCESSIVE/DEMANDING.
- In addition, pay no attention at all to the dog when it barks unless you know it's for a legitimate reason (e.g., the dog really needs to go out).
- The dog should also be put in a Crate at night so it gets out of the habit of waking you to go out.

Problem 2: When a dog that's left alone outdoors barks hysterically it's probably because of Separation Anxiety, which may be exacerbated by territoriality.

- The immediate first step to take is to leave the dog indoors instead of out in the yard where it disturbs the neighbors. If the dog isn't properly trained and you don't want to give it the run of the house, put it in a Crate indoors. Don't let the dog think you're rewarding it for barking by moving it indoors; rather, start the dog off indoors. Without the stimuli of passing people, dogs, cars, and so forth, the dog may remain quiet inside the house.
- If you want to train the dog to remain quietly outdoors or in when you're out, begin by feeding and exercising it before you go so it will be tired and full when you leave.
- One effective training method is what I call the "startle" approach. For this you have to be at home during the day. With the dog wherever you want it, outdoors or in, prepare to leave in your usual fashion. Go out, away from the dog's sight, and sneak back. As soon as the dog begins to bark excessively, toss a Noisemaker, Throw Chain, or Water Balloon at it, or if the weather's warm, squirt it with a jet of water from a hose. If possible, don't let the dog know you are the culprit. The aim is to startle the animal and distract it from barking. Do this each time the dog begins to bark too much. Some animals may need only one or two "treatments" to stop barking excessively.

■ For most dogs, however, the startle approach probably won't work that quickly. If you can't be at home and the dog is allowed to get away with excessive barking most of the time, it will remain a habit. Try to enlist the help of a reliable friend, or hire a neighborhood youngster who's willing to sit outside your house while you're gone. Your substitute can then perform the startling actions.

■ If you decide to keep your dog indoors, a Crate will often make an animal feel secure and may eliminate the barking problem.

■ When a dog continues to bark even when it's in the crate, you may want to try one of the sound-activated devices that's on the market. It will emit a high-pitched noise when a dog barks. I do not believe in the use of electronic collars that shock dogs—we don't know the degree of discomfort they cause an animal. *(See box,* ELECTRONIC DEVICES AS BEHAVIOR MODIFIERS, p. 107.)

■ Last, if all else fails and your dog's an otherwise well-trained animal, take it to work with you, or see if your neighbor will let the dog stay with her while you're not there. Then you can continue to work on the barking problem when you're at home. *(See* WORK, TAKING A DOG WITH YOU.)

Problem 3: If the problem is clearly a case of an overterritorial dog, *see* TERRITORIAL AGGRESSION, Problem 1.

TEACHING A DOG TO BARK ON SIGNAL

Problem: Jane lives alone and would like to teach her extremely friendly Labrador retriever to bark when strangers come to the door instead of welcoming everyone with obvious joy.

DIAGNOSIS
Some very friendly dogs view all people as part of the family and greet them happily with tail wags.

TREATMENT
To teach your dog to bark on signal you'll need one other person's help.

- With the dog on leash, sitting by your side, have your helper knock on the door or ring the bell.
- As soon as you hear the signal, call excitedly, "Who's there??" or "What is it?" The dog may bark. If it does, praise it lavishly and give it a treat.
- If the dog doesn't bark, have the person come to the door again, and this time act very alarmed and move around waving your arms in an agitated manner.
- If the dog still doesn't bark, try making panting, huffing sounds—"huf, huf, woof, woof"—just as an adult wolf does to teach a cub to bark.
- When the dog does bark, praise it and then tell it to stay while you open the door. Greet your friend, and ask him or her to praise the dog too.
- Repeat the entire routine until the dog learns to bark automatically whenever anyone comes to the door.

BATHROOM STATION See *box,* INDOOR COMFORT STATION, p. 157.

A BED FOR A DOG

All dogs, like wolves, like to have a special nest they can go to sleep in. A nest of some kind is not only comfortable, but helps an animal feel secure and safe. Elaborate beds are not necessary—most dogs will welcome a soft towel or an owner's discarded sweater or blanket.

For some dogs, a Crate can become a welcome bed. In the absence of a bed of their own many dogs will adopt a piece of furniture or their owner's bed as a nest.

See also DIGGING: DIGGING INDOORS/MAKING A NEST; JUMPING PROBLEMS: JUMPING ON THE BED, JUMPING ON CHAIRS OR COUCHES.

BEDROOM, BEHAVIOR IN See JEALOUSY: JEALOUSY OF AN ADULT PERSON; JUMPING PROBLEMS: JUMPING ON THE BED.

BEGGING

BEGGING FOR ATTENTION See AFFECTION, EXCESSIVE/ DEMANDING; BARKING PROBLEMS: EXCESSIVE BARKING, Problem 1; CHEWING PROBLEMS; HOWLING; LAMENESS, SYMPATHY; LICKING PROBLEMS; MOUTHING; NIPPING; WHINING; YAPPING/ YIPPING BEHAVIOR.

BEGGING FOR FOOD

Problem: Pookie has become a real pest. Every time people sit down to eat, there he is sitting by their side, whining, barking, and finally pawing at them to give him a tidbit. It isn't so bad when it's just the family, but it's very annoying and embarrassing when company comes for dinner.

DIAGNOSIS

Begging is a completely natural canine behavior. Wolves and dogs often watch each other eat, hoping for the chance to steal a bite. When a puppy watches people eat it's hoping they'll drop a morsel of food or perhaps even let it have a piece of their meal. If you cave in to your pet's silent pleas and let it have even one small bite from your plate, you'll be on the way to establishing a very bad habit. Remember, what's cute in a puppy can become very annoying in an adult dog.

TREATMENT

- The best and easiest treatment is to avoid the problem in the first place by never allowing anyone to feed a dog at the table.
- If the begging occurs only at dinnertime, feed your dog its own dinner just before you eat. This way it won't be hungry and may go to sleep.
- Tell the dog "NO!" each time it begins to beg. This may be effective for some animals.
- With a persistent beggar, leash the dog and attach the leash to a doorknob or a chair leg that's out of reach of the dining table. Tell the dog to stay and proceed with your meal.
- Alternatively, if your dog is crate-trained, put it in the Crate in the room with you while you eat.
- If none of these steps works or if the dog continues to whine and plead throughout the meal, your only alternative is to close it out of the room while you eat. If you have an enclosed yard, put it outdoors, or use a pressure Gate to keep the dining area closed off.

BEHAVIOR CHANGES

Behavior changes in a dog can have several causes. A dog's behavior may change if it has a traumatic experience such as a serious illness, an injury, or a frightening trip. The loss of a favorite companion may make a dog become listless and disinterested. A move can also confuse or disorient a sensitive or elderly dog so badly it becomes fearful and unsure of itself. Most often, however, a sudden change in a dog's behavior has a physical cause. An older dog naturally slows down, but so does a dog that doesn't feel well, is losing its sight or hearing, or is in pain. A dog can also seem to undergo a personality change if it isn't getting the proper nutrients from its food. Always consult your veterinarian if your dog's behavior changes in any way.

See also OLDER DOG PROBLEMS.

BEHAVIOR MODIFICATION

To modify behavior means literally to change it to make it less extreme or strong. The term "behavior modification" is used by animal behaviorists to describe a technique in which a dog's behavior is conditioned or reconditioned, usually from an undesirable to a more desirable mode. The technique is also referred to as "behavioral engineering."

I prefer to use the terms "programming," "deprogramming," and "reprogramming," because I feel they are more descriptive of the process that takes place. Obedience Training in all of its aspects and on all levels is an example of behavior modification, or programming. Breaking a dog of a bad habit, such as chasing cats, is a more complex example. In this case the dog must first be taught *not* to indulge in the unwanted behavior and then taught *what it is acceptable to do*. In other words, it will have been Deprogrammed and then reprogrammed. Its behavior will have been modified, or changed to be more acceptable.

See also box, DEPROGRAMMING AND DESENSITIZATION, p. 88; *box,* ELECTRONIC DEVICES AS BEHAVIOR MODIFIERS, p. 107; *box,* ELIZABETHAN COLLARS AS BEHAVIOR MODIFIERS, p. 108; *box,* LIQUIDS AS AIDS IN BEHAVIOR MODIFICATION, p. 196; *box,* PRAISE TO MODIFY A DOG'S BEHAVIOR, p. 244; *box,* SETUPS, p. 264.

BICYCLE CHASING See CHASING PROBLEMS: CHASING BICYCLES.

BICYCLING WITH A DOG See JOGGING WITH A DOG.

BITING PEOPLE

Problem: At the recent ASPCA-sponsored Dog Walk to benefit homeless dogs held in New York City's Central Park, thousands of dogs and their owners met without incident. One problem did arise, however. One of my clients who owns a Welsh terrier was standing with her dog by the sign-in table next to a man with a handsome rottweiler. The rotty looked at my client sweetly and she extended her hand toward him to say hello. Immediately, he snapped and bit her fingers. Fortunately, the wound wasn't serious, but there was a lot of blood and confusion. The rottweiler's owner was naturally upset. Although his dog did have a biting problem, he was normally under complete control. Apparently both owner and dog became distracted with all of the dogs and people in close proximity.

DIAGNOSIS

A well-trained, well-treated, socialized dog should *never* feel the need to bite a person under any circumstances. Puppies should be taught from the beginning never to nip anyone.

However, dogs do sometimes bite. An overly fearful dog has the potential to bite, and so do dogs that have been mistreated or teased. The scenario above is a very commonly seen situation involving a highly territorial dog that is very protective of its owner. Its territoriality was exacerbated because there were a lot of strange dogs and people around. In this case the dog perceived the approach of a stranger as a threat and reacted in what was, for it, a natural way. Because the bite it gave was not serious, it was probably intended to be a warning only— "Stay away from my master, or else."

For discussions of other reasons a dog may bite, *see* AGGRESSION (all types cross-referenced); CHILDREN AND DOGS; NIPPING; *box*, RAGE SYNDROME, p. 252; *box*, TERRITORIAL BEHAVIOR, p. 289.

TREATMENT

- When any dog bites or threatens to bite, the underlying cause must be discovered and appropriate training steps taken to cure the problem.
- The responsible owner of a highly territorial dog such as the one above will usually train the dog well and have it under control at all times, especially in crowds.
- In an extreme case such as the one above, with thousands of dogs and people milling around nearby, the owner should have been particularly vigilant and tuned in to his dog's reactions. If he had acted quickly he would have been able to avert the problem. Dogs often give clues when they're about to bite: laid-back ears, lowered tail, and bared teeth are all clear signals that a dog is not happy with a situation and may be about to go one step further. *(See* HOW TO INTERPRET YOUR DOG'S BODY LANGUAGE, FACIAL EXPRESSIONS, AND VOCALIZATIONS, p. xi.)
- On the other hand, if my client had heeded the advice never to reach out to any dog without asking first if the animal is friendly, the incident would never have happened.

BITTER-TASTING LIQUID *See box,* LIQUIDS AS AIDS IN BEHAVIOR MODIFICATION, p. 196.

BLINDNESS, SIGNS OF *(See also box,* BEHAVIOR CHANGES, p. 33; OLDER DOG PROBLEMS.)

Problem: Pat Kelly's concerned that her dalmation, Spot, is undergoing a personality change. Twice in recent days he has acted frightened and almost nipped her when she came into a room and reached down to pat him. She's worried he might nip at their daughter or one of her friends.

DIAGNOSIS

If the dog nips and acts startled only when someone approaches suddenly, it may be an indication the animal is losing its sight. Most blind dogs do very well once they become accustomed to their condition and as long as they're in a familiar place. But initially a dog that's going blind won't understand what's happening and will be jumpy, especially if it's startled by an unexpected touch.

TREATMENT

- First, the dog should be examined by a veterinarian. There are treatments for some kinds of canine eye disease and blindness.
- If the dog's eyesight is failing or has already failed, there is no need to change its life-style. But you and all other family members should be aware that the animal may be easily startled if you come upon it suddenly or touch it unexpectedly. Family and friends should make it a habit to speak to the dog as they approach it so they don't take it unawares.
- Finally, if it's necessary to move the furniture in your home or to take the dog to new surroundings, take time to orient your pet carefully so it won't be confused. With a leash on, walk the dog around and let it sniff and explore as much as it wants. When you go from room to room, be sure the dog knows where you've gone. At first, when you go out, confine the dog in a small area where it feels comfortable so it doesn't wander off looking for you and become lost.

BOARDING A DOG

Many people are loath to get a dog because they travel extensively and don't like the idea of boarding their pet. Nowadays there is little basis for concern—the old days of dirty kennels and careless keepers are mostly a thing of the past. Clean, modern, spacious kennels and personal care are now the norm.

Before you decide on a kennel for your pet, visit several facilities if possible and talk to the owners. Responsible kennel owners are only too happy to show you around and answer questions. Ask about veterinarian care, the policy about immunizations and physical checkups, and any other topic you want. The American Boarding Kennels Association (ABKA) is a trade organization that sets standards for boarding facilities. It can help you locate an approved kennel in your area. You can contact ABKA at 4575 Galley Road, Suite 400-A, Colorado Springs, CO 80519.

Before you leave your pet in a kennel for any length of time, it's a good idea to take the dog for a couple of practice sessions. Leave your pet overnight and come back for it the next morning. Do this several times so the dog becomes conditioned to the fact that when you leave it alone in a strange place, you always come back for it. *(See box,* SOCIALIZATION, THE KEY TO A WELL-ADJUSTED DOG, p. 271.)

Calm, highly social dogs often seem to enjoy staying in a kennel. Others only tolerate it. But if you've shopped carefully and prepared your pet ahead of time, rest assured the dog will be perfectly all right in a well-run kennel while you're away.

BOATS, BEHAVIOR ON *(See also* SWIMMING PROBLEMS.*)*

Problem: Sue and Jim spend most summer weekends on their fifty-foot motorboat. When it was time to get the boat in order in the spring, they took their nine-month-old bloodhound, Rocky, out to the boatyard with them. They wanted him to get used to the boat while it was still at the dock, because they expected to take him out on the water with them every week. The minute he set foot on the boat deck, Rocky panicked. He ran to the side of the boat away from the dock, jumped into the water, and swam around in circles, barking. He had to be hauled into a dinghy and taken to shore. Sue and Jim are amazed at his reaction and know they'll need help in turning Rocky into a good boat companion.

DIAGNOSIS

Some dogs take to the water and to boating like ducks. Others don't like any part of it—the slippery deck, the rocking boat, and the water all around sends them into a panic.

TREATMENT

A dog that's fearful of new things in general and of boats, docks, and water in particular has to be carefully programmed to accept its new surroundings and taught how to behave properly.

- The dog should be leashed at all times at first. Not only does a leash help you control the dog, but it gives the animal a sense of security.
- With the leash held firmly, walk the dog all around the boat, paying particular attention to the perimeters of the vessel. If the dog goes to the edge or starts to lean over, say "NO" sharply and give a leash correction.
- If the deck is slippery and the dog slips and slides on it, consider covering it with indoor-outdoor carpeting, or at least putting down a small square of something the dog can get a purchase on. Remember, when the deck gets wet it will be even more slippery. This can be

a big problem with a large, ungainly animal or an older dog.

- Some people, especially those with sailboats that heel in the wind, put netting up between the rail and the deck to keep an animal (or small child) from slipping into the water.
- Even though your dog may be a good swimmer, it's a good idea to have it wear a life preserver, at least until you're sure it won't jump or fall off the boat when you're under way.
- If you plan to stay on the boat overnight, you'll have to teach your dog how to get in and out of a dinghy to go ashore to relieve itself. Agile dogs such as poodles can often learn to climb ladders with ease. Others have more difficulty. I've even seen a boat rigged up with a winch and canvas sling made just to get a large dog on board and off again!

BODY LANGUAGE See HOW TO INTERPRET YOUR DOG'S BODY LANGUAGE, FACIAL EXPRESSIONS, AND VOCALIZATIONS, p. xi.

BOLTING

BOLTING FROM EXUBERANCE (See also PULLING ON A LEASH.)

Problem: Patsy thinks one of these days her giant schnauzer is going to make her fall flat on her face. Every time she puts his leash on and opens the door to take him out, the dog bolts ahead of her as if he's been shot from a cannon, down the steps and the path out to the road.

DIAGNOSIS
Large, very energetic dogs that love to run often bolt out of the door in sheer exuberance as if they were not on a leash, especially when they're young.

TREATMENT

- You have to remind a dog such as this that it *is* on a leash this time. Anticipate the dog's actions and hold the leash firmly so you can immediately give a sharp Leash Correction. Give the correction, saying "No" very firmly. Praise the dog lavishly when it walks nicely by your side.
- Be sure a large energetic dog has the opportunity to get sufficient exercise so it's not so ready to explode out of the door each time you want to go for a walk. *(See also,* EXERCISE, DOGS' NEED FOR.)

BOLTING FROM THE HOUSE

Problem: Phoebe is a well-behaved little terrier that's been trained to walk nicely on the leash, and seems to be happy indoors with her owners all of the time. That is, until someone opens the front door. When Phoebe's mistress goes to the door to take in the newspaper in the morning, or to let a friend in—*whoosh*—Phoebe flies past her and bolts out of the door and down the street without a backward look. The dog has narrowly escaped being hit by a car on several occasions, and has almost knocked down a couple of visitors.

DIAGNOSIS

Dogs such as this are very energetic and curious, and sometimes seem to be purposefully mischievous. An indoor dog that continuously bolts out of the door may not get enough vigorous exercise on a regular basis and finds it exhilarating to tear out and around. Usually a dog will outgrow the tendency to bolt out the door.

Sometimes, this type of bolting can be related to Chase Behavior. If a dog sees a child or bicycle passing as it looks out the door, it may dash out to do a bit of chasing.

TREATMENT

Whether or not you think your pet will outgrow the tendency to bolt out the door every time it's opened, this is a behavior you'll have to stop before the dog gets hurt, or knocks someone over as it hurtles outdoors.

- If your dog has been well trained, have it sit or tell it to sit/stay before you open the door. Praise the dog when it obeys.
- If your dog is not trained well and you don't trust it to remain in a sit/stay, you can try the leash trick. Put a short leash on your dog while it's in the house and let it drag the leash around. (Note: only do this when you're at home—a leash could become caught and choke the animal when no one's around.) When you want to open the door, put one foot on the handle of the leash. Tell the dog to stay; if it bolts anyway the leash will stop it from going far. Snap the leash and tell the dog "No" at the same time. Again, give the animal positive reinforcement with praise when it learns to stay still on its own.

There are two other methods that you can use to condition a dog not to run out an open door. Both require extreme care so you don't hurt your pet. The aim is to make it see the door as a possible threat.

- Crack the door open. Wait until your naturally curious dog begins to stick its nose out of the crack, then *gently* push the door closed while you say "No" at the same time. After a few "lessons" the dog will usually decide it's not worth having its head squashed to go out the door.
- Open the door when the dog is across the room while you watch the dog carefully. As soon as it begins to move toward the door, slam it. At the same time, say "No" very firmly. Praise the dog if it stays still.

BOLTING IN FEAR (See also FEARFULNESS; FLIGHT BEHAVIOR PROBLEMS.)

Problem: Colin regularly jogged in the park with his collie, Misty, running along with him off leash. Misty was perfectly behaved and never left his side as they ran along, even when other dogs came near. But one day as they jogged, a big truck rumbled by and backfired very loudly just as it was opposite them. Misty panicked and bolted off.

DIAGNOSIS

A loud startling noise such as a backfire can cause even the best-behaved dog to bolt in fear. This type of bolting is a form of Flight Behavior—the principal difference is that a dog that bolts in fear will come back as soon as the frightening event is over while a dog exhibiting full flight behavior will keep right on running for some time.

Although a bolting dog will return, it is in serious danger if there are moving vehicles nearby.

TREATMENT

- For a dog's safety, you should never allow it to be unleashed anywhere near traffic. No matter how well behaved your pet is, you can never really predict when something may trigger it to bolt.
- If an unleashed dog does bolt you must be prepared to respond quickly to control it. Make it refocus on you by clapping your hands and shouting to it to stop and stay. When it freezes, call it back to you and reassure it that everything's all right. (*See also box,* NOISEMAKERS, p. 217; *box,* THROW CHAIN, p. 290.)

BONDING

Pack animals such as wolves and dogs form very strong bonds with other pack members. As young animals grow from puppyhood and develop within the pack, adult pack members always nurture and care for them. The bond they form is based on physical closeness and touch as well as social hierarchy.

I often speak of "bonding" with your dog. This is a very important aspect of your relationship with your pet. When you adopt a puppy or dog and bring it into your household, you become that animal's pack. Your puppy or dog will bond with you when you are affectionate with it, interact with it in play and training, and show it you care for it and will not only nurture it but lead it and show it what you expect it to do.

See also box, PACK BEHAVIOR, p. 230.

Daisy, a mixed-breed terrier, enjoys a favorite Bone. (Bruce Plotkin)

BONES FOR DOGS

All dogs love to chew bones, but be sure to check with your veterinarian before you give your dog any kind of natural bone. *Never allow a dog to chew poultry bones*—they splinter very easily and could cause serious physical damage. The same is true of lamb, pork, and veal bones to a lesser degree. The only safe "real" bone to give a dog is a well-boiled beef knuckle bone. Nylon and other composition dog bones provide good chewing exercise, but don't contain the calcium natural bones do. For rawhide bones, *see box,* CHEW TOYS FOR DOGS, p. 61.

BOREDOM *(See also* CHEWING PROBLEMS; DESTRUCTIVE BEHAVIOR; DIGGING; EXERCISE, DOGS' NEED FOR; SCRATCHING PROBLEMS; SEPARATION ANXIETY.)

Problem: Every time the Magees leave their Irish setter, Pat, alone in the house, the dog acts very restless. He doesn't do anything really bad, but he always seems to have been poking around. One day when they left a closet door open, Pat took all of the shoes out of the closet and piled them in the middle of the living-room floor. They wonder if Pat is bored when they leave him alone.

DIAGNOSIS

A dog may act in a way we characterize as being "bored." This is really a human emotion. What a dog may be suffering from is a mild form of Separation Anxiety. When left alone some dogs seem to have a lot of displaced energy, move around a lot, indulge in Exploratory Behavior, cry or bark. Sometimes this escalates into actual Destructive Behavior in the form of Digging, or Chewing. Other dogs display their "boredom" by acting mildly depressed and disinterested in the world around them. Owners of dogs such as this often feel guilty about leaving their pets. Some people even go so far as to leave the television or a radio on to "keep the dog company."

This behavior often surfaces at the stage when a puppy is maturing into an adult dog. At this time the dog's owners no longer feel the need to nurture the animal as much as they did when it was growing up, and often cut back on exercise and playtime. This can be a difficult transition period for a young dog, especially one with a lot of energy.

TREATMENT

- The best way to offset boredom in a dog is to be sure it's relaxed and tired out when you go out. Give it an extra-long, extra-vigorous exercise session before you leave it alone.
- Be sure to provide your dog with a couple of favorite

Toys or tasty Bones to keep it occupied while you're gone.

■ It's questionable whether a television or radio playing will do anything to relieve a dog of boredom. The only thing it may relieve is your sense of guilt.

BOWING See PLAY-BOWING.

BRAIN DISORDERS

The term "brain disorder" is often used by lay people to refer to neurologic diseases and disorders that affect a dog's brain or brainstem. There are many different kinds of neurologic disorders that dogs can suffer from. A large number of them are genetic, but they can also be caused by an injury, poisoning, or metabolic imbalance. Genetic neurological disorders often don't surface until a dog reaches maturity.

Brain disorders or dysfunctions can take various forms. They can be manifested by abnormal physical signs and/or behaviors such as loss of balance, circling, head tilts, staring into space, and snapping at invisible objects. Epileptic seizures are a common and serious form of neurological disorder in dogs, but can often be successfully treated with drug therapy. Idiopathic Aggression is believed to be caused by a brain disorder.

If you suspect your pet is suffering from any kind of neurologic dysfunction or disorder, seek veterinary help right away.

See also box, SEIZURES IN DOGS, p. 259.

BRUSHING PROBLEMS (See also box, MASSAGE FOR DOGS, p. 200; box, PATTING A DOG, p. 235.)

Problem 1: Susie read it was a good idea to groom a dog regularly, even when it had short hair. So she put her eight-month-old border terrier on a towel on the kitchen counter, got out an old hairbrush, and began to brush the dog. At first, he seemed to like it when she gently brushed the top of his head and shoulders, but as she moved along his body he began to get tense, and all of a sudden he turned around and nipped her hand.

Problem 2: The soft-coated wheaten terrier had always enjoyed being brushed, but because her owner had been away, she hadn't been groomed for a while and had developed some bad mats in her coat. When her owner tried to brush her, the dog snarled, showed her teeth, and ran away. Now every time the owner gets the brush out, the dog growls and runs off.

DIAGNOSIS

Although these problem reactions have different causes, both dogs are defending themselves in an automatic way from something that either frightens or hurts them.

Brushing should be a regular part of every dog's life, and is usually a routine that's enjoyed by both dog and owner. If a puppy is regularly brushed gently while it's growing up, it will learn to enjoy it. But if a half-grown dog has never before been brushed, like the border terrier above, it may be afraid and apprehensive because it doesn't know what's going on.

Even a dog that loves to be brushed, like the wheaten terrier, will react badly if it's in pain. When fur becomes matted it eventually tightens the skin and makes it very tender. Any attempt to brush a badly matted dog will hurt the animal, and it may well defend itself by nipping.

TREATMENT

Problem 1: To accustom a nervous dog to brushing, there are several steps you can take. *(See also box,* MASSAGE FOR DOGS, p. 200.)

- Some dogs are fearful of unknown objects, so the first thing you should do is allow your pet to investigate the brush. Put the brush on the floor and let the dog sniff it. Then pick up the brush and let the animal sniff it while you're holding it.

- With the leash on, lift the dog up onto a table or counter. A leash not only restrains a dog but gives it a sense of security at the same time. Working on a counter or tabletop prevents the dog from trying to escape.
- Start off by stroking the dog gently all over its body. Then repeat the process, using your fingertips and nails to "brush" the dog. Do this every day until the animal relaxes and begins to enjoy the attention. Talk soothingly to your pet all the time and tell it how good it is and give it a treat at the end of the session.
- Now bring the brush out and allow the dog to sniff it again. After petting and stroking the animal to relax it, begin to brush it very gently all over. Talk soothingly all the while. Be firm—don't allow the dog to decide it doesn't want you to brush certain areas of its body, but gently insist. Soon the dog will realize that you're not going to hurt it and will remain calm. There are often certain parts of the body that your dog will never like having touched, but it should be able to learn to at least tolerate being brushed in these areas.

Problem 2: When a dog has become badly matted like the wheaten terrier above, you must be especially careful.

- The best thing to do is take the animal to a professional groomer to be dematted and cleaned up. This way the dog won't associate you with a bad experience and you can continue its brushing sessions at home.
- However, if the dog was frightened or hurt when you tried to remove the mats it may take a while to regain its trust. Go slowly and, if necessary, follow the treatment for Problem 1 to desensitize the animal and reprogram it to again enjoy being brushed by you. It will help if you give the dog a food treat after each brushing session so that the experience will have pleasant associations.

BULLYING/BOSSINESS *See* DOMINANCE-RELATED AGGRESSION.

BUMPING INTO PEOPLE See FACE RUBBING; HERDING BEHAVIOR PROBLEMS; LEANING ON PEOPLE.

BURYING FOOD/BONES (See also DIGGING: DIGGING OUTDOORS.)

Problem: Every time the Days give their Boston terrier a dog biscuit, he runs outdoors, digs a hole in the edge of the flower bed, and carefully buries it. The dog never seems to go back for the buried biscuits but keeps asking for more. They've found literally hundreds of half-decayed biscuits, plus a few beef knuckle bones, in the flower bed and thrown them out.

DIAGNOSIS

Burying bones and other food is an instinctive form of hoarding or food storage that dogs have inherited from their ancestors the wolves. Wolves regularly bury small prey to go back to when their primary food supply is low for some reason. Although some dogs have retained the burying instinct, a pet dog has no need to call on this reserve food, so it usually remains buried until it rots away.

TREATMENT

- There is no foolproof treatment for this habit, except to be sure the dog doesn't have access to the yard until it's eaten its biscuits.
- If you want to try a Setup, here's how. Buy a mouse trap, dig a hole in the dog's favorite burying spot, set the trap, place it in the hole with a sheet of newspaper on top, and cover it gently with earth. When the dog begins to dig, the trap will go off and startle it. The dog will probably forget about burying, but there's no assurance that a persistent burier won't simply find another location for its hoarding.
- Some people advocate burying chicken wire just under the surface of the earth so a dog can't dig far. If a dog is a dedicated burier this might require an entire chicken-wired yard in order to succeed.

■ Alternatively, if your yard is fenced so other dogs can't get in, you can put the dog outside leashed to a trolley. Put the trolley in an area where there are no flower beds or valuable bushes, and make the lead short enough so the dog can't reach the beds but can still run around and get some exercise.

C

CAGE See *box*, CRATES FOR DOGS, p. 78.

CAR PROBLEMS

NOTE: *Never leave your dog alone in a parked car. It could be dog-napped, but more important it could die if the sun heats the car too much. A dog cools itself by panting—a very inefficient method—and will soon suffer from heat stroke and brain damage in a hot car. In weather as cool as seventy degrees it takes only a few minutes of sun to heat the interior of a car to well over a hundred!*

CAR CHASING See CHASING PROBLEMS: CHASING CARS.

CAR MANNERS

Problem: Oscar narrowly missed a head-on collision in his car when he was taking his Airedale, Shandy, to the veterinarian's office for a checkup. He was driving along with Shandy on the front seat next to him when a girl with a big Newfoundland walked by on the driver's side of the road. Just as a small red truck came around the corner in the opposite direction, Shandy leaped onto Oscar's lap to scream and bark at the Newf out of the half-open window. Oscar momentarily lost control of his car and swerved into the oncoming lane. Fortunately, the truck driver was able to stop, averting a serious accident. Shaken, Oscar scolded Shandy severely and drove slowly on.

DIAGNOSIS
Most dogs enjoy car riding, but serious automobile accidents can and do occur when dogs that haven't been taught car manners jump on their owners or become tangled between their feet when they're driving. A dog has no way of knowing how to act in a moving car unless it's been taught. Added to this, many dogs ride in cars only once or twice a year—to go to the doctor or groomer, for instance—so have no opportunity to practice good car manners. It does no good to scold a dog after it's caused a problem in a car. That only serves to confuse the animal and make it nervous.

TREATMENT
You must be absolutely sure your dog is under control if you're going to drive alone with it in the car, no matter how small the animal is. This is for the dog's sake as well as yours.

- Never drive with car windows all the way down if your pet's in the car. The dog might take it into its head to jump out. Or flying dust or debris could severely damage a dog's eyes.
- Even if you don't think you'll often take your dog in the car with you, the most practical thing to do is teach it how to ride in a moving car when it's a puppy. First, put the puppy in the car and tell it to sit. It can ride in the front with you or in the backseat, but it must learn to stay quietly until you tell it it's all right to move around. *(See also box,* SOCIALIZATION, THE KEY TO A WELL-ADJUSTED DOG, p. 271.)
- Take the puppy with you on short trips, around the block or up to the corner. Go to the park, get out and

take a short walk, then get back in the car. This will help to socialize the puppy to car travel. Then you can graduate to longer trips in busier areas until you're sure the dog knows what's expected of it no matter what the distractions are.

- Take practice runs from time to time to reinforce your pet's car manners.
- At first, always hold your dog's leash when you're riding in the car. This will give you control over the animal. The minute it begins to act excited or upset, snap the leash and say "No."
- Alternatively, special car-riding "seat belts" for dogs are available in pet stores and by mail order. Adjustable harnesses that come in various sizes, they attach to a car's existing seat belt. One of these devices will keep an animal from harm in case of a hasty stop or even an accident, and also keeps a dog quiet and in its place as you drive.
- An overly excitable small dog may travel better in a carrying case. The case will keep the animal safe and quiet and also prevent it from becoming upset at outside sights. This method of car travel can also help a carsick dog—see below.
- If you have a station wagon or van, a large dog that's accustomed to a Crate can ride in one in the back. There are also wire barriers on the market to close off the back of a wagon. These, too, provide the animal with security and prevent any interference with the driver.

CAR SICKNESS

Problem: The Carpenters had anticipated driving to their new country cottage every weekend with their basset hound, Pete, but they find they have a bad problem. They get no farther than the corner when Pete begins to pant rapidly and whine piteously, and before long he throws up all over the back of the car. They're at their wits end— they can't leave him home every weekend, but they really can't stand to take him with them in the car.

DIAGNOSIS

Dogs get carsick for several reasons. If a dog hasn't been socialized to car riding when it's young, nervousness may cause it to become upset enough to vomit. Other animals seem to be particularly susceptible to motion sickness. Puppies in particular are apt to become nauseated in a car; they often outgrow this tendency. *(See also box,* SOCIALIZATION, THE KEY TO A WELL-ADJUSTED DOG, p. 271.)

TREATMENT

- Don't give a puppy or dog anything to eat or drink for several hours before a car ride. An animal with an empty stomach usually won't vomit. Wait until you get to your destination to let your pet drink and have a snack.

- If your dog is an adult that hasn't been socialized to car riding, suspect nerves as the primary cause of its trouble. Try socializing it gradually to the car just as you would a puppy. Follow the steps in the discussion of car manners, to do this. Once the dog realizes nothing bad will happen when it goes in the car with you and that it will end up in a nice place with you at the end of the trip, it may overcome its nervousness and become a good car rider.

- When a puppy or dog continues to become sick in the car despite your efforts to calm it, the next step is to put it in a carrying case or covered crate in the car. Motion sickness is often closely related to vision, and it may be that the rapidly passing landscape makes the animal nauseated. It may feel better if it can't see outside the car.

- If none of these steps does the trick, consult your veterinarian. It's possible that a mild tranquilizer may help your dog relax and get over its nervousness and nausea.

CAR TRAVEL *(See also* VISITING WITH A DOG.)

Problem: Vicki wants to take her Maltese, Whitey, on a four-day car trip. The dog loves to ride in the car and is very well behaved, but Vicki wants to be sure everything will go smoothly.

DIAGNOSIS

Car travel with a well-behaved dog usually presents no problems as long as you prepare ahead of time. If your dog has barking problems, is especially nervous, or suffers from extreme Separation Anxiety, it's best to make other plans. It can be very difficult if not impossible to deal with behavior problems when you're away from home, and a bad-mannered or excitable dog will make your trip miserable.

TREATMENT

To make sure your trip goes smoothly, follow these steps:

- Even a well-socialized, calm dog may be a bit stressed in strange surroundings, and stress makes any animal more susceptible to disease. So be sure your dog's immunizations are up-to-date.
- Take along an ample supply of your dog's food, any medications it currently uses, and some familiar toys and chewies. Also take a thermos of water and a bowl so you can offer the dog water while you're on the road.
- If you are going to stay in a motel or hotel along the way, be sure to make reservations ahead of time and ascertain the motel or hotel does take animals. A bed or familiar article of your clothing will make it easier for your dog to stay quietly alone in a strange room when you go out to eat.
- Be especially careful to keep your dog under complete control in any strange place. Walk only in designated areas and be sure to clean up after your pet.

CASTRATION OF MALE DOGS—FACTS & MYTHS

Castrating, or neutering, a male dog can prevent many behavior problems from developing and can also help to ameliorate or even solve existing behavior problems. Castration will reduce a dog's aggressiveness, territoriality, tendency to roam, mounting behavior, and other sexually motivated behaviors that are not desirable in a pet. It can also prevent many hormone-related disorders such as testicular cancer and prostate abscesses that often develop in older, unneutered male dogs. Finally, it is the most effective and permanent means of birth control for a male animal.

The operation itself is relatively uncomplicated and poses little danger to a dog. It can be performed at any age. Puppies are usually neutered at around six or seven months of age, depending on their size and breed.

Fortunately, more and more people now accept this preventive surgery as a normal part of responsible pet ownership. The old myths about castration making a dog less brave or masculine, or causing it to become fat, have been dispelled. Most owners now realize the operation has long-lasting physical and behavioral benefits for a male dog.

See also box, MALE DOGS' BEHAVIORAL CHARACTERISTICS, p. 198.

CATS, AGGRESSION TOWARD See PREDATORY AGGRESSION.

CHASE BEHAVIOR

Chase behavior is a very strong canine instinct. In the wild, a wolf must immediately chase an animal that's running away or it will go hungry. This automatic reaction has been inherited by all dogs, and has been highly developed in some breeds, such as greyhounds. A dog that's concentrating on a chase can be extremely difficult to stop. Once a chasing dog reaches its prey it often tries to stop it or make it go in another direction by nipping at its heels in a classic herding action.

See also HERDING BEHAVIOR PROBLEMS; NIPPING.

CHASING PROBLEMS

CHASING ANIMALS *See* PREDATORY AGGRESSION.

CHASING BICYCLES

Problem: Ebony, a shaggy black mixed-breed, is well mannered in every respect but one. Whenever she sees a bicycle going by on the road in front of her house, she races out to chase it. Adults can quickly outride her and soon she drops back and returns to her lawn, but several neighborhood children have fallen when she leaped up against their bicycles, nipped at their feet and ankles, and knocked them over. Ebony's owners know it's only a matter of time until a child suffers from a broken bone or worse.

DIAGNOSIS

A bicycle's turning wheels are guaranteed to trigger Chase Behavior in most dogs.

TREATMENT

There are two approaches to use to stop a dog from chasing anyone or anything that goes by the house. The first treatment is aimed at startling the dog out of the behavior. This requires the cooperation and help of the "chasee." In the case of a bicycle rider, it goes like this:

- Arm the rider with a Water Balloon and have him pedal along the road past the dog. As soon as the dog begins to give chase, the rider throws the balloon right in the animal's face. At the same time, you and the rider both shout "NO!" in your loudest, harshest voices.
- Repeat the water balloon treatments until the dog decides to give up bicycle chasing.
- Another method is gravel-tossing by both the rider and you. As the dog begins to give chase, the rider throws a handful of gravel at it while shouting "No! Go home!" Or you can rush out and toss the gravel at the dog at the same time you shout "No!" Be very careful the gravel doesn't hit the dog in the face.

The second treatment method is aimed at reprogramming the dog and depends to a certain extent on your knowing when the rider will go by your house. It goes like this:

- Put the dog on a leash and go outside with it when you know the rider is about to go by. The minute the dog begins to give chase, give a quick Leash Correction and say "No."
- After you've done this for several days, put the leash on the dog but don't hold it. As the bicycle appears, say "No." If the dog obeys, praise it lavishly.
- The next step is to remove the leash and rely only on the verbal command. Again, tell your dog how good it is when it acts correctly.

- If you can enlist the aid of the rider, ask him or her to say "NO, GO HOME!" to the dog as it nears the edge of your property. This will serve to reinforce your training.

CHASING CARS

This problem has the same roots as Chasing Bicycles. The major difference is that car chasing can be much more dangerous for a dog. The diagnosis and treatments are the same as those for chasing bicycles.

CHASING PEOPLE

Again, the problem is rooted in traditional Chase Behavior. If a dog regularly chases a jogger, say, who goes by your house at the same time every day, you can treat the problem in the same way as you would if the dog chased a bicycle rider.

Zack, a bulldog, accepts a rawhide Chew Toy from his owner. Note the Chew Toy is just the right size for his mouth. (Bruce Plotkin)

CHEW TOYS FOR DOGS

Dogs should be given toys to chew for the health of their gums and teeth and to provide needed chewing exercise. Puppies in particular need appropriate items to chew when they're teething to prevent them from chewing household objects. *(See also box,* TEETHING BEHAVIOR, p. 283.)

There are a number of different kinds of dog chew toys available. Rawhide chew toys are generally considered safe for dogs, as long as they are the correct size. Too-small or too-soft rawhides will break down into small pieces that could cause choking. Well-made latex or vinyl toys with squeaks inside are also safe as long as they are strong enough so your dog can't get at the squeak. A relatively new item on the market is cotton rope, designed to actually "floss" a dog's teeth. Rope chew toys come in various shapes to please a dog.

Some dogs prefer one kind of chew toy, some another. Offer a variety of toys at first. Then when your dog indicates a preference for one type, buy several so a chew toy is always on hand whenever your pet has the urge to chew.

Most dogs take immediately to chew toys, but some may require encouragement. If your puppy or dog doesn't seem to know what to do with a chew toy, hide a food treat inside the toy, or rub the toy with soft cheese or peanut butter to give the dog the idea. Once your dog begins to chew the toy, praise it lavishly.

See also box, BONES FOR DOGS, p. 45; TOYS FOR DOGS.

CHEWING PROBLEMS *(See also* DESTRUCTIVE BEHAVIOR; SEPARATION ANXIETY.)

CHEWING OBJECTS/CLOTHING (See also EXPLORATORY BEHAVIOR; PICA.)

Problem: Now that Jo-Jo, her nine-month-old beagle, was completely house-trained, Melissa thought it was safe to give the dog the run of the apartment when she went to work. But she was in for a terrible shock! When she walked into her apartment in the evening, the first thing she noticed was a couple of her shoes lying on the hall floor. The shoes were badly chewed. Then when she went into the living room, she was really shocked. The sofa cushions were on the floor, stuffing poking out of them, and the leg of her favorite footstool was chewed almost in half. Jo-Jo was nowhere to be seen until Melissa looked in the bedroom. There was the dog, happily gnawing on Melissa's favorite sweater. Melissa was so upset she didn't know what to do.

DIAGNOSIS

Chewing is a normal canine behavior. Dogs use their mouths and noses to explore their environments; they also chew because it feels good to them and relieves tension and anxiety, and because they simply enjoy it. All puppies chew, especially when they're teething. Chewing helps puppies relieve the pressure and pain of erupting teeth, just as it does for babies and toddlers. They also chew things such as rocks and sticks in an effort to obtain extra calcium.

Owners often think it's not necessary to teach a puppy not to chew household objects because it will "outgrow" the habit. This is a big mistake. A puppy that's allowed to chew its owner's possessions will grow up to be a dog that chews its owner's possessions.

Sometimes an owner unwittingly creates a problem when he gives a puppy something such as an old sock or slipper to chew. Later, when the puppy chews on a good pair of socks or new shoes, the owner is horrified. But if he stopped to think about it, he would realize he shouldn't expect a dog to know the difference between an old shoe and a new one.

A dog that's feeling especially stressed or anxious sometimes takes to chewing, even though it's never chewed before. So may a dog that's suddenly left alone for long periods of time. In this case, the chewing is one of many symptoms of Separation Anxiety.

TREATMENT

Because chewing is an ingrained, normal habit of dogs, you shouldn't try to prevent your dog from chewing. You should redirect your dog's chewing instinct so it chews what you want it to. Punishment or scolding rarely help prevent a dog from chewing. As a matter of fact, harsh punishment can make a chewing problem worse by causing a dog to feel anxious and stressed. In all cases, provide your pet with acceptable Chew Toys or Bones.

- One way to stop a dog from chewing a forbidden object is to catch it in the act and startle it into stopping by shouting "NO!" and clapping your hands, or tossing a Noisemaker at it.
- At the same time, redirect your dog's chewing behavior by handing it a Bone or Chew Toy and praising the animal when it begins to chew on the toy. If the pet doesn't chew on the toy, try the steps mentioned in *box*, CHEW TOYS FOR DOGS, p 61.
- Some dogs can be prevented from chewing if you spray the forbidden object with a nasty-tasting liquid (*see box*, LIQUIDS AS AIDS IN BEHAVIOR MODIFICATION, p. 196). This only works, however, when a dog's chewing behavior is directed at only one object or type of object. Otherwise, a determined chewer will simply go to work on something else in the house.
- If you're not going to be at home, don't give a chewing dog the opportunity to reinforce its bad habit. Confine it in its Crate or in a room where there's little or nothing to chew, such as a kitchen or bathroom. Be sure to provide a confined dog with several Chew Toys and/or Bones.
- Finally, when a dog persistently chews inappropriate objects despite all of your efforts to redirect its actions,

suspect a physical problem. Tooth pain (see box, TEETH-
ING BEHAVIOR, p. 283), stomach problems, and nutri-
tional imbalances can all create the desire to chew.
Take your pet to the veterinarian for an evaluation.

CHEWING SELF See box, ACRAL LICK DERMATITIS/GRANU-
LOMA, p. 4; box, FLANK SUCKING, p. 125.

CHILDREN AND DOGS

BABIES AND DOGS See JEALOUSY: JEALOUSY OF A NEW BABY.

TODDLERS AND DOGS (See also FEAR-INDUCED
AGGRESSION; FOOD-GUARDING AGGRESSION; OBJECT-GUARDING
AGGRESSION; PAIN-INDUCED AGGRESSION; box, TERRITORIAL
BEHAVIOR, p. 289.)

PROBLEM:

The Smiths are worried. Maisie, their ten-year-old otter
hound, accepted their child, Sam, calmly when he was a
baby. But now that Sam's beginning to walk around, it's
a different story. Whenever Maisie's asleep and the
youngster toddles over to her, the animal growls. And
when Sam grabs onto her fur with his little hands, Maisie
turns around as if to nip him. So far, nothing bad has happened, but the Smiths are afraid Sam may be bitten. They
love their dog and don't want to have to give her up,
however.

DIAGNOSIS

An older dog that calmly accepts an infant can easily feel
threatened when the child becomes a toddler and begins
to walk around and invade the animal's territory. A dog
that allows the adults in its family to handle its food
bowls, bed, and toys may perceive a small toddler as another animal and become territorial. At the same time, a
toddler can frighten or hurt an animal with loud steps, a
high-pitched voice, and grasping hands. A toddler who

startles a sleeping dog by stepping on it or stumbling over it might even be bitten.

TREATMENT

As a baby grows into a toddler it must be carefully taught how to behave around a dog. At the same time, the dog must be watched carefully and shown what's expected of it. Although a child will soon outgrow the toddling stage, the lessons it learns now will form the basis of its interaction with animals throughout its lifetime. By the same token, a dog that's learned to accept one toddler calmly should be able to behave properly around all young children.

Here are some steps you can take to smooth the way toward a good dog-toddler relationship.

- Until you're completely sure your dog can be totally trusted with a toddler and vice versa, never leave the two alone, even for a minute. Supervise any child-dog interactions.
- Find a time when you can sit quietly in a room with the dog while the child plays nearby so the dog understands the child is part of the family group, or pack.
- The dog should be obedience-trained (*see box,* OBEDIENCE TRAINING, p. 218), know the meaning of "No," and be able to respond to down/stay, or Go to Your Place. A dog that's well trained has a built-in safety valve and is more able to be trusted around all children than a nondisciplined animal.
- Now is the time to teach the dog not to jump up on people if it hasn't already learned this lesson. For how to do this, *see* JUMPING PROBLEMS: JUMPING ON PEOPLE IN THE HOME IN GREETING. If the dog should accidentally knock a toddler over it could cause the child to become fearful of all dogs.
- Take time to spend some quiet moments every day with the dog alone, playing or simply petting it so it still feels secure and loved by you.
- Teach the child never to disturb the dog when it's sleeping, eating, or chewing on a bone or toy, and show

it how to be careful when walking around the dog so it doesn't accidentally step on it. Even if your own dog is completely trustworthy in this respect, these are valuable safety lessons for a child and can never be learned too young.

- Show the child how to approach the dog slowly, hold a hand out to the animal, and pet it nicely on its back or underneath the chin. Don't allow the child to grasp the dog's fur, ears, or tail. These actions could hurt a dog enough so it might snap.
- All the while you're working with the child, talk to the dog softly and tell it how good it is.
- Allow the dog to be present when you're performing everyday actions with the child. Have it in the room during toilet training or diaper changing, while the child is bathed, dressed, and put to bed. All of these parent-child interactions will help the dog understand this is still a baby who needs to be nurtured and treated gently.
- An older dog that doesn't feel well or is in pain may never learn to relax around small children. If you have a dog such as this you'll have to separate child and dog, at least until the child is old enough to understand the animal's moods and needs.

DOGS AND OLDER CHILDREN

Problem: Ten-year-old Ruthie and her family moved out of the city to the suburbs over the summer. In the fall, Ruthie wanted her parents to let her walk the short distance up a hill to school by herself. Most of the children from the block walked to school, and she wanted to be "one of the crowd." Although there was a town ordinance requiring that dogs be confined or leashed, several large dogs regularly ran loose in the neighborhood first thing in the morning. Ruthie's parents feared the dogs might bother the child, who had little experience with dogs.

DIAGNOSIS

It's very important for a child to learn how to act around strange dogs, especially if she's apt to be alone outdoors. According to statistics, school-age children are the most frequent victims of dog bites. They can be bitten because they tease or threaten a dog, but most often it's because they don't understand how to act around dogs and are perceived as a threat by a dog. Parents and other adults need to learn as much as they can about canine behavior and pass the information along to their children.

Although most pet dogs won't do anything to harm a child, a highly territorial animal may take umbrage if anyone walks on its property. Also, a loose dog that joins an informal pack of other dogs will often revert to pack behavior and act in a less civilized way than normal.

TREATMENT

Learn how to interpret dogs' body language and teach this important skill to your child (see How to Interpret Your Dog's Body Language, Facial Expressions, and Vocalizations, p. xi). All children should be taught the following, even if it's unlikely they will ever meet up with a strange or unfriendly dog. Only one bad incident may thoroughly frighten a child or result in injury.

- *Never* approach a dog you don't know without asking the owner first. If there's no owner present, don't approach the dog.
- Even with an owner's permission, *never* run up to a dog, raise your arms or wave them around, or jump up and down in front of the dog. A dog may interpret any of these actions as threats. Stay calm and quiet when you approach a dog that doesn't know you.
- If you want to make friends with a dog that doesn't know you, extend your hand slowly toward it, with the palm facing down and your fingers curled underneath. Allow the dog to sniff your hand. If the animal seems calm and friendly, then you can turn your hand over slowly and gently begin to stroke the animal on its

back. *Never* put your hand over a dog's head; this may be seen as a threatening gesture by a dog.

- If you see two dogs fighting, *never* get between them or try to stop them, even if one of the dogs is your own. You could easily be bitten accidentally. Get adult help.

- *Don't lean or squat down to a dog's eye level* when you greet a strange dog. Aggressive dogs stare into each other's eyes as a challenge to fight *(see* EYE CONTACT; NEGATIVE EYE CONTACT). In addition, if you assume a position that's lower than the dog's it is a signal to the animal that you're submissive to it—this is a clear-cut invitation to a dog to be aggressive. *(See box,* AGGRESSIVE BEHAVIOR IN DOGS, p. 7; *box,* DOMINANT BEHAVIOR, p. 98; *box,* SUBMISSIVE BEHAVIOR, p. 276.)

- If a dog runs toward you, *don't run away.* Running will trigger a dog's chase instinct. *(See box,* CHASE BEHAVIOR, p. 58; *box,* FLIGHT BEHAVIOR, p. 126.)

- Instead, hard as it may be, *stay still.* Stand quietly with your arms at your side, or lie facedown on the ground and stay still. Don't wave your arms around—again, the dog may think you're threatening it, which will make it angry. If you stay quiet, almost all dogs will lose interest in you in a few moments and go away. If more than one dog is present and the animals form a circle around you, do the same thing and wait until all the dogs back off before you move.

- If you're carrying something you don't want a dog to get, your lunch for instance, the temptation is to raise it above your head out of reach. *Don't lift anything up away from the dog,* because this is a clear play signal and most dogs will jump up to grab an object that's held aloft.

- If you can muster up a strong-sounding voice, tell the animal in firm tones, "Go home!" Many dogs are so well trained to respond to this command they'll stop in their tracks and go off toward home.

DOGS AND VISITING CHILDREN (See also TERRITORIAL AGGRESSION; *box*, TERRITORIAL BEHAVIOR, p. 289.)

Problem: Schatzi, the Kellys' Doberman, grew up with the two children in the family and was sweet as could be with them. Problems arose, however, when the children grew up and went to school. When one of the youngsters brought a friend home to play, Schatzi became very aggressive toward the visitor. As soon as the children walked in the door, the dog began to bark aggressively, growl, and even approach the visiting child on stiff legs, hackles raised. The first time it happened, Mrs. Kelly immediately grabbed Schatzi by the collar, led her off to the bedroom, and closed the door. But now she's worried. What if she hadn't been right there when the children came in?

DIAGNOSIS

A highly territorial dog may perceive a visitor as a threat, especially if the animal has been raised with children and considers them part of her pack. Schatzi was protecting *her* youngster against a stranger.

Dogs may carry this type of protective behavior a step further and go after anyone who walks too close to the family on the street.

TREATMENT

A dog that goes too far with its protective instincts must be desensitized and taught to accept friendly visitors in its home, children or adults.

- Until you have desensitized the dog *(see box, DEPROGRAMMING AND DESENSITIZATION, p. 88)* and are sure it won't attack visiting children, always keep it confined whenever visitors are expected.
- To teach a dog to accept visitors you must show it that you accept them. Put the dog on leash and take it into the room where the visiting child is playing. Sit down and talk to the children and let the dog watch them play. Speak softly and calmly to the dog and tell it how

good it is. Pet it and see if you can get it to relax. Stay in the room for at least a half hour and then leave with the dog. Do this every time there's a visiting child until the dog learns to relax while you keep it by your side.

- Once the dog has learned to relax in the presence of visiting children, walk it directly over to where the children are playing. If the dog begins to tense, growls, or barks, correct it immediately with a snap of the leash and "No." Take it back to the chair and sit down.
- Go through these steps as often as needed. Once the dog is able to approach a visiting child with no problem, sit down right next to the children with the dog still leashed. Invite the visiting child to pet the dog. Always keep a close watch and tight lead on the animal until you're sure everything's all right.
- Once the dog is able to accept a visiting child while the child plays with your youngster, you have to be sure it will be friendly when a visiting child comes into the house. Sometimes a highly territorial dog will be fine with visitors once they're inside, but will try to bar them from entering in the first place. Again, use the leash and your verbal corrections to teach the dog it's all right to allow visiting children into the house. You may have to continue to keep the dog leashed for some time to be sure it understands. If you think a child might come to visit when you're not at home, close up the dog until you're certain it won't cause a problem.

CHOKE COLLARS See *box*, TRAINING COLLARS, p. 299.

CIRCLING BEHAVIOR (See *also* BALL-PLAYING FETISH; *box*, BRAIN DISORDERS, p. 47; *box*, OBSESSIVE-COMPULSIVE BEHAVIOR IN DOGS, p. 222.)

Problem: Bonzo, a beagle mix, is driving her owners crazy. Every time anyone in the family gets up and moves to walk to another room, pick something up, or whatever, the dog runs around and around in circles, nonstop. If someone sits down, the dogs sits by his side, but as soon as he stands up the circling begins again. The dog is wearing everyone out with her continuous, frenzied circling activity and is completely unheeding of commands to stop.

DIAGNOSIS

Dogs that indulge in this type of compulsive, mindless behavior usually have some type of brain damage. They become overexcited whenever anyone stands up or moves, don't know what to do, and simply end up going in crazy circles. Circling shouldn't be confused with more normal types of hyperactivity *(see* ABNORMAL ACTIVITY LEVELS: HYPERACTIVITY*)* or with Tail-Chasing/Biting.

TREATMENT

There is often nothing to be done to eliminate this behavior, but it can be brought under control to a certain extent.

- The first thing you should do is take the dog to the veterinarian. Sometimes drug therapy can help calm down a dog that becomes frenzied on a regular basis.
- You can curtail the behavior through Obedience Training. Once the dog is taught to walk on a leash you can use the leash to calm it down. When it starts to circle mindlessly, take out the leash, snap it on, and tell the dog to heel *(see box,* HEELING, p. 148*)*. Then walk around for a few minutes until the dog is calm. After you do this a few times, some dogs will learn to calm down immediately as soon as they see the leash.
- If the dog is calm only when the leash is on, leave the dog leashed in the house and attach the end of the leash to a nearby doorknob, for instance, so the dog can remain in the room with you.
- Alternatively, keep the dog in a Crate in the room with you.

COLLARS FOR DOGS

There are a number of different kinds of dog collars. Some are designed to be used for training and others for everyday walking, and still others are primarily decorative.

Lightweight elastic collars are made for puppies. Although they are good first collars, they don't last very long.

Leather collars come in different colors. They can be flat or rolled and are put on with buckles. Rolled collars have no edges to fray and are sturdier than flat ones. Lightweight leather is a good material for a puppy's first collar.

Nylon is very light and durable. Nylon collars with buckles are also used for puppies and small dogs. Training collars are now made in nylon as well as chain and work well for animals with long coats that might get tangled in a chain, or those with sensitive necks.

Training collars are also made of a variety of materials and come in various weights and lengths to suit any size dog. These collars are straight with large rings on each end. For more about how to put on and use this type of collar, *see box,* TRAINING COLLARS, p. 299.

Whatever type of collar you choose, it is essential that it fit your dog correctly. A too-small collar will choke the animal, while a too-large collar will slip off right over the dog's head. To determine the proper collar size, measure your dog's neck where it joins the shoulders and add two or three inches. If the collar you choose has an adjustable buckle, purchase one a size too big so your puppy won't outgrow it too fast. Check the size of a puppy's collar once a week—puppies grow very fast!

COLLAR, TEACHING PUPPY TO WEAR

Problem: Mary bought a pretty red collar for her three-month-old Scottie puppy. But when she put it on and set the puppy on the floor, the animal had a violent reaction. It ran around in circles, shook its head vigorously, and repeatedly rubbed its neck on the carpet and furniture.

DIAGNOSIS
A puppy may not like the feeling of a collar around its neck the first time one is put on and will go into frenzies trying to get the collar off.

TREATMENT

- When a puppy becomes frantic with a collar on, take the collar off immediately.
- Next day, sit down and put the puppy on your lap. Pet it and talk to it soothingly as you buckle the collar on. Keep the puppy in your lap with the collar on for a few minutes so it can get the feel of it.
- As soon as you put the puppy on the floor, initiate a favorite game or give it a wonderful new toy to explore. This will take the pup's mind off the collar.
- Another ploy is to feed the puppy immediately after you put the collar on. This will not only serve as a distraction but give collar-wearing a pleasant association.
- When the puppy has worn the collar without a bad reaction for a few minutes, take the collar off and then put it back on again so the animal becomes used to the process.
- Never leave a puppy alone with a collar on. It could easily catch the collar on something and hurt itself. But do put the collar on every day so the puppy is completely comfortable in it when it's time to teach it to walk on a leash.

COMMANDS, HOW TO GIVE See *box,* TALKING TO YOUR DOG, p. 282.

COMMUNICATING WITH YOUR DOG See *box*, TALKING TO YOUR DOG, p. 282.

COMPULSIVE BEHAVIOR See *box*, OBSESSIVE-COMPULSIVE BEHAVIOR IN DOGS, p. 222.

CONDITIONED BEHAVIOR

Conditioned behavior, sometimes called conditioned response, is behavior that has been taught over a period of time until it has become automatic. The behavior may be bad or good and can be learned through repetition or reward and reinforcement. For example, when a begging dog is regularly given a piece of food from the table, begging behavior is reinforced and becomes a conditioned behavior. To recondition or countercondition an undesirable habit, a dog must be systematically desensitized and taught a new set of responses.

On the positive side, Obedience Training on all levels relies on conditioned behavior for its success. A well-trained dog has been conditioned through repetition and reward in the form of Praise to respond to signals and commands in a certain way.

See also box, DEPROGRAMMING AND DESENSITIZATION, p. 88; *box*, REINFORCEMENT—REPETITION AND REWARD IN TRAINING, p. 253.

CONVULSIONS See *box*, SEIZURES IN DOGS, p. 259.

COPROPHAGIA (Feces-Eating, Stool-Eating)

Problem: Chuck is totally disgusted with his English bulldog, Daphne. When he lets her out in the yard, she sniffs all around until she finds a piece of her own feces that Chuck hasn't cleaned up yet, and eats it. He's sure it isn't good for her to eat her own wastes, but more important, he finds himself avoiding her doggy kisses and licks. He can't help remembering what she's just eaten when she puts her face near his.

DIAGNOSIS

Coprophagia, or stool-eating, is very common among wolves as well as dogs and is probably related to two normal canine behaviors. Mother wolves and dogs always consume their pups' wastes until the youngsters are old enough to leave the den. Also, dogs and wolves in the wild often eat the droppings of large hooved herbivorous animals. This manure contains undigested nutrients.

Some animal behaviorists feel it's simply an unpleasant behavior that has become a bad habit when adult domestic dogs regularly eat their own or other dogs' droppings. In my opinion, both types of coprophagia arc nutritional in origin. If a dog's digestive system is unable to absorb certain nutrients from its food, these dietary elements are passed out of its body in the stool. Then the animal's natural instinct is to eat its own stool in an effort to supply its body with these nutrients. When it eats other dogs' stools, it's also trying to make up for nutritional deficiencies. It also stands a good chance of picking up the eggs of intestinal parasites when it does so. Fortunately, now that poop-scoop laws are enforced in most communities it's more difficult for a dog to find other animals' leavings.

A puppy left alone for long periods of time in a small area with its own wastes may take to playing with and even eating its stools out of Boredom.

Whatever the reason or reasons for coprophagia, it's considered a disgusting habit by most dog owners.

TREATMENT

When a dog has a well-developed habit of coprophagia, scolding will do no good, nor will strong repellents. The only way to solve the problem is to prevent it or get at the root of it.

- The first step should be to take the dog to the veterinarian to discuss the dog's diet. The availability of nutrients—their ability to be absorbed in an animal's body—differs among foods. Usually, once an animal is eating a nutritionally complete, readily absorbable diet the problem will solve itself.
- Sometimes, vitamin and/or mineral supplements are also helpful, but don't give a dog supplements without a veterinarian's advice. Oversupplementation can cause a nutritional imbalance that can result in serious physical problems.
- When a dog eats its own feces, keeping its run or yard scrupulously clean will eliminate the problem.
- If your dog finds and eats feces outdoors, keep it on a short leash when you walk it.
- Be sure your dog has plenty of acceptable things to chew on. (*See box*, BONES FOR DOGS, p. 45; *box*, CHEW TOYS FOR DOGS, p. 61.)

CORRECTING A DOG

When we speak of correcting a dog there are two steps: first, stop it from doing something; then, show it what you want it to do.

Timing is essential if a correction is going to be effective. The dog must be stopped in the act the minute it starts to misbehave. Once it has stopped and focused on you, you can then continue with the right action.

If a dog is on leash, use a Leash Correction. If the dog isn't leashed, startle it with a Noisemaker, Throw Chain, or Water Balloon to make it stop in its tracks and look at you. Then emphasize your action with a strong "NO!"

See also box, PUNISHMENT, p. 247.

CRATES FOR DOGS 77

COUPLERS

A coupler is a leash that can be used to walk two dogs at the same time. It has one handle and two ends that form a V, each leg of which is attached to a dog's collar. A coupler is especially helpful if one of your dogs is a laggard and/or one always wants to get ahead of you. It keeps both dogs in the same position and forces them to walk at the same pace. It also enables you to easily control both animals instead of being pulled in two different directions.

CRATES FOR DOGS

I refer to crates for dogs throughout this book. When used correctly, a crate is an extremely useful tool for training, retraining, housebreaking, and travel. Many, many dogs become so accustomed to their crates that they go to them voluntarily and use them exclusively for sleeping.

You can create your own wire divider for a Crate so it won't be too big for a puppy. Orsina, a Shar Pei puppy, is confined in a space just large enough for her in one end of a large Crate. As your puppy grows, move the Crate divider to create a larger and larger space. Eventually remove the divider altogether as we've done for Wrinkles, an adult Shar Pei. (Bruce Plotkin)

Crates and cratelike travel cages come in all sizes. If a crate is going to be used to help a puppy become house-trained, it should be large enough to be comfortable, but not so large there's room for the puppy to establish a bathroom area inside it. If you don't want to have to purchase larger and larger crates as your puppy grows, get a crate with an adjustable wire dividing wall that can be moved as a puppy grows, or create your own divider with wire. Don't use anything for a divider that's chewable, such as wood or cardboard, and be sure there are no sharp edges a puppy could hurt itself on.

To figure the proper size for a crate, find out how big your puppy will be as an adult and get a crate that will allow the adult animal to lie down comfortably on its side and sit or stand without hitting its head on the top. If you have doubts, consult your breeder, trainer, or veterinarian as to the right size crate to get for your puppy or dog.

A crate should never be used as a means of punishment or as a prison for a dog. Never scold a dog at the same time you put it in the crate, and try to make the crate as pleasant to be in as possible by putting in a blanket, toy, water, and so forth. Your dog should consider its crate a safe "den" to relax and feel comfortable in.

CRATE PROBLEMS

CRATE DEPENDENCY (See also box, A BED FOR A DOG, p. 31.)

Problem: Anne is upset because her Dalmatian, Snoopy, seems to like being in his crate better than being in the room with her. Every time she sits down in the living room to read, Snoopy sits with her for just a few minutes. Then he gets up and goes into the kitchen where his crate stands with the door open, goes in, curls up, and goes to sleep.

DIAGNOSIS
Like wolves, dogs like a "den" to sleep in. Some dogs have highly developed denning instincts and feel secure only when they're sleeping in a cozy enclosure such as a crate.

TREATMENT
It's difficult to change a dog's desire for a safe den in which to sleep. But you can modify the habit.

- You can reach a compromise with your dog so it will sleep in the room with you and still feel secure. Purchase an airline travel crate in the correct size for your dog. Take the door and the top half off and place the bottom of the crate near your favorite chair or your bed. It will form a cozy, high-sided "nest" for your dog to sleep in. At first you may have to lure your pet into its new bed with a favorite treat, but soon it should learn to enjoy it.

CRATE DESTRUCTION (See also DESTRUCTIVE BEHAVIOR.)

Problem: A five-year-old Shar Pei had become extremely destructive because of Separation Anxiety. He had ripped a hole in the wall by the front door and torn up the carpet. When his owners closed the dog in a bathroom he tore the wallpaper off the walls. In desperation, the owners bought a sturdy crate and put the dog in it. To their amazement, when they came home the dog was loose. He had literally destroyed the crate by chewing and prying the wire apart. They bought a stronger crate and the dog destroyed that too. Needless to say, the Shar Pei's owners are becoming desperate.

DIAGNOSIS
An older dog that's never been closed up may have a severe reaction to a crate, especially if the animal is already

badly stressed with Separation Anxiety. A really hysterical, strong dog is able to destroy even the sturdiest crate.

TREATMENT
In a case such as this, the animal must be reprogrammed to accept the crate. *(See box,* BEHAVIOR MODIFICATION, p. 34.)

- To help an older dog accept a crate, you have to create a sense of well-being for the animal. To do this, begin by crating the dog only when you're at home in the room with it. Also have it sleep in your bedroom in the crate.
- When the dog accepts this calmly, begin to feed it its meals in the crate.
- After a while the dog should be calm and happy in the crate and you should be able to leave it alone there for short periods of time.
- Gradually increase the length of time you leave the dog alone in the crate until you can be away all day with no problem.
- Once your dog is able to stay calmly without attempting to destroy the crate you can begin to leave the door of the crate open. Usually, all signs of destructiveness will have disappeared. If they recur, continue to leave the crate door closed when you're not home. After a while, try opening it again.

CRATE PROTECTION

Sometimes a dog becomes so attached to its crate that it won't allow anyone to come near it. To solve this problem, *see* TERRITORIAL AGGRESSION, treatment steps.

CRATE SOILING

Problem: Gene was confused. He'd read that a great way to house-train a puppy was to put it in a crate. So he bought a big crate, lined it with paper, and put his puppy in it. Much to his distress, the next morning the puppy had soiled all over the crate, sat in it, and made a complete mess of himself and the crate. Now Gene had to give the puppy a bath as well as clean up the mess before going to work.

DIAGNOSIS

A puppy that's been house-trained to paper has no way of knowing the paper inside a crate is *not* intended for a bathroom. It's exhibiting Conditioned Behavior when it soils the crate.

Most dogs won't soil the area in which they sleep, but if a crate is too big for a puppy, the puppy will soil in one corner and sleep in the opposite corner.

TREATMENT

- First, don't put paper in a crate.
- Second, be sure the crate is not too large. It should be just big enough for the puppy to stand and lie down comfortably. *See box,* CRATES FOR DOGS, p. 78, for how to determine the proper crate size.

D

DANCING DOBERMAN SYNDROME

Problem: Pinka, a five-year-old female Doberman pin-scher, has begun to do the oddest thing. When she stands she appears to be "dancing" as she flexes each back leg and lifts each foot in turn. She performs the action continuously whenever she's standing still. Her owners wonder why she does this. They also worry that she might be in pain.

DIAGNOSIS

This disorder has been dubbed "Dancing Doberman Syndrome" because it affects only dogs of that breed. It may occur in either sex and can begin at any age. The syndrome is only evident when a dog is standing up, and most animals with the disorder are able to walk perfectly well. As reported in the November 1991 *Animal Health Newsletter,* published by Cornell University College of Veterinary Medicine, studies conducted at the University of Florida show the condition progresses in severity. There's currently no known cause or cure, but apparently no pain is associated with it.

This shouldn't be confused with the "dancing" on hind legs often performed by agile dogs such as poodles and terriers that are very theatrical by nature.

TREATMENT

- There is no known or necessary treatment for this condition. If a dog in the advanced stages of the disease seems upset or uncomfortable, reassure the animal and see that it doesn't have to stand for long periods of time.

DEAFNESS, SIGNS OF *(See also box, BEHAVIOR CHANGES, p. 33; OLDER DOG PROBLEMS.)*

Problem: Florence is becoming very cross with her Bedlington terrier, Lambie, who seems to have undergone a complete personality change. All of a sudden the dog ignores her when she calls, and doesn't even look up to greet her when she comes home. The other day, Lambie snapped at her when she leaned down to pet him— something he's never done before. Florence thinks maybe Lambie is annoyed with her because she's been out so much lately.

DIAGNOSIS
A dog that suddenly fails to pay attention to verbal commands or one that seems frightened or startled when it's touched is probably losing its hearing or is possibly even completely deaf. Although a dog can go deaf suddenly from an injury, most lose their hearing very gradually, and it may not be until a dog is completely deaf that an owner notices the change.

Elderly dogs often suffer from gradual hearing loss, but puppies can be born deaf and young dogs may develop hearing problems because of congenital defects, injury, illness, poisoning, ear canal blockage, or the prolonged use of some medications.

TREATMENT

- First, take the dog to the veterinarian for an assessment. There is usually nothing to be done medically for a deaf dog, but you should make certain there is no blockage of the ear canal or an infection that should be treated.

- A dog that's lost its hearing will rely on its other senses to function. Learn to use exaggerated body language to communicate with your pet. Don't allow your dog to use its deafness as an excuse to misbehave. If it was a well-behaved dog before it lost its hearing it should continue to be a well-behaved dog.

- Be careful not to startle a deaf dog. If the animal's asleep when you walk into a room, stamp your feet on the floor so it can feel the vibrations and know you're coming. This works well if you have wooden floors, but if you live in a house with nonvibrating concrete floors you'll have to figure out some other way to warn your dog of your approach.

- Never touch a deaf dog until you're sure it knows you're there or it may react with a nip. Warn visitors or houseguests about this important safety precaution.

- Be especially aware of your pet's safety. Don't allow it to go outdoors alone unless your yard is securely fenced. If the dog is elderly, consider the possibility that its eyesight may be failing too, and be sure it doesn't become disoriented. If you take it to a strange place for a visit or to stay, keep it leashed by your side until you're sure it knows the lay of the land.

DEFECATION, EXCESSIVE *(See also box,* DIARRHEA, p. 91.)
Problem: Sherri can't believe how many times her basenji defecates. The dog goes every time she's walked, four times a day, and then goes again out in the yard at least five more times. Sherri is getting a little bit tired of scooping all that poop.

DIAGNOSIS

A normal, healthy adult dog usually defecates no more than three or four times a day. Often a dog will go a couple of times on a walk because of the stimulation of other dogs' odors. When a dog defecates too often or its feces are excessively large, suspect intestinal parasites or a dietary problem.

Worms can cause a dog to have loose, frequent stools, but are not common in adult dogs that don't run loose and don't eat garbage and small prey. More frequently the reason for excessive stools is a poor diet. An improper diet that contains too much bulk and not enough usable nutrients or one from which the nutrients are not readily absorbed will create a lot of waste that the dog will have to get rid of in its feces.

TREATMENT

- Take a stool sample to the veterinarian to be sure the animal doesn't have intestinal worms.
- Talk to your veterinarian about your dog's diet. High-quality dog foods are available from veterinarians and pet specialty stores. They provide readily utilized, complete nutrition without a lot of excess bulk and other fillers that can cause voluminous stools.

DEFIANCE—FACTS & MYTHS

An owner sometimes attributes a dog's disobedience to "defiance," a deliberate, challenging resistance to her authority. She may think something like "Rex is defying me when he won't get off the couch when I ask him to."

This is an example of Anthropomorphism—assigning a human trait to a dog. In reality, dogs simply don't think this way. They aren't capable of the complex reasoning that would lead them to deliberate defiance.

Usually the reason for a dog's seeming "defiance," or apparent refusal to obey its owner's wishes is that it simply doesn't understand what's wanted. The owner may give an unclear command or say too many things at once, or the dog may not hear the entire command because there's a lot of confusion in the room.

So-called defiant behavior should not be confused with Stubbornness, which stems from different circumstances.

See also box, MIXED MESSAGES, p. 203; *box,* SPITE—FACTS & MYTHS, p. 273; *box,* TALKING TO YOUR DOG, p. 282.

DENTAL CARE See TOOTH CARE PROBLEMS.

DEPROGRAMMING AND DESENSITIZATION

When I talk of "deprogramming" a dog I mean undoing previously learned behavior. For example, if a dog regularly chases cats and its owner now wants to get a pet cat, the dog's cat-chasing response has to be deprogrammed before the dog can learn not to chase the new cat.

The word "desensitize" means, literally, to make less sensitive. When I speak of desensitizing a dog I'm referring to a gradual process through which the animal will become less sensitive to certain stimulants and learn to tolerate them calmly. For example, a dog that's terrified of thunder or a hunting dog that can't stand the sound of a gunshot can be gradually desensitized until it can accept these sudden loud noises without panicking.

See also box, BEHAVIOR MODIFICATION, p. 34; FEAR-FULNESS; *box,* SETUPS, p. 264.

To help prevent your dog from engaging in Destructive Behavior when you're not home, reserve a special toy to give it when you go out. Here Spanky, a soft-coated wheaten terrier, holds his favorite toy. (Bashkim Dibra)

DESTRUCTIVE BEHAVIOR (See also BOREDOM; CHEWING PROBLEMS; CRATE PROBLEMS: CRATE DESTRUCTION; DIGGING; EXERCISE, DOGS' NEED FOR; SCRATCHING PROBLEMS; SEPARATION ANXIETY.)

Problem: Whenever the Lewises leave their year-old setter alone in the house all day, the dog pulls everything apart. He takes all the cushions off the sofas and chairs, dumps over the wastebaskets, pulls the bedspread off the bed, knocks over the plants, scratches the hardwood floors, and generally makes a complete mess. They're getting pretty sick of the destruction he wreaks.

DIAGNOSIS

There can be several causes of destructive behavior in dogs. It may be due to Separation Anxiety; I'll deal with this separately. In the case above, the problem may be rooted in Boredom. Young, normally active dogs that are left alone a great deal may become "itchy" and restless. Lacking anything better to do, they often resort to destructive behavior.

TREATMENT

- A dog that's tired out won't feel much like running around destroying things in the house. Take the dog for a good run or have a vigorous play session outdoors before you go out for any length of time *(see box,* GAMES TO PLAY WITH DOGS, p. 134). Praise the dog lavishly if all is well when you get home.
- Find a Toy or chew item that especially appeals to the dog. Buy several of them, but don't give them to the dog. Reserve them for times when you are going to be out. Then the toy becomes a special treat the dog has only when it's left alone. Sometimes this will entertain and distract a dog enough to prevent it from becoming destructive. Again, give the dog lots of Praise if it's behaved well in your absence.
- Another way to treat destructive behavior is to use a Setup. Go out as usual. After five minutes, burst back in the house so you can catch the dog in the act. Tell it "No" very strongly, give it a toy, and leave again. Do this again and again until the dog realizes it's just not worth the effort to be destructive and goes to sleep. If everything's in shape when you return, tell the dog how good it is.
- If all else fails, to prevent the dog from doing further damage get a suitable Crate and leave the dog in it when you're out. Don't make the dog think the Crate is

a punishment, but treat the whole thing matter-of-factly. Exercise the dog before you leave and be sure there's ample water, a treat or two, and some toys in the Crate. Give the dog a lot of attention and exercise when you get home. Once the destructive habit has been broken, many dogs are able to graduate from the Crate after a period of time.

DIARRHEA

Although it is a medical problem, diarrhea is often considered a behavior problem by owners because a puppy or dog with diarrhea is virtually impossible to house-train.

Stress because of a change in ownership or home or because of Separation Anxiety can cause any dog to suffer from a temporary bout of diarrhea. So can a sudden change in diet. A diet lacking in sufficient bulk may cause some dogs to develop chronic diarrhea. Some dog breeds have an intolerence for soybeans, a source of bulk in many dog foods. They will develop chronic diarrhea on the wrong diet. A dog's digestive tract can also be badly upset if it chews or eats inappropriate things, such as wallpaper, paste, carpeting, and so forth.

If a puppy or dog with diarrhea acts lethargic or ill, has diarrhea for more than twenty-four hours, or the diarrhea is accompanied by vomiting, seek veterinary help right away. Intestinal worms can be the culprits in young dogs, and some systemic diseases will cause diarrhea.

See also DEFECATION, EXCESSIVE; VOMITING.

DIGGING *(See also* BURYING FOOD/BONES; DESTRUCTIVE BEHAVIOR; *box,* TERRITORIAL BEHAVIOR, **p. 289.**)

DIGGING INDOORS/DESTRUCTIVE DIGGING

Problem: The little Cairn terrier has done so much damage you'd think it was a mastiff! Whenever anyone walks in the apartment hallway outside the front door, the dog becomes frenzied trying to get out and at the person and digs and digs and digs. So far the terrier has destroyed the rug, the hardwood floor, the walls on either side of the door, and the door itself.

DIAGNOSIS
This is a case of a highly territorial dog that's destroying the entry of an apartment trying to dig itself out to defend its turf. Dogs also dig destructively indoors for all of the same reasons they dig outdoors.

TREATMENT
Follow the same treatments listed in the discussion of digging outdoors, p. 93.

DIGGING INDOORS/MAKING A NEST *(See also box, A BED FOR A DOG, p. 31; box, FEMALE DOGS' BEHAVIORAL CHARACTERISTICS, p. 122.)*

Problem: At first Sunny thought it was cute when her little silky terrier, Toto, "made a bed" for herself in the bedroom carpet next to Sunny's bed at night. The little dog scratched and scratched and then turned around a couple of times and lay down on the spot. But a year later, the carpet's worn bare and Sunny doesn't think Toto's bed-making is so cute anymore.

DIAGNOSIS
This is a classic case of natural nest-making activity. Some dogs make nests on the floor; others choose chairs, beds, even people's laps. In this instance the action has become somewhat obsessive.

TREATMENT

Scolding or yelling will do nothing to stop a dog such as this from its continual bed-making; it will only serve to make both dog and owner miserable.

- The best solution to this problem is to provide the dog with a Bed of its own. A flat cushion-type bed or even a piece of old carpeting can be put down right on top of the spot the dog usually digs. Then the dog can scratch and dig to its heart's content without damaging the carpet.

DIGGING OUTDOORS *(See also* BURYING FOOD/BONES; *box,* SCENT MARKING, **p. 256.)**

Problem: The Levines are at their wits' end. Their beautiful grassy backyard has been turned into a dust bowl by their little dachshund. The dog just digs and digs and digs. Now he's starting in on the vegetable garden!

DIAGNOSIS

Digging is a natural canine behavior. Wolves and dogs have scent glands on the bottoms of their feet, and they dig to leave both visual and olfactory marks. Wolves also dig to make burrows or nests for young, and to bury food.

Some dog breeds have a tendency to dig more than others, but any dog that's left alone outdoors for long periods of time may dig for several reasons. It may dig in an attempt to get under a fence just to escape, or to follow loose dogs running by in a natural pack reaction. If it's especially hot or cold, a dog may dig a hole to get relief from the weather—to cool off or stay warm.

But a dog that digs and digs in a mindless fashion is probably suffering from Separation Anxiety, Boredom, and/or excess energy.

TREATMENT

- One way to treat a digging problem is to take away the dog's opportunity to dig. Create a dog run—one area in which the dog is confined. Either accept that the area will be full of potholes or put down concrete.

- When a dog spends a lot of time outdoors in the yard, be sure it has shade in the summer and shelter in cold weather. Be sure, also, it has plenty of fresh drinking water.
- If yours is a high-energy dog you may be able to stop its urge to dig if you make sure it has a great deal of Exercise before it's put out in the yard.
- As for Destructive Behavior indoors, providing the dog with something special to chew or play with while it's in the yard may help distract it from digging.
- The startle method may also work. Let the dog out in the yard and watch it. As soon as it begins to dig, rush out beating a pot or shaking a Noisemaker, shouting "NO, NO, NO!" in your loudest, strongest voice. When the dog stops digging, give it a Chew Toy and go back inside and watch. As soon as it begins to dig again, repeat the action. After a while most dogs will give up and stop digging.
- Alternately, if its warm out, you can startle the dog into stopping by suddenly squirting it with a hose or bombing it with a Water Balloon. Again, say "NO!" repeatedly each time you squirt or bomb the dog.

DISPLACEMENT—WHAT DOES IT MEAN?

Displacement is a term used in human psychology to describe a situation in which a person redirects an emotion such as anger from the thing or person that angered him to something else. For example, a man who's upset at his friend may punch the wall instead of his friend.

Dogs engage in displacement too. A dog that's distressed and frustrated at being left home alone may "displace" its emotional upset by engaging in Destructive Behavior. Owners often think a dog does something destructive to "get even," but this assumes a thought process no dog can have. For how to redirect displacement behavior, *see* CHEWING PROBLEMS; DIGGING; DESTRUCTIVE BEHAVIOR; SEPARATION ANXIETY. *See also box,* ACRAL LICK DERMATITIS GRANULOMA, p. 4; *box,* FLANK SUCKING, p. 125; *box,* OBSESSIVE-COMPULSIVE BEHAVIOR IN DOGS, p. 222; SCRATCHING PROBLEMS: SCRATCHING SELF; TAIL CHASING/BITING.

DOG FIGHTING See INTER-DOG AGGRESSION; INTERMALE AGGRESSION.

DOMINANCE-RELATED AGGRESSION *(See also box,* DOMINANT BEHAVIOR, p. 98; *box,* PACK BEHAVIOR, p. 230.)

Problem: Kathy bought an eight-week-old bull mastiff pup and called him Tuffy. From the first moment it was clear he had a very strong "personality." Kathy laughed when she told her friends, "Tuffy certainly has a mind of his own. Whenever we go for a walk, he goes wherever he wants, sometimes blocks out of our way. It's as if *he's* walking *me.*" As the dog grew and became stronger, Kathy was surprised to find she occasionally felt a little uneasy around him. He was affectionate most of the time and nice to everyone who came to the house. But he began to make it very clear to her that he would do as he pleased. He began to run the household and strongly resisted all attempts to direct his actions. What Kathy had thought of as amusingly "bossy" behavior was no longer funny now that Tuffy had grown to be a powerful adult dog.

Then one day Kathy was hurrying to clean up the apartment for company and gave Tuffy a gentle shove to move him out of the way of the vacuum. He jumped up, stared at her, and growled menacingly, baring his teeth. Kathy was frightened. She quickly turned off the vacuum and backed out of the room, closing the door behind her.

DIAGNOSIS

This is a classic case of dominance-related aggression toward a person, based on pack mentality. Dogs treat humans as they do canine pack members, and in a one-dog household, the owner is the only other member of the pack.

In every pack there is a clear-cut leader. If an owner fails to assume leadership with a dog when it's young, the dog will take over the dominant role. If necessary, the dog will resort to aggression in order to get its way and maintain its leadership. Most of these dogs will remain friendly with visitors because they constitute no threat to their leadership—they are not members of the pack.

TREATMENT

As in all cases of aggression, this situation will only become worse with neglect and may escalate to a dangerous point, especially when a dog is large and powerful. It's important to act quickly before something bad happens and a dog bites someone. I strongly recommend enlisting the help of both a veterinarian and a professional trainer when a dog shows clear signs of aggression, particularly if it has been allowed to become more and more aggressive over time.

The dog will have to be programmed to recognize its

owner as leader. At the same time, the owner needs to learn how to take a leadership role—the Alpha Position.

- It is vital for you to assume leadership over the dog. You can only do this through Obedience Training. In the dog's eyes you can then maintain a logical leadership position.
- Use a strong, firm tone of voice to give commands to the dog. Sound stimulants or Noisemakers are very useful to make a dog such as this focus on you.
- Exaggerate your body language to make your meanings crystal-clear. *(See* HOW TO INTERPRET YOUR DOG'S BODY LANGUAGE, FACIAL EXPRESSIONS, AND VOCALIZATIONS, p. xi.)
- Never resort to harsh physical treatment of a dog *(see box,* PUNISHMENT, p. 247). Hitting or threatening to hit a naturally aggressive dog will cause the animal to feel it must rise to the challenge—a potentially dangerous reaction.
- A High Collar will help control a strong dog during training and while on walks.
- A Crate can be a positive factor in reprogramming an aggressive dog. When used properly, it can become a haven for the dog and at the same time provide security for the owner during the training process.
- Because of the traditional pack hierarchy in which males are always dominant over females, male dogs are naturally more aggressive than females. Neutering a male dog will help ameliorate this inherent dominance; as the testosterone level in the dog's body gradually becomes lower, he will usually begin to act less "macho." *(See box,* CASTRATION OF MALE DOGS—FACTS & MYTHS, p. 57; *box,* MALE DOGS' BEHAVIORAL CHARACTERISTICS, p. 198.)

DOMINANT BEHAVIOR

Within a wolf pack there is only one dominant (Alpha) pair of animals. All of the other animals are subordinate to the Alpha male and female in descending order, ending at the bottom with the youngest pups.

A dominant animal always holds its head and tail high, stands tall, walks with assurance, and stares aggressively at all other animals. It expects them to respect its dominance by acting submissive. A dominant dog will often mount a less dominant individual.

If a dominant wolf or dog is challenged by another animal, a fight will ensue. The fighting will continue until one animal admits defeat by acting in a submissive manner.

A naturally dominant dog will attempt to run everyone else, including its owners. A special section in the beginning of this book, HOW TO INTERPRET YOUR DOG'S BODY LANGUAGE, FACIAL EXPRESSIONS, AND VOCALIZATIONS will help you learn how to communicate with your pet and make your leadership role clear.

See also box, ALPHA POSITION, p. 12; EYE CONTACT: NEGATIVE EYE CONTACT; INTER-DOG AGGRESSION; INTERMALE AGGRESSION; MOUNTING BEHAVIOR; *box,* PACK BEHAVIOR, p. 230; *box,* SUBMISSIVE BEHAVIOR, p. 276.

DOWN/STAY

When a dog is in down/stay position it will stay quietly in place, lying down, until you tell it to get up. It will be able to do this wherever it is, whatever the distractions. This is an especially useful command for a dog to learn if you entertain a lot, or plan to take your dog to work with you, for example. Down/stay is always used when you teach your dog to Go to Your Place.

DRAGGING See BOLTING: BOLTING FROM THE HOUSE; PULLING ON A LEASH.

DREAMING

Problem: Lynn worries about her Australian terrier, Kanga. The little dog always whines and twitches in her sleep, and lately she's taken to making little grunting noises and moving her legs back and forth as if she's running. Lynn doesn't know if she should leave the dog alone or wake her up when she does this.

DIAGNOSIS
Just as people do, dogs need to dream when they sleep. There's a stage in deep sleep called REM (rapid eye movement) in which many individuals move around and even make sounds. During this stage most animals dream. If a dog (or human) is deprived of this stage of sleep repeatedly it can cause severe behavior problems ranging from depression and hyperactivity to aggression.

Some dogs seem to dream more actively than others, as some people do. Sometimes the overt activity occurs only when the animal has been overstimulated or has become overtired, but some animals exhibit outward signs of dreaming all of the time.

TREATMENT

- No matter how tempting it may be, by no means wake a dog when it shows outward signs of dreaming. Let it sleep on. It's nothing to worry about.
- If the animal's sounds and motions disturb you, have it sleep in another room.

DRINKING PROBLEMS

DRINKING EXCESSIVELY/TOO FAST (See also VOMITING.)

Problem: Whenever Max, a bloodhound, comes indoors, he goes to his water bowl and quickly drinks and drinks and asks for more. After he's finished, he throws up.

DIAGNOSIS

An active dog, especially a large breed, works up a tremendous thirst when it runs around outdoors. The problem is, dogs don't have a clue that drinking too much too fast will cause them to throw up.

TREATMENT

- In this case, the treatment is easy. Limit the amount of water you offer a dog when it first comes in after exercising. After the dog has cooled down and calmed down, you can refill its bowl without worrying that it will drink too fast.
- Some people advocate putting a few ice cubes in an overheated dog's dish instead of water. The dog can cool its mouth off and obtain some moisture from licking the cubes without danger of overdrinking.

DRINKING OUT OF THE TOILET BOWL

Problem: James finds it disgusting that his Great Dane regularly drinks out of the toilet bowl.

DIAGNOSIS

A large, thirsty dog will drink water anywhere it can find it. Many big dogs seem to think toilets were made just to serve as large water bowls for them.

TREATMENT

- Be sure the dog has plenty of fresh water available in one or more drinking bowls all of the time.
- Don't use poisonous chemicals in the tank or bowl of your toilet.
- To prevent a dog from drinking from the bowl, keep the door of the bathroom closed, or be sure to shut the toilet lid.

DROOLING

Problem: Ajax, a Great Pyrenees, has a very bad habit. Whenever anyone comes to the house to visit, he puts his large head in the person's lap, asking to be petted. The problem is, Ajax drools a lot. Many visitors have been visibly upset when the large, friendly dog deposited strings of saliva all over their good clothes.

DIAGNOSIS

Drooling is not really a behavior problem, but it's hard not to view it as one. Certain dog breeds have loose, pendulous lower lips that form pockets, or jowls, in which saliva collects. When enough saliva collects, it overflows, and the dog drools. The dog has no control over this excess saliva. Males usually have larger heads and jowls than females; therefore they drool more.

TREATMENT

- If you have a breed of dog that drools a lot, you can keep things neater by teaching the animal to allow you to wipe its face and jowls to get rid of the excess saliva.
- Start when the dog is young and wipe its entire face off with a towel several times a day. A good time to do this is immediately after the dog has had a drink of water, when its face and jowls are likely to be good and wet. Tell it how good it is when it stands still for the wiping. Soon this will become a regular part of the dog's daily routine.
- Train the dog to wait for an invitation from you or a visitor before it puts its head on the furniture or in anyone's lap. You can then wipe the dog's face and jowls off ahead of time and and prevent the drooling damage to a certain extent.

DROP IT!

Drop it! is one of the most useful commands you can teach your dog and should be among the first things your puppy learns. It can prevent a puppy or dog from chewing or eating something you don't want it to, and, more important, it can protect your pet's life if it should happen to pick up something dangerous or poisonous.

To teach a puppy to respond to this command, wait until it picks something up in its mouth. Lean over and put your hand on either side of its jaw, where the hinges are. While you apply gentle but firm pressure on the animal's jaw, say "Drop it!" and take the object out of the puppy's mouth with your other hand. When you have the object in your hand, tell the puppy how good it is and pet it. At this point you can give the puppy a small food treat as a reward. (*See box,* FOOD REWARDS AS TRAINING TOOLS, p. 132.)

If the puppy doesn't cooperate, tries to pull away, or growls, you'll have to take strong measures. Don't give up or you'll be giving the puppy the message that it can get away with resisting you. Press harder on the animal's jaw with the fingers of one hand at the same time you grasp the top of its jaw with the other hand and literally pry the mouth open. Grasp the object and pull it out of the puppy's mouth. Then praise the animal and give it a treat.

With a stubborn dog, use a Setup. Place an intriguing object on the floor and let the dog pick it up. Then repeat the lesson immediately so the puppy knows you mean business. Continue to repeat the lesson until the puppy responds to your command immediately the first time you give it.

DRUGS AND DOG TRAINING

Many dog trainers advocate the use of drugs as aids when working with especially difficult or aggressive dogs. They reason that a tranquilized dog will be easier to work with and will present less of a challenge to owner and trainer. In my opinion this is not only ineffective, but can also be dangerous.

Animals metabolize medications and drugs at different rates, according to their own makeup. If you drug a dangerous, highly aggressive dog you have no way of knowing when the drug will take effect or how long it will last. Reactions to drugs can be extremely unpredictable, and some drugs may even cause strange side effects. For instance, I've seen a formerly well-behaved dog act in an uncharacteristically aggressive manner because its body chemistry had become unbalanced by drugs.

Even if a drugged dog does do what you want it to, there's no guarantee at all it will respond correctly once the drug wears off. You won't have modified the dogs's behavior and corrected it, you will have simply stifled it momentarily, for the duration of the drug's efficacy. All the drug therapy will accomplish is to give you a false sense of security. The problem won't have been solved, just contained.

The only time drug therapy might be useful is if a dog has a medical or neurologic problem that's causing undesirable behavior.

See ABNORMAL ACTIVITY LEVELS: HYPERACTIVITY, PROBLEM 2; *box,* SEIZURES IN DOGS, p. 259.

E

EAR CARE

Problem: The veterinarian told Millie to put drops in her cocker spaniel's ears three times a day to clear up an infection. He showed her how to do it, and she went home, drops in hand. But when Millie tried to medicate the dog at home, the animal tried to run away. When Millie grabbed him he turned around, snarled, and acted as if he was going to nip her.

DIAGNOSIS

Whether pendulous or erect, a dog's ear flap, or pinna, is laced throughout with veins and nerves and is therefore very sensitive. If a dog has an inflamed ear canal the surrounding neck area may also become sore to the touch. Too-rough or incorrect handling when cleaning a dog's ears or trying to medicate a dog with an infected ear may hurt the animal enough to make it react with a defensive snap or nip. (*See* PAIN-INDUCED AGGRESSION.)

TREATMENT

- Like any grooming or care routine, your task will be much easier if you accustom your pet to being handled when it's still a puppy. A dog that's learned to allow you to touch its ears and trusts you not to hurt it will

be easy to treat or groom. *(See box,* SOCIALIZATION, THE
KEY TO A WELL-ADJUSTED DOG, p. 271.)

- If you are at all tentative or unsure when you begin to
clean or treat a dog's ears, the dog will sense it and try
to get away to avoid the unpleasant procedure. If
you're really nervous about medicating a dog, enlist the
aid of a friend or family member the first couple of
times. The other person can hold the dog and pet it
while you work on the ears. You'll avoid a struggle that
will only serve to upset both you and your pet and
make it more difficult to handle the next time.

- There are several ways to be sure the dog can't back
off or run away while you're working on its head. If
it's a small puppy or dog, sit down and place the animal on your lap, rear end against your body. Hold it
firmly around the chest with one hand while you work
with the other. Or, place the dog sideways and hold its
head against your body. A larger dog should be put up
on a table or countertop. The slippery surface will dis-
arm it and prevent it from obtaining a firm footing to
escape. Again, press its rear end against your body with
one hand, or hold its head against you, leaving the
other hand free to work on the animal. Very large dogs
can be backed into a corner with a leash and collar on
for control, while you kneel or sit down to their level.
If you hold the ear flap gently it will keep the dog from
trying to pull away and escape, but whatever you do,
don't grab the ears if the dog starts to run off.

- Place medicines or cleaning materials right at hand. It
will do no good to have the dog nicely in place if you
have to let go to scrabble around for your equipment.

- Speak to the dog soothingly and tell it how good it is
as you work on it. No matter how wiggly or nervous a
dog seems, don't let your temper get the better of you
or you'll simply confirm the animal's suspicions that
this is *not* going to be a pleasant experience. Stay calm
and firm.

- If your dog continues to struggle and to try to bite, you
can fashion a temporary Muzzle. Take a length of soft
cloth such as old panty hose or a strip of gauze. Wrap

it around your dog's nose, cross it under the chin, and bring it around the neck. Tie it at the top of the dog's neck. Now you can work on your dog without fear of a bite.

EATING PROBLEMS See APPETITE PROBLEMS; GULPING FOOD.

EATING FECES See COPROPHAGIA.

EATING NONFOOD See PICA.

ELECTRONIC DEVICES AS BEHAVIOR MODIFIERS

There are a great many electronic devices on the market designed to deter dogs from barking, jumping on furniture, entering rooms, running away, and so forth. Most of them give a dog a mild shock to startle it and make it stop whatever it's doing. Others emit a loud noise that's also meant to stop a dog in its tracks.

In general these devices are merely "Band-Aids" and do nothing to actually solve behavior problems. I feel they also have great potential for misuse and mistreatment. However, humane electronic devices *may* be useful as behavior modifiers when used in conjunction with other training steps. For instance, something that's activated when a dog barks such as a box that makes a loud noise or a tape recording of your own voice shouting "NO!" may help cure a dog with a severe barking problem.

See also box, BEHAVIOR MODIFICATION, p. 34; *box,* FENCES: INVISIBLE, p. 123.

ELIMINATION PROBLEMS See CRATE PROBLEMS: CRATE
SOILING; DEFECATION, EXCESSIVE; DIARRHEA; HOUSE-TRAINING
PROBLEMS; *box*, HOUSE-TRAINING TIPS, p. 152; URINARY
PROBLEMS.

ELIZABETHAN COLLARS AS BEHAVIOR MODIFIERS

An Elizabethan collar is a cone-shaped device made
of plastic or stiff cardboard that can be tied around a
dog's neck in back of its ears. It looks something like
an upside-down lampshade and is often used by veterinarians to prevent an animal from scratching its
head or biting other parts of its body, especially after
surgery.

But an Elizabethan collar can also be used to help
teach a dog not to jump by blocking its peripheral vision so it can't judge height or depth and is afraid to
try. Unlike some anti-jumping devices sold commercially, the collars are completely safe to leave on an
unattended animal for hours and don't prevent normal
locomotion, eating, or drinking. They're available
from veterinarians and come in various sizes to suit
any dog.

See also box, BEHAVIOR MODIFICATION, p.34; JUMP-
ING PROBLEMS: JUMPING ON THE KITCHEN COUNTER OR
DINING TABLE; JUMPING OVER FENCES.

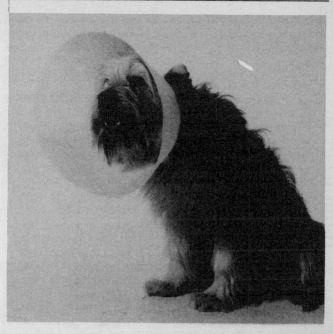

Daisy wears an Elizabethan Collar that blocks her peripheral vision and will prevent her from attempting to jump over a fence. (Bruce Plotkin)

EMOTIONS—DO DOGS HAVE THEM?

Are we being anthropomorphic when we assign emotions to our pet dogs? Yes and no.

No, because dogs do have well-documented emotions. They react to people, things, and events and clearly show their feelings with body language and facial expressions. This is part of their pack orientation. Members of a pack must be able to let other pack members know how they feel. We, too, can recognize such feelings as fear, aggression, anxiety, loneliness, dislike, pleasure, and happiness in dogs. Or to be exact, we recognize feelings to which we have assigned these human terms.

Yes, when we attribute more complex emotions to dogs. Defiance, Jealousy, and Spite, for example, are feelings based on reasoned cause-and-effect beyond the ability of a dog to devise. They are human emotions. When a dog is a well-loved member of the family it's only natural to anthropomorphize and believe it's feeling the way we do. There's no harm in this as long as it doesn't lead to spoiling and behavior problems.

See also box, ANTHROPOMORPHISM, p. 13; *box,* PACK BEHAVIOR, p. 230; HOW TO INTERPRET YOUR DOG'S BODY LANGUAGE, FACIAL EXPRESSIONS, AND VOCALIZATIONS, p. xi.

ENERGY LEVELS See ABNORMAL ACTIVITY LEVELS.

ENTERTAINMENT See BOREDOM; *box,* GAMES TO PLAY WITH DOGS, p. 134.

EPILEPSY See *box,* SEIZURES IN DOGS, p. 259.

ESCAPING See BOLTING; *box*, FLIGHT BEHAVIOR, p. 126; JUMPING PROBLEMS: JUMPING OVER FENCES.

ESP—DO DOGS HAVE IT?

Stories attributing extrasensory perception or supernatural powers to dogs abound. Dogs are known to be able to predict earthquakes, thunderstorms, and floods. They can find their way home across hundreds of miles of unknown terrain, are capable of tracking down lost people under extremely difficult conditions, and can locate individuals buried under many feet of rubble or snow.

Dog owners often like to think their pets have special powers, but the reality is more down-to-earth. Dogs' "ESP" is due to their exceptionally acute senses. They can hear, see, and smell things we can't. This accounts for their ability to "predict" meteorological events and home in on lost or buried people and faraway locations. Supernatural powers don't allow them to do these things. Rather, their highly developed senses give them the ability to perceive things we humans can't.

See also box, HEARING: PROBLEM SOLVING USING A DOG'S KEEN SENSE OF HEARING, p. 147; *box*, SMELL, DOGS' KEENEST SENSE, p. 268; *box*, TOUCH—THE TACTILE SENSE IN DOGS, p. 297; *box*, VISION IN DOGS, p. 314.

ESTRUS See *box*, FEMALE DOGS' BEHAVIORAL CHARACTERISTICS, p. 122; *box*, SPAYING OF FEMALE DOGS—FACTS & MYTHS, p. 272.

EXCITABILITY See ABNORMAL ACTIVITY LEVELS: HYPERACTIVITY.

EXCITEMENT URINATION See URINE LEAKING/DRIBBLING IN A YOUNG DOG.

EXERCISE, DOGS' NEED FOR

Problem: Three Dandie Dinmont terriers, a mother and two of her sons, lived together in the same house. Their owners loved watching them romp around and play together. The problem was that when the owners were out the three dogs got into all kinds of destructive mischief. They ran all over the house, knocking things down and creating a lot of mess.

DIAGNOSIS

Exercise is a necessity for dogs. Just like wolves, they need to move around a lot. Some dogs require more daily exercise than others, and a number of dog behavior problems stem from lack of sufficient exercise. When high-energy dogs like terriers don't get enough exercise they will often lapse into unconsciously Destructive Behavior out of sheer high spirits. When several dogs live together each animal's high spirit plays off the others and the result can be chaos.

TREATMENT

- If you can't provide a high-energy dog with at least two hours of walking time each day, engage a dog walker to help.
- An alternate form of exercise that works very well for people who can't get out to exercise their dogs every day is to give the animal a daily turn on a Treadmill. *(See also box,* GAMES TO PLAY WITH DOGS, p. 134.)

EXPLORATORY BEHAVIOR *(See also* VISITING WITH A DOG.)

Problem: The Goldsmiths were amazed at their two-year-old Tibetan terrier's behavior when they took him to a summer cottage they'd rented. He went from room to room, rooting in corners, poking behind chair cushions and underneath sofas, and nosing into each closet, cupboard, nook, and cranny. When he came to a closed door he barked as if to say "Open this." He didn't settle down until he'd checked everything out.

DIAGNOSIS

This is an example of canine exploratory behavior. A wolf will naturally explore a new environment to be sure it's free from hidden danger, and it's perfectly normal for any dog to give a new dwelling a thorough going-over. It's not that it doesn't trust its owners, but there's an instinctive need to be sure a previously unknown area is safe. A dog needs to look at everything in a new place before it can relax.

Chewing, Licking, Mouthing, and Nipping are other forms of exploratory behavior engaged in by puppies.

TREATMENT

- As long as a dog isn't doing any damage, allow it to explore to its heart's content. If you stop it, it will only go back and continue with its rounds later on.
- When you go to a new place with your dog, always take along a supply of the animal's favorite toys and bones, and a familiar bed or cushion for it to sleep on.

EYE CARE

Problem: The little Maltese has to have her eyes flushed out every day to prevent tears from running down her face and staining the white fur on the sides of her nose. The difficulty is that she hates the process and snarls and fights her owner each time he tries to work on her eyes.

DIAGNOSIS

Many white, long-haired dogs such as Maltese, bichons frisés, poodles, and so forth need to have their eyes and faces cleaned regularly to prevent permanent staining.

The process rarely hurts a dog, but it is unpleasant and can be frightening if the dog isn't used to it.

TREATMENT

- If you know your dog will require regular eye care, begin to accustom it to the routine when it's a young puppy.
- Steps for performing eye care are the same as those for Ear Care.

EYE CONTACT

POSITIVE EYE CONTACT See *box*, FOCUSING, p. 128.

NEGATIVE EYE CONTACT (See also *box*, AGGRESSIVE BEHAVIOR IN DOGS, p. 7; *box*, DOMINANT BEHAVIOR, p. 98; *box*, PACK BEHAVIOR, p. 230; *box*, SUBMISSIVE BEHAVIOR, p. 276.)

Problem: Freddie adopted a grown male keeshond from a shelter. The dog seemed well behaved, although he was a bit reserved and never looked at his new owner. Freddie didn't worry about it. He figured it might take a while for the dog to become used to him. Then one day Freddie was sitting at his desk with the dog lying nearby. He looked up from his work and caught the dog's eye. The dog stared hard at Freddie and growled menacingly, deep in his throat.

DIAGNOSIS

Eye contact is a form of communication between dogs. When aggressive puppies are very young they learn that they can easily stare down their more submissive brothers and sisters. As they mature, if two aggressive male dogs meet, they often challenge each other's dominance by staring at each other. If one dog doesn't back down, the staring match will end in a fight. A naturally aggressive dog that hasn't been obedience-trained may try not to make eye contact with a person to avoid a confrontation.

But if eye contact does occur it will attempt to dominate its owner by staring him down. For more about this, *see* HOW TO INTERPRET YOUR DOG'S BODY LANGUAGE, FACIAL EXPRESSIONS, AND VOCALIZATIONS, p. xi.

TREATMENT

- If an adopted older dog shows signs of aggression by staring at you in a challenging way, drop your eyes. This is not a cop-out, but a way to avoid a confrontation until you can deal properly with the dog's aggression.
- Immediately take a dog that shows aggression to a well-established trainer who will help you teach the dog obedience and at the same time show you how to establish a leadership role with your pet. *(See box,* ALPHA POSITION, p. 12.)
- Once you have begun to train the dog, don't allow it to challenge your authority.
- Don't deliberately challenge any aggressive dog by looking it directly in the eyes, whether the animal belongs to you or not. The old theory that you should "stare down" an aggressive dog probably led to a lot of dog bites.

F

FACE-RUBBING *(See also* SNIFFING PEOPLE AND OTHER DOGS IN GREETING.)

Problem: The Halseys' bearded collie, Susie, has a very annoying and embarrassing habit. Whenever people come into the house she greets them happily with wags and then goes up to them and rubs her face against their clothes. When a visitor has pants on, she often puts her nose between the person's legs and rubs her face in his crotch.

DIAGNOSIS

There are several possible reasons for face-rubbing. A dog may rub its face against people in a gesture of affection and as an invitation for a pat. But when the rubbing becomes insistent and involves the animal's poking its nose into cracks and crevices, it's probably because a dog needs to clean its face off. Some dogs irritate their owners by continually rubbing their faces on upholstered furniture or rugs. A dog with lots of long facial hair may have difficulty removing debris from its muzzle and around its eyes and find it satisfactory to perform this cleaning job against a convenient person or piece of furniture.

When a dog's continual face-rubbing seems to have nothing to do with cleaning—if, for instance, it doesn't have much facial hair—the animal may be suffering from an allergy that's making its nose or face itch. A dog suffering from a contact allergy will usually have a skin rash. Dogs with food allergies or seasonal inhalant allergies caused by pollen or other airborne irritants will simply itch. For more about allergies in dogs, *see* SCRATCHING PROBLEMS: SCRATCHING SELF.

TREATMENT

- If the face-rubbing is clearly affectionate in nature, a pat and "All right, enough" will usually stop the action.
- If, however, the rubbing is more intense and insistent, suspect an ulterior motive on the part of the dog. First, stop the action immediately with a firm "No," and a hand clap or other attention-getting sound.
- Take over the job of face-cleaning. Teach your dog to stand still while you thoroughly wipe off its face and muzzle. Do this on a regular basis immediately after the dog eats or drinks and if necessary when it comes indoors or first thing in the morning. Whenever the dog begins to go into its face-rubbing routine, tell it to sit, and wipe its face off yourself. After a while most dogs will learn to come to you for a face-wiping whenever they need it.
- If none of these things helps, take your pet to a veterinarian for assessment. A dog that's suffering from an allergy can be treated either medically or through a change in diet.

FEAR BITER See FEAR-INDUCED AGGRESSION.

FEARFULNESS (See *also* BOLTING; FLIGHT BEHAVIOR PROBLEMS.)

Problem: When the Cantors moved to New York City from a farm upstate, they didn't anticipate the terrible time they would have with their Bernese mountain dog, Helen. The dog was completely attached to them and their family and seemed very calm and accepting of anything they did. So it came as a complete surprise to them when she reacted violently the first time they tried to take her for a walk in the city. No sooner did they get to the sidewalk than Helen froze in her tracks and then turned and tried to bolt off. Straining frantically at her leash, her eyes rolled back in her head, she seemed not even to hear her owners when they spoke to her. After a few minutes, they gave up and took her indoors, thankful that at least they had a fenced-in yard in the back of the house where she could relieve herself.

DIAGNOSIS

This is an example of extreme fearfulness. A dog that has lived in a calm environment with few loud noises or strange people to contend with may react with terror when confronted by city sights, sounds, and smells. Cars, trucks, and buses driving by, strangers rushing along the street, and so forth provide more stimulants than the dog can handle all at once.

Dogs are often especially fearful of loud noises such as thunder, backfiring cars, and fireworks.

TREATMENT

A fearful dog's behavior can be modified with careful step-by-step desensitization *(see box,* DEPROGRAMMING AND DESENSITIZATION, p. 88) to whatever stimulants it is afraid of. Then the dog's confidence must be built up to a level at which it can accept and deal with the fear-producing events.

- First of all, give your pet a refresher course in basic obedience. An obedient dog will be better able to focus on you when the need arises. *(See box,* OBEDIENCE TRAINING, p. 218.)
- One way to desensitize a fearful dog is to make a tape of the sounds it's afraid of. With the dog sitting calmly by your side in a quiet room, begin by playing the tape softly. If the dog reacts in fear, speak to it, make it look at you, and tell it everything's all right. Pet it and give it a treat while the tape continues to play. Do this every

day until the dog stays perfectly calm. Then gradually increase the volume of the tape each day until the dog is able to remain calm and quiet when it's played at full volume. Always praise and reassure the dog throughout the process.

- Once a dog is able to tolerate a feared noise inside the house, take it to a spot where the actual noise will take place. Make the animal Focus on you and speak to it just as you did indoors. Once you think everything's all right, begin to walk with the dog. Keep a careful eye on the animal, and if you see it begin to tense or act afraid, squat down and make it focus on you again. Continue to do this until the dog is able to tolerate whatever noise and/or other stimulant it was afraid of.
- If a dog is fearful of thunder or firecrackers or some other noise that may occur when you're not there, you should carry the simulation one step further. Time the recording to begin after you've left, and go outdoors. During the playing of the tape, go back inside. If the dog has remained calm, do nothing. Don't make a fuss or the dog may wonder what the excitement is all about. But if it's still acting fearful, go back and repeat the steps above until the animal becomes so familiar with the noise it doesn't panic, even when you're not there to reassure it.

FEAR-INDUCED AGGRESSION

Problem: Tippy, the Jacobses' two-year-old Lhasa apso, has always been a sweet, good-natured dog ever since they adopted her from a shelter. That's why they were so surprised and horrified when she growled at their next-door neighbor. Mrs. Jones was gardening when she walked over to talk to the Jacobses. She leaned down to greet Tippy and the dog backed off, hackles up, growling and showing her teeth. Startled, Mrs. Jones stood up. "Maybe my gardening hat frightened her," she said a bit shakily. The Jacobses apologized profusely and took Tippy indoors. They decided to try an experiment. Mr. Jacobs got an old sun hat out of the hall closet, put it on, and bent to pat Tippy. The dog had the same reaction to him she'd had to Mrs. Jones. They were amazed—how come she didn't recognize her own master?

DIAGNOSIS

This is an example of a dog that's been badly frightened or mistreated by someone wearing or carrying something. It could be anything—a hat, black shoes, a uniform, an umbrella, or something else. Especially in the impressionable early months, one bad incident can be enough to imprint itself on an animal's consciousness so it becomes terrified of anyone in a big hat, black shoes, etc. A dog such as this is so sensitized all it sees is the feared object. Everything else is blanked out. In the animal's extreme fear, it will strike out aggressively to protect itself from what it perceives as the "enemy."

Fear-induced aggression may also be directed toward *all* humans. This can occur if a naturally timid puppy is treated very harshly. It will grow up to be a dog that's afraid of all people and will act aggressive if anyone comes too near or tries to touch it. This kind of dog may easily become a fear biter. It will take a great deal of professional treatment to help a dog such as this.

TREATMENT

A dog that's fearful of an object has to be desensitized so it's no longer frightened of anyone wearing or carrying the feared object.

- Place the feared object or item of clothing on the floor in a central but neutral location (e.g., the living room, not the room in which the dog regularly eats or sleeps). Encourage the dog to explore the area near the object and sniff at it, but don't force it.
- Once the dog is able to walk past the object without a problem, gradually put it nearer and nearer the dog's usual eating area.
- Let the dog become used to seeing you with the object. Carry it around in your hand or draped over an arm as

you go about preparing the dog's dinner, putting its leash on, taking a walk, and so forth.

- Continue allowing the dog to sniff the object and see you with it until it accepts the item calmly.
- Once the dog accepts you with the object, enlist the help of a neighbor or friend and have her go through the same routine. Have her hold the object or wear the clothing while she sits and talks to you. If the dog reacts aggressively, wait a while before trying it again.

A dog that's fearful of people must also be desensitized and socialized to strangers so it doesn't regard everyone it meets as a potential threat. (*See box,* DEPROGRAMMING AND DESENSITIZATION, p. 88; *box,* SOCIALIZATION, THE KEY TO A WELL-ADJUSTED DOG, p. 271.)

- A dog such as this is often helped a great deal by attending an obedience class. It helps accustom it to strange people and other dogs and also teaches it to rely on you, its owner and leader, to keep it safe.
- Put the dog on a short leash and take it into areas where there are a lot of people walking around—a mall, busy street, etc. Have the dog heel beside you, and if it becomes frightened, stop and make it focus on you immediately until it calms down.
- Group walks with other dogs and their owners can also help socialize and desensitize a fearful dog. The presence of the other dogs will take the animal's focus off the people and help it relax.
- If you're not successful desensitizing an overly fearful dog, seek professional help before your pet bites someone out of terror.
- Always keep an overly fearful dog under tight control when children are around.

FECES-EATING See COPROPHAGIA.

FEEDING PROBLEMS See APPETITE PROBLEMS.

FEMALE DOGS' BEHAVIORAL CHARACTERISTICS

Unspayed female dogs are often subject to hormone-induced cyclical mood swings and behavior changes. In most breeds the heat, or estrus cycle, occurs twice a year. Some breeds cycle less often. Just before a cycle begins, a female dog will often display nesting behavior. Some animals become really involved in nest building and collect things from all over the house with which to line their nests. They may also dig excessively. *(See* DIGGING: DIGGING INDOORS/ MAKING A NEST.)

At this point a female dog will urinate frequently in an attempt to attract a mate. This can present a problem for an owner who's not prepared to walk a pet more often than usual. There are several stages in the cycle, and when a female is not yet receptive to mating she may become very "touchy" and snap at people or other dogs if they approach her from behind or touch her on the rear.

When a dog has been neutered as a puppy, sexual characteristics are not especially noticeable: spayed females and castrated males behave in much the same way. In this case differences between individual animals are generally due to genetics and handling rather than sex.

See also box, SPAYING OF FEMALE DOGS—FACTS & MYTHS, p. 272.

FENCE JUMPING See JUMPING PROBLEMS: JUMPING OVER FENCES.

FENCES: INVISIBLE

Invisible fences to keep dogs from leaving their home property have become very popular in recent years. The devices consist of two parts. Electronic sensors are buried in the ground at the edge of a dog owner's property. The dog wears a special collar that produces a small electric shock if the animal crosses the invisible buried sensors. A dog has to be programmed to realize what triggers the shock and how to avoid it.

An invisible fence can be very useful if you live way out in the country and want to prevent your pet from dashing off to chase deer, rabbits, or other game. But it can present a problem in more populated areas. Although an invisible fence will keep a dog *in*, it does nothing to keep other dogs *out*. This can put a dog at a distinct disadvantage if loose dogs regularly come around. Also, if the temptation is very strong, some dogs will simply break through an invisible fence, ignoring the shock. Once a dog has done this no amount of further programming will convince it the invisible fence is invincible.

FEROCIOUSNESS See AGGRESSION; *box,* RAGE SYNDROME, p. 252.

FETCHING PROBLEMS

Problem: Claire loved it when her golden retriever, Clyde, ran to bring her a toy whenever she came home. She thought it was cute that the dog wanted to please her so much, and she praised Clyde lavishly whenever he brought her something. But as Clyde got older, his fetching habit turned out not to be so cute. One day when Claire went out to get her newspaper from the driveway, there were *five* papers, and Clyde, wagging vigorously, was just returning home with another newspaper in his mouth. Horrified, Claire scolded Clyde and put him indoors. Then she sat down to call any of her neighbors whom she thought subscribed to the morning paper. At least Clyde had a nice soft mouth and hadn't torn the papers.

DIAGNOSIS

It's the nature of some dogs, retrievers in particular, to enjoy fetching things and bringing them to you. When you praise a dog that has a natural bent for fetching things, you're encouraging it to go to further and further lengths to please you. When the fetched items belong to you, the behavior is perfectly acceptable, but problems arise if a dog begins to fetch other people's possessions.

TREATMENT

You can modify a dog's behavior so it understands it's all right to fetch certain items and not others.

- To let a dog know you're not pleased when it fetches a particular item, put your hand around the dog's muzzle and squeeze it firmly as you say "No." Take the forbidden item from the dog, put it well out of reach, and give the dog something it's all right for it to have.
- If a dog begins to fetch other people's belongings, see if you can enlist the aid of at least one victim to perform a Setup. Ask the person to leave her paper in the driveway and let her know when you let the dog out. Have her watch, and the minute the dog begins to pick up her paper, tell her to rush out shouting "NO!" If the dog drops the paper, have her praise it and give it a treat or a bone. If, on the other hand, the dog runs off with the paper, have her call you immediately so you can deal with it when it comes home. Most dogs will get the idea after one or two surprises.

FIGHTING See *box*, AGGRESSIVE BEHAVIOR IN DOGS, p. 7; INTER-DOG AGGRESSION; INTERMALE AGGRESSION.

FINICKY-ACTING See APPETITE PROBLEMS: LOSS OF APPETITE/ACTING FINICKY.

FITS See *box*, SEIZURES IN DOGS, p. 259.

FLANK SUCKING

Flank sucking is an obsessive neurologic behavior that's characteristic of Doberman pinschers. Because the behavior is confined to one breed of dog, it is thought to be an inherited condition.

Affected animals continually lick and suck on one rear thigh to the extent that the fur wears completely off and the skin eventually becomes thickened and shiny-looking.

As in Acral Lick Dermatitis/Granuloma, onset occurs at five years of age or older. Treatments and prognosis are similar.

See also box, OBSESSIVE-COMPULSIVE BEHAVIOR IN DOGS, p. 222.

FLATULENCE

Problem: The Petersons really didn't know what to do about their boxer, Joe. He's a sweet animal but is so gassy and flatulent they can't stand to have him in the room with them. When company comes they always have to close Joe in another room to avoid embarrassment.

DIAGNOSIS

Flatulence is caused by excess gas, air, or a combination of the two in an animal's digestive tract. Although it can be caused by disease, it's usually the result of eating too much gas-producing food and/or swallowing air. Dogs with pushed-in (brachycephalic) faces often swallow air when they eat, so are especially apt to become flatulent.

TREATMENT

- Have a flatulent dog looked over by a veterinarian to be sure there is no physical cause for the problem.
- Ask the veterinarian to prescribe a diet that won't produce excess stomach gas. Sometimes several diets will have to be tried, because food that prevents flatulence in one individual may not work for another.

FLIGHT BEHAVIOR

Flight behavior is an instinctive canine reaction. It occurs when an animal feels threatened and either doesn't want to fight or is fearful. The animal runs off headlong in an effort to get far away as fast as possible. It differs from Bolting in that a dog that has bolted will usually return to its owner when called, once it realizes there's no real danger. A dog exhibiting flight behavior is heedless to calls and won't stop until it has to because of exhaustion.

See also FEARFULNESS.

FLIGHT BEHAVIOR PROBLEMS *(See also* FEARFULNESS.)

Problem: On a crisp fall day, Andrew took his saluki, Zelda, to the woods five miles from home for a long walk. Holding the leash lightly, Andrew let the big dog run ahead of him, kicking up leaves in the path. All at once Andrew heard hoofbeats, turned, and saw a horse and rider trotting up behind them. Before he could tighten his hold on Zelda's leash, the dog broke loose and took off through the woods at top speed, never pausing to look back. Hours later, exhausted and worried, Andrew finally found the big dog loping slowly along the side of the road toward home.

DIAGNOSIS

The anecdote above is a classic example of Flight Behavior, brought about by intense Fearfulness.

TREATMENT

As for Fearfulness, an animal that exhibits flight behavior needs to be desensitized to whatever triggers its flight.

- For its own safety, a dog that's prone to flight behavior must be securely collared and leashed at all times outdoors.
- Hand in hand with firm leash control, you must let the dog know you're there and in command all of the time. Speak to it and reassure it at the same time you're keeping it by your side.
- When one particular stimulus or type of stimulus causes the dog to flee, you can gradually desensitize it a step at a time. If the problem is horseback riders, for example, take the dog to a nearby riding stable. With it under firm control, first let it see some horses as they stand quietly. Have a horsey-smelling rider pet the dog. Then let it see some riders and horses walking slowly around the ring. Little by little, one day at a time, have the dog become used to the horses and riders as they move around, faster and faster from walk to trot to canter. Finally, take the dog with you into the woods when you know a horse and rider will be coming by. Once you have your dog desensitized to horses it should be able to stand by your side calmly and watch as horse and rider go by.
- You can go through the same steps to desensitize a dog that exhibits flight behavior when a bicycle or truck passes. Whatever it is the dog is frightened of, allow it to become used to the stimulus gradually.

FOCUSING

I often use the phrase "Make your dog *focus* on you." What I mean is to make your dog stop what it's doing and look directly at you so you can tell it what you want it to do.

This can be accomplished in several ways. You can use body language. Clap your hands, snap your fingers, slap your thigh. You can make clicking or kissing noises with your mouth or use a Noisemaker or Throw Chain. If you hold up a Food Reward, a dog will look up at you. All of these things will make a dog stop what it's doing and focus on you.

A friendly, responsive dog may frequently look up at you and make Eye Contact. A dog that focuses on you without being asked is either seeking your approval or wants to find out what you'd like it to do next.

See also EYE CONTACT: NEGATIVE EYE CONTACT.

FOOD-GUARDING AGGRESSION (*See also* box, FOOD-GUARDING BEHAVIOR, p. 131.)

Problem: The Hayses can't figure out what's going on with the lovely year-old springer spaniel they got for their eleven-year-old daughter, Jenny. Affectionate, well mannered, and obedient most of the time, the dog turns into a snarling, threatening monster as soon as he's fed. The first time Jenny fed her new dog, she sat on the floor next to him to watch him eat. Instead, she got the surprise and scare of her life. Her new "friend" lunged toward her, teeth bared, growling and snarling ferociously. Horrified, Jenny let out a yell, scooted across the floor into the hall, and slammed the kitchen door.

After comforting the frightened girl, Jenny's parents went to see if they could figure out what was wrong. When they opened the kitchen door a friendly, wagging dog ran to greet them. This seemed to be the same delightful dog they'd brought home.

DIAGNOSES

Sometimes when an older dog is adopted it may have already developed behavior problems you will have to cope with. For other types of problems, *see* OLDER DOG PROBLEMS: ADOPTING AN OLDER DOG.

If a dog is so highly protective of its food that it becomes aggressive, the behavior has been caused by past experience. It may be impossible to know the exact cause with an older dog. If a dog has been living in a kennel or shelter with a lot of other dogs and the owners or keepers haven't properly supervised the feeding, it's possible the animal has had to fight for its share of food. Or perhaps it was the smallest in a large litter of pups and its food-guarding behavior necessarily became very strong. In other cases, small children may have been allowed to tease a dog and take away its feeding dish. In each instance the dog's latent food-guarding instinct has been amplified until it became aggressive around food. Dogs such as this usually remain perfectly friendly at all other times. A dog may exhibit food-guarding aggression toward another pet in the household as well as toward people.

TREATMENT

If a young puppy shows signs of food-guarding behavior you can prevent it from escalating by feeding the pup directly out of your hand. When an older dog has already developed food-guarding aggression you must teach the dog to trust you so completely it will allow you to touch its food bowl, pat it while it eats, and even pick up the food while it's eating. The dog has to learn to understand you won't ever take its food away. Then it should learn to tolerate strangers around while it eats. The steps below involve the cooperation of at least two family members.

■ Before you feed the dog, attach a long leash to a training collar and put it on the animal. While holding the leash, stand across the room and let the dog go to its bowl. When the dog begins to eat, have a family member approach. If the dog growls or acts aggressive in any way, snap the leash and shout "NO!" in a loud voice. (For how to do this, *see box*, LEASH CORRECTIONS, p. 192.) Repeat this over and over day after day until the dog learns to allow one of its owners to come and stand near the food bowl while it's eating.

- Next, go through the same steps while someone pets the dog as it eats; moves the bowl as the dog eats; sits on the floor beside the dog as it eats; and even picks the bowl up for a minute as the dog is eating.

- Once the dog calmly accepts these actions from a family member, it's time to get it used to having strangers around while it eats. To be on the safe side, leash your dog when you ask a friend to help you check it out. Go through the same steps described above until you're sure your dog will remain perfectly calm no matter who approaches while it's eating. This is especially important if there are children in the household who might bring friends home.

- Until you are absolutely certain your dog can be trusted, make sure to send any visiting children out of the kitchen and close the door before you feed it.

FOOD-GUARDING BEHAVIOR

Food-guarding is a very strong instinctive canine behavior that dogs have inherited from their ancestors the wolves. In order for any wild animal to survive it's necessary for it to guard its share of food or it will go hungry. In lean times a wolf will even guard its food from other family members. This instinct eventually ends in the survival of the strongest, fittest animals.

A highly territorial dog may have especially strong food-guarding instincts that can escalate into aggression unless they're controlled early in the animal's life.

See also FOOD-GUARDING AGGRESSION; *box,* TERRITORIAL BEHAVIOR, p. 289.

FOOD REWARDS AS TRAINING TOOLS

Food rewards/treats can be useful training tools when used properly, in the right context. But many dog owners continuously give their pets treats. They toss a biscuit to a dog when it wakes up, goes out, comes in, or just looks pleadingly at them. This accomplishes nothing except to eventually make the dog an overweight beggar.

To be a useful training tool, a food treat should be a reward for good behavior. *After* a training exercise has been successfully completed, you can give a dog a biscuit along with praise and a pat. But do the exercise first, without using food as a bribe.

Food rewards can be especially useful when you're training a puppy. Puppies are always hungry, and a proffered treat can help a youngster focus on you while you're working with it.

The only other time a food reward is useful during an exercise is if you're working with a performing animal that may need a little encouragement and extra energy to continue repeating an action over and over.

See also OBESITY; *box,* PRAISE TO MODIFY A DOG'S BEHAVIOR, p. 244; *box,* REINFORCEMENT—REPETITION AND REWARD IN TRAINING, p. 253; *box,* TIMING—ITS IMPORTANCE IN ALL ASPECTS OF DOG TRAINING, P. 292.

FRISBEE-CATCHING See *box,* GAMES TO PLAY WITH DOGS, p. 134.

FURNITURE, JUMPING ON See JUMPING PROBLEMS: JUMPING ON THE BED; JUMPING ON CHAIRS OR COUCHES.

G

GAMES TO PLAY WITH DOGS

One of the most satisfying ways to interact with your dog is to play with it. Dogs of all ages like to play games; even older animals benefit from the stimulation of modified game-playing. Playing with a dog has more than entertainment value; it helps offset Boredom and Destructive Behavior by tiring a dog out and relaxing it. Here are a few types of games you can play with a dog—you may think of others.

- Retrievers and other bouncy, high-energy dogs especially enjoy vigorous *fetching and catching* games with a ball or Frisbee. As your dog ages you can adapt a fetching game so the ball is rolled rather than tossed.
- Very active energetic dogs love to play *chase* with their owners, racing from one point to another outdoors.
- Scenting and *hide and search* games are fun for dogs of all ages. For a scent game, put a food treat inside a favorite bone or chew toy, hide the toy, and tell the dog to find it. Or simply hide a favorite toy or bone somewhere to be found. Nothing

can match the pleased-as-punch attitude of a dog that's just found a hidden object.

- *Jumping* is also a great activity for dogs. Encourage your dog to run and jump over hurdles, fences, and other obstacles outdoors.

See also BALL-PLAYING FETISH; PLAY PROBLEMS; TOYS FOR DOGS; TUG-OF-WAR.

Bouncy, high-energy dogs like Sally, a border collie mix, especially enjoy fetching/catching Games such as Frisbee. (Bruce Plotkin)

GARBAGE STEALING/DUMPING *(See also* APPETITE PROBLEMS: EXCESSIVE APPETITE; GULPING FOOD.)

Problem 1: Rex is an adorable Manchester terrier with one very bad habit. Every time his owners leave the kitchen, Rex immediately goes over to the garbage pail, stands up on his back legs with his paws on the rim of the pail, and dumps it over. When his owners come back, there's a mess all over the floor and Rex is sleeping in the next room looking like a little angel.

Problem 2: For the fourth time this month, Lucy's neighbor has called to complain about Lucy's Lab mix, Oscar. It seems that on the mornings the garbage collector comes, Oscar goes down the road and tears open the plastic bags the neighbor has put out, strewing garbage all over the road. Lucy wishes her neighbor would buy some strong-lidded cans for her garbage, but knows she has to do something about Oscar.

DIAGNOSIS

Any dog, no matter what size, has a natural instinct to find and eat available food. In the wild, a wolf would soon go hungry if it didn't do this. A dog has no way to know garbage is not there for it to eat. To a dog, garbage smells and tastes delicious.

Dogs that run loose outdoors can get into big trouble if they steal garbage from unknown sources. The food they find may be rotten and make them sick. It could even contain poison put there by unthinking people to get rid of vermin.

TREATMENT

To modify garbage-stealing behavior you have to make the experience become a negative one.

- If you can catch a dog that regularly dumps over an indoor garbage pail in the act and scold it, the scolding may do the trick. You'll be letting it know this is not an acceptable action.
- If a scolding doesn't work, there are several steps you

can take to modify a garbage-stealing dog's behavior *(see box,* BEHAVIOR MODIFICATION, p. 34). You can use a Setup. Buy some balloons and blow one up. Put it in the garbage can and bring the dog over to the can. Then pop the balloon to startle the dog. After you've done this, leave another blown-up balloon in the garbage can. Most dogs will then shy away from a possibly popping balloon.

■ You can also modify a dog's behavior if you put a mousetrap underneath a couple of sheets of newspaper in the bottom of the garbage can. As soon as the dog begins to put its nose in the can, the trap will snap and startle it. If you decide to use a mousetrap, be sure to put it underneath paper so the dog's nose won't be hurt.

■ Another method is to spray some bitter-tasting liquid directly on top of the garbage in the can *(see box,* LIQUIDS AS AIDS IN BEHAVIOR MODIFICATION, p. 196). As soon as the dog attempts to bite into the garbage it will get a mouthful of a nasty taste and give up the whole idea.

■ A free roaming dog that steals garbage is more difficult to foil unless you can enlist the aid of a neighbor. Provide her with some bitter-tasting liquid to spray her garbage with. Or better yet, you or the neighbor can keep watch, and as soon as the dog begins to knock over the garbage cans or root in the bags, rush out, startle it with a Noisemaker, Throw Chain, or Water Balloon, and shout "NO!"

While you're in the process of modifying a garbage-stealing dog's behavior, you should keep it from getting at garbage, either indoors or out.

■ To foil outdoor garbage stealing, the safest and most sensible course is to keep a roaming dog indoors. If you're unwilling or unable to do this, try to convince neighbors who put garbage out in bags or unclosed cans to purchase containers with tightly fitting spring-type lids.

■ You can prevent an indoor dog from stealing garbage if you take your garbage out right away, buy a tightly closed container, or place it somewhere where the dog can't get it.

GASEOUSNESS See FLATULENCE.

GATES TO CONFINE DOGS

A gate that fits in a doorframe by means of pressure or suction can be very useful to keep a dog in, or out, of an area while you're training it. Some owners prefer a gate to a Crate, and a gate can help gradually introduce a previously crated dog to the rest of the house. Because these gates are made of mesh and are see-through, they don't give a dog the feeling it's being shut out, away from the family. A gate enables a dog to see and hear what's going on on the other side and is far better in most instances than a closed door.

A gate can be used during house-training, when you're teaching a dog not to beg at the table, to stay off upholstered furniture, or not to take toys away from children. One of the most important uses of a pressure gate is when you're in the process of introducing a dog to a baby or new animal in the household. With a gate in place the dog can become accustomed to the newcomer's looks, sounds, and smells without making direct contact.

Bulldog Zack can see and hear what's going on while he's safely contained behind a pressure Gate. (Bruce Plotkin)

GETTING EVEN *See box*, SPITE—FACTS & MYTHS, p. 273.

GO TO YOUR PLACE!

"Go to your place," or "Go to your bed," is among the most useful commands you can teach a dog, especially if the animal is large and/or very energetic. A dog that responds to this command will never become a nuisance underfoot and won't have to be closed up or kept behind a gate.

It will be easier to teach a dog this command if it has learned Off-Leash Obedience so it will respond to your signals. Choose an out-of-the-way spot under a table or in a corner, for instance. You can put the dog's bed in the spot, or not, as you choose. Put the dog's leash on and have it heel. Then walk it over to the spot you've chosen, take off the leash, say, "Go to your place," and give a Down/Stay signal. When the dog lies down, praise it. Then walk away. If the dog begins to follow you, take it back and make it lie down again. Then move around the room in your usual fashion while the dog stays quietly. After a while, signal it to sit and then come.

GRABBING OBJECTS OR CLOTHES See TUG-OF-WAR.

GRASS-EATING (See also VOMITING.)

Problem: Every once in a while, the Danielses' poodle goes out in the backyard and chews and swallows blades of grass. When she comes in, she invariably throws up the undigested grass on the hall rug.

DIAGNOSIS

Wolves and dogs both eat grass, although they are by nature carnivorous animals. All dogs seem to feel the need to eat grass from time to time. No one really knows why they do this, but there are several theories.

One theory is that the grass fills some unknown nutritional need. Some who believe this point out that wolves always eat the contents of the stomachs of their prey, and their prey are usually grass-eating animals. Therefore, they think there may be traces of some nutrients in the grass that canines instinctively seek.

Another theory is the grass provides needed fiber in a dog's diet. If a dog is usually fed a commercially prepared diet, however, this doesn't make sense, because all commercial dog foods contain fiber.

Yet another explanation is that since the grass is indigestible it acts as an emetic to induce vomiting when a dog's stomach is upset. This would explain the seemingly erratic nature of the grass-eating, but it doesn't seem to be entirely valid, because dogs are usually able to vomit at will without the help of grass.

TREATMENT

- Whatever the reason for it, grass-eating seems to be a strong instinctive action of almost all dogs, and you shouldn't attempt to stop it.
- If you see your dog eating grass you can anticipate the results and put the animal in the kitchen or bathroom until the vomiting occurs.
- When a dog constantly eats grass it may be due to a dietary need. Check with your veterinarian to be sure the food you're giving your pet meets its nutritional needs.
- If your dog is a regular grass-eater, be sure there are no poisonous chemicals on your lawn. If it's necessary to use chemicals for some reason, keep your dog away from the lawn for at least twenty-four hours after the chemicals are applied.

GROOMING See BRUSHING PROBLEMS; EAR CARE; EYE CARE; box, MASSAGE FOR DOGS, p. 200; NAIL-CLIPPING PROBLEMS/ TECHNIQUES; TOOTH CARE PROBLEMS.

GROWING PAINS See LAMENESS, SYMPATHY.

GROWLING *(See also box,* AGGRESSIVE BEHAVIOR IN DOGS, p. 7; FEAR-INDUCED AGGRESSION; PLAY-GROWLING; HOW TO INTERPRET YOUR DOG'S BODY LANGUAGE, FACIAL EXPRESSIONS, AND VOCALIZATIONS, p. xi; TERRITORIAL AGGRESSION.)
Problem: Bitsie was a perfectly trained Welsh terrier, loving and gentle with her family. But when she was out on a walk or in the park and a stranger or friend of the family put out a hand as if to pat her, Bitsie let out a low-pitched growl.

DIAGNOSIS
In dog-to-dog communication a serious growl is a clearly understood warning: "Back off, or I may bite you." It is one of the first signs of aggression. Fearful, badly socialized, or highly territorial dogs may growl at humans for the same reason. A fearful dog growls because it doesn't want to be touched by a stranger. A badly socialized dog may growl because it was never exposed to a lot of different people as a puppy. *(See box,* SOCIALIZATION, THE KEY TO A WELL-ADJUSTED DOG, p. 258.) A highly territorial dog growls because it mistakenly thinks it must protect its owner against a stranger. Growling in anger at a friendly person for any reason at all cannot be tolerated.

TREATMENT
It's easier to treat a growling problem if you can ascertain what's triggering the behavior.

- When a dog acts fearful and uncomfortable around anyone who's not a family member, it must gradually be desensitized. Follow the treatment steps given for Fearfulness and Fear-Induced Aggression to accomplish this, substituting people of all sizes and shapes for noises or other stimuli.
- It's possible a dog that growls at strangers was not properly socialized as a puppy. When a puppy is handled and touched by a number of friendly people

throughout its growing-up stages it will learn to tolerate strangers well. If an adult dog hasn't been socialized as a pup, the process must be done now. With the dog under tight control, ask a friend or neighbor to come near and attempt to pat the dog. Greet the person warmly as he comes close to you and the dog. If the dog growls, give it a Leash Correction, say "No," and make it sit and stay. Again, have the person approach. Continue to do this until the dog accepts the person's pat. Have the person then give the dog a treat and praise it. Do this as many times with as many people as is necessary for the dog to calmly accept anyone who comes near it.

- If the dog is highly territorial and protective of you, go through the same steps you would with a badly socialized dog to show it you are not in need of protection.

GUARD DOG See LEARNED AGGRESSION.

GUARDING BEHAVIOR:

GUARDING FOOD See FOOD-GUARDING AGGRESSION.

GUARDING OBJECTS See OBJECT-GUARDING AGGRESSION.

GUARDING PEOPLE/PLACES See TERRITORIAL AGGRESSION.

GUILT—FACTS & MYTHS

Guilt, like Defiance and Jealousy, is an emotion that is dependent on reasoning beyond the ability of any dog. When we say a dog feels or is acting "guilty," we are anthropomorphizing. In order to feel guilt a person must go through a complex thought process: he must feel responsible for something he's done wrong either on purpose or through carelessness, realize that this act has either harmed or displeased someone, and then proceed to feel remorse for the act.

People often reason a dog is feeling "guilty" because it acts in a cringing manner when they come home and find a mess or house-training mistake. In reality, the dog is afraid it's displeased it's owner and is acting submissive in hopes of offsetting a scolding.

See also box, ANTHROPOMORPHISM, p. 13; *box,* SUBMISSIVE BEHAVIOR, p. 276.

GULPING FOOD (See also APPETITE PROBLEMS: EXCESSIVE APPETITE.)

Problem 1: Ned, a big Saint Bernard mix, practically inhales his dinner every night. His owners wonder if they're feeding him enough because he gulps his food so fast.

Problem 2: Whenever Sheila walks her pointer, Rosie, the dog manages to find a scrap of food in the curb or by some garbage cans, and before Sheila can react, Rosie gulps the food down.

DIAGNOSIS

Food-gulping is another instinctive canine behavior dogs have inherited from wolves. In the wild an animal will often gulp its food in order to prevent another animal from stealing it. Sometimes large or very active dogs become very hungry and feel the need to gulp their food down especially fast. This can result in a very serious problem. Gastric (stomach) dilation or torsion, popularly called bloat, can occur when a large dog eats a lot of food too quickly, drinks water, and then exercises.

When some dogs are walking on leash outdoors, they'll grab food they see on the street and gulp it down quickly. In this case, they want to prevent you from taking the food away.

TREATMENT

- To prevent food-gulping indoors, especially with large dogs, divide the daily rations into two meals and feed the animal morning and night instead of once a day. You can also add a few biscuits as snacks throughout the day so the dog doesn't become so hungry it feels the need to gulp down its food.
- Teach your dog the "Drop it!" command to prevent it from gulping down possibly dangerous or tainted food when you're walking outdoors. In the meanwhile, keep the dog on a tight leash when walking near garbage pails or bags to prevent it from finding any food to gulp.

H

HAND-SHYNESS

Problem: Whenever Rob reaches out to pat his puppy, the dog acts frightened, cringes, backs away, and growls.

DIAGNOSIS
A dog that shies away from a friendly hand is suffering from what's commonly called hand-shyness. Naturally sensitive dogs are more apt to develop this problem than their bolder cousins.

You can inadvertently create a hand-shy dog if you correct a Mouthing or Nipping puppy with a slap on the nose or face. Or if you punish a puppy after the fact with a slap or rolled-up newspaper, the puppy won't know what it's being hit for. (Remember, Timing is everything when you correct a dog of any age. *See also box,* PUNISHMENT, p. 247.) These actions will teach a dog to be fearful of your hand. It doesn't know whether to anticipate a hit or a pat when you put your hand out toward it.

A dog such as this will often bite your proffered hand if you persist in trying to pat it, or if it feels cornered. This is one form of Fear-Induced Aggression.

TREATMENTS
A hand-shy dog must be carefully desensitized until it learns to enjoy, rather than fear, hand contact.

- When the dog is calm and relaxed, slowly put your hand underneath its chin and stroke it very gently, as you talk to it in a soothing way. Repeat this day after day. When the dog is completely comfortable as you do this, very gradually move your hand until you can stroke it all over. *(See also box,* PATTING A DOG, p. 235.)
- Sometimes a Food Reward will help you get close to a very hand-shy dog. Hold a treat out in your hand and, when the dog comes to get it, stroke the animal gently underneath the chin.
- It may take a lot of time and patience to desensitize an extremely hand-shy dog.

HARNESSES FOR DOGS

People sometimes mistakenly think a harness is more suitable for a dog than a collar, especially when the dog is small. But although a harness may be attractive-looking, it gives you absolutely no control over a dog and is useless when you are training your pet.

There are a couple of circumstances in which a harness is acceptable for everyday use. A harness can be substituted for a collar once your dog is so perfectly trained to respond to your verbal commands it never requires a Leash Correction. Veterinarians also recommend using a harness rather than a collar to reduce pressure on the windpipe of a dog with tracheal problems.

In addition, harnesses are always used for tracking dogs. These dogs can't have their necks restricted by collars because they have to stretch their heads down to the ground to sniff while pulling their handlers along on a trail. For the same reason, working sled dogs are also harnessed, not collared.

See also box, COLLARS FOR DOGS, p. 72; *box,* TRAINING COLLARS, p. 299.

HEADCOLLARS *See box,* MUZZLES FOR DOGS, p. 207.

HEARING: PROBLEM-SOLVING USING
A DOG'S KEEN SENSE OF HEARING

A dog's sense of hearing is extremely well developed. It's well known that dogs can hear many things we can't. You can utilize this keen sense when you want to capture a dog's attention and make it stop what it's doing and Focus on you so you can correct it.

Throughout this book I refer to Noisemakers and Throw Chains as useful tools when correcting a dog. But if you don't have any of these things handy, a hand clap, slap on your thigh, sharp whistle, clicking or kissing noise, or shouted "NO" will all be easily heard by a dog, even from far away.

See also DEAFNESS, SIGNS OF.

HEAT CYCLE *See box,* FEMALE DOGS' BEHAVIORAL CHARACTERISTICS, p. 122; *box,* SPAYING OF FEMALE DOGS— FACTS & MYTHS, p. 272.

HEEL NIPPING *See* HERDING BEHAVIOR PROBLEMS.

HEELING

Heeling is an important obedience lesson that enables you to walk comfortably with your dog without the animal lunging ahead of you, lagging back, or becoming tangled up in your feet and ankles.

When a dog is in proper heel position, it's on your left side with its front feet in line with your feet. As you walk with the dog on or off leash, the dog stays even with you at all times, speeding up or slowing down as you do. A dog that has learned to heel correctly will be able to follow you as you turn corners in either direction, or walk around objects.

HERDING BEHAVIOR PROBLEMS

Problem 1: Josie's briard is a big, gentle dog that loves to run in the fields around the house. But every time Josie's ten-year-old niece comes to visit, the dog continuously bumps into the child with his shoulder as if he's trying to turn her in another direction. At first this seemed amusing, but it's beginning to drive the child crazy. She can't walk across the room or the front yard without the dog bumping into her. The dog has even taken to bumping schoolchildren as they walk along the road. Although this doesn't hurt them, it does upset them.

Problem 2: The Randalls' two corgis are very playful and love to run around in the yard with the children. The only problem occurs when the Randalls' oldest son and his friends play touch football. The dogs run around and around, nipping at the boys' heels as if to get them to stop running and gather them into a circle.

DIAGNOSIS

Dogs sometimes bump into people with their heads in an attempt to get attention. But the kind of bumping the briard is indulging in is clearly misdirected herding behavior, as is the nipping of the two corgis.

Herding behavior stems from the action taken by wolves when they hunt cooperatively as a pack. One or two animals usually go forward, up to the prey, and circle and heel-nip the victim to drive, or herd, it toward the rest of the waiting pack. Herding is especially well developed in some dog breeds such as briards and corgis. A dog with a strong herding instinct feels compelled to herd anybody who comes onto its property, or perhaps to gather up children or adults who are running. Depending on the type of dog, it may do this with either bumping or nipping. (*See also* NIPPING for other types of nipping behavior.) If herding is allowed to get out of hand it can become a problem and may even turn into aggression with some dogs.

The herding instinct of dogs can also have a positive side when there are toddlers in a family. Many a herding dog has become a "nanny" for children, successfully keeping them away from dangers such as roads, streams, and the like.

TREATMENT

- To avoid the bumping or nipping behavior with children, don't allow the dog to run loose when there are apt to be children around. Keep it under leash control until it's properly obedience trained, at which time you can tell it to stay, or Go to Your Place when children are around.
- You can desensitize a dog's strong herding instinct around children if you can enlist the aid of some neighboring youngsters and their parents. Ask the children to form a circle in your yard and walk the dog, on leash, all around the circle, inside and outside the diameter. The minute the dog begins to bump or nip, give it a Leash Correction. Then, when you're sure the dog is under control, try the same thing with it off-leash. When the dog is able to walk around the youngsters and not bump or nip them, praise it lavishly.

- You can also go into areas where there are a lot of people walking or running—a park or school track, for instance. With the dog under strict leash control, let it become desensitized to this activity until it no longer feels the need to herd everyone who walks or runs by.
- A group obedience class, too, will help a dog with a strong herding instinct to get the urge to herd everyone out of its system.

HIGH COLLAR

What professional dog handlers call a "high collar" provides excellent control over very strong, willful, or aggressive dogs.

Instead of putting a Training Collar around a dog's neck in the usual position, place it high, around the sensitive area just behind the dog's ears. This allows you to correct and control the dog without using a lot of strength or applying undue pressure.

HIGH-STRUNG BEHAVIOR See *box*, ANXIETY IN DOGS, p. 14; FEARFULNESS.

HOTEL, STAYING IN See CAR PROBLEMS: CAR TRAVEL.

HOUSE-TRAINING PROBLEMS *(See also* CRATE PROBLEMS: CRATE SOILING; DEFECATION, EXCESSIVE; DIARRHEA; *box*, HOUSE-TRAINING TIPS, p. 152; OLDER DOG PROBLEMS; SEPARATION ANXIETY; URINARY PROBLEMS; URINE LEAKING/DRIBBLING; URINE MARKING.)

BREAKING TRAINING

Problem: The little six-year-old bichon frisé had always been perfectly house-trained until recently. Now, whenever her owners come home they find a puddle and a "package" right inside the front door.

DIAGNOSIS

It's unusual for a previously well-trained dog to suddenly break house-training when all of the factors in its life remain the same.

In a case such as the one above, the most obvious answer is that the sudden breaking of training has a physical cause. As dogs age it can be difficult for them to wait as long as before between outings. They can also develop various disorders that create an urgent need to urinate or defecate. In addition, older dogs may not be able to assimilate their food as well as they could when they were younger.

TREATMENT

- When a dog of any age suddenly develops house-training problems and there is no obvious change in its life-style, seek veterinary help right away to rule out a physical cause.
- If you can, arrange to walk the dog more frequently, or hire a dog-walker to do this. Alternatively, teach your dog to use an Indoor Comfort Station you've prepared ahead of time.
- A change to a diet specifically designed for older dogs is often helpful in reducing an animal's need to defecate too often.

HOUSE-TRAINING TIPS

- *Absorbent pads*, similar to disposable diapers, are sold at pet supply stores and through mail-order catalogs. They soak up and hold moisture much better than newspaper and are neat and easy to pick up.
- A *Crate* of the right size can be a positive aid in house-training and will help a puppy or dog learn to wait until the appropriate moment to relieve itself. *(See box,* CRATES FOR DOGS, p. 77; CRATE PROBLEMS: CRATE SOILING.)
- An *Indoor Comfort Station* is a very useful device to use if you will not be home all the time to take or let a puppy or dog outdoors.
- *Inducers*, in the form of suppositories made for infants, will give a puppy or dog the idea to defecate outdoors. This method is especially useful if an older dog hasn't been properly house-trained and doesn't understand why it's being taken out. After inserting a suppository, immediately take the animal outside, where it will naturally defecate to eject it. Then praise the dog lavishly so it knows it's done the right thing.
- A *plastic drop cloth* such as painters use to protect furniture from splashed paint will protect your rug or carpet while house-training a puppy. Staple the plastic tightly over the entire carpet. Then place paper, an absorbent pad, or an Indoor Comfort Station in the corner you want the puppy to eliminate in. The plastic will keep the carpet dry and clean while the puppy is house-trained.
- A *Schedule*, strictly adhered to by you, is one of the best tools in house-training. When a puppy or dog knows what to expect and when, it's able to learn much faster than if it has no idea when it may be fed, walked, or let out of the Crate to relieve itself.

HOWLING (See also BARKING PROBLEMS: EXCESSIVE BARKING; *box,* VOCALIZING BEHAVIOR, p. 318.)

Problem: When the Cooks decided to get a malamute, it was on the understanding that she'd spend most of her time outdoors. They'd been bothered by raccoons raiding their garbage and thought the dog's presence would scare them off. Besides, Sue Cook didn't want all that fur in the house. Much to their distress, however, the minute it got dark, the dog began howling. Although their nearest neighbors were some distance away, the penetrating sound of the howls made them think they'd better put the dog inside.

DIAGNOSIS

Wolves howl to communicate with each other and to make contact in the wild. Although it's in the nature of all canines to vocalize, most dogs don't howl as much as their cousins the wolves. But some dog breeds are more apt to howl than others, malamutes among them. Dogs like this will often bark and bark until the bark turns into a howl.

TREATMENT

■ To treat a howling problem, follow the same Behavior Modification techniques given for barking; *see* BARK-ING PROBLEMS: EXCESSIVE BARKING.

HUNTING See PREDATORY AGGRESSION.

HYPERACTIVITY See ABNORMAL ACTIVITY LEVELS: HYPERACTIVITY.

HYPERKINETICISM See ABNORMAL ACTIVITY LEVELS: HYPERACTIVITY, PROBLEM 2.

—————— **I** ——————

IDIOPATHIC AGGRESSION (See also box, BRAIN DISORDERS, p. 47; box, RAGE SYNDROME, p. 252.)

Problem: Although George, a huge shaggy Saint Bernard, always acted somewhat aggressive toward strangers who approached the house, he was the soul of gentleness with his family. Obedient and well behaved, the big dog was a joy to have around. Then one day George was lying at his mistress's feet as his owners sat around the fire talking to some friends. The dog suddenly woke up from his nap, stared into space for a minute, and without warning lunged at his mistress's face, growling and snarling. Fortunately his master, Jim, was able to grab George by the collar, drag him away, and shove him out the door. Shaken, the dog's owners and their friends stared at each other, horrified and stunned. After a few minutes they decided George must have had a particularly vivid nightmare—it was the only way to explain his sudden bizarre behavior. When the dog came back inside, he ambled over to his mistress and plopped his head in her lap to be petted. They all laughed and forgot the incident.

Two weeks later, George attacked again. He suddenly leaped at Jim as the man walked into a room. Jim was badly bitten on the arm as he fended the dog off. This time there was no logical explanation, and all Jim could think was, "Thank heavens it wasn't a child who was bitten!" After the attack, George walked away as if nothing had happened.

DIAGNOSIS

Dogs such as this are often called psychopathic or brain-disordered animals. Medically, this type of aggression is labeled idiopathic because there is no known clinical or behavioral cause for it. It is believed by some to have a genetic predisposition. The behavior is characterized by sudden, unprovoked, viciously aggressive attacks that occur sporadically, often weeks or months apart. Just before an attack a dog may look glazed, and directly afterward most animals act as if nothing unusual has happened. The attacks are usually directed toward family members or close family friends. Dogs that exhibit this behavior are often very friendly, pleasant animals at other times.

TREATMENT

There is never a discernible specific medical cause for this puzzling behavior and the unprovoked nature of these kinds of aggressive attacks makes it impossible to diagnose them behaviorally. Therefore, there is no successful way to treat a dog with this syndrome. Drug therapy *(see box,* DRUGS AND DOG TRAINING, p. 104) and electric collar treatments have been tried by some veterinarians, but because the attacks are always so sporadic, these methods are necessarily hit-or-miss.

The only safe, realistic solution to this tragic problem is to have the dog euthanized before it hurts someone seriously.

IGNORING COMMANDS *See* DEAFNESS, SIGNS OF; *box,* DEFIANCE—FACTS & MYTHS, p. 87; STUBBORNNESS.

INCONTINENCE *See* OLDER DOG PROBLEMS; URINE LEAKING/DRIBBLING.

This easy-to-clean homemade Indoor Comfort Station consists of a large plastic picture frame lined with an absorbent pad. It's the perfect size for a toy dog like Kimberly the Yorkie. (Bruce Plotkin)

INDOOR COMFORT STATION

An indoor comfort station is a spot you set up in your home for your dog to use as a bathroom. Some owners train a dog to use this instead of going outdoors; others provide an indoor area for a dog to use only in emergencies; still others who travel a great deal with their pets use an indoor comfort station regularly when they stay in hotels, motels, or other people's homes. In these cases an indoor comfort station provides both pet and owner with a secure sense that no accidents can occur.

Whatever the reason for creating an indoor comfort station, you can't assume your dog will understand what it's for unless you teach it. A dog can learn to use both the outdoors and an indoor comfort station if it's trained young. If you know you're going to want your dog to use an indoor comfort station on a regular basis, it's best to start training the dog to use it from the very beginning. Large dogs in particular may have difficulty adapting from one system to another if they've been well taught to use the outdoors.

Indoor comfort stations take many forms and can be homemade or bought from pet-supply stores. Some people simply put layers of newspaper on the floor or devise various trays or holders for paper or absorbent training pads. Pet stores and mail-order pet-supply companies carry comfort stations with fake grass and posts for males to raise their legs on.

Whatever system you choose, an indoor comfort station must be easy to clean and large enough to accommodate your dog comfortably. Most dog owners place a comfort station in an out-of-the-way area such as a basement or seldom-used bathroom.

INFANTS AND DOGS See CHILDREN AND DOGS:
TODDLERS AND DOGS; JEALOUSY: JEALOUSY OF A NEW BABY.

INJURED BEHAVIOR *(See also* LAMENESS, SYMPATHY.)

Problem: Ginny was driving along a country road when
she spotted a large dog lying on the grass next to the
pavement. The dog looked odd to her, so she stopped her
car, got out, and went to see if something was wrong. As
she got close to the animal she could see its leg sticking
out at an angle, obviously broken. She wanted to help,
but when the dog saw her it suddenly began to growl and
snarl at her. Ginny backed off, got into her car, and hoped
she could find a phone nearby to call for help.

DIAGNOSIS
A dog that's in pain will often act aggressively, even toward its owners. (*See* PAIN-INDUCED AGGRESSION.)

A badly injured dog may be in shock. In this case the
animal is often literally out of its mind and will lash out
furiously at anyone who comes too close.

TREATMENT
In the anecdote above, Ginny acted correctly.

■ Never go near a dog that's obviously injured, even if
the animal appears to be unconscious. Don't allow your
desire to help to get in the way of your common sense.
■ Get help in the form of a veterinarian or animal control
officer. If you're in an unfamiliar area, call the police,
who can locate the proper people.
■ If you have to leave the dog to call for help, try to find
a landmark for the rescuers. Even a badly injured dog
is capable of dragging itself for some distance if it feels
threatened or wants to get home.

INTELLIGENCE IN DOGS

Owners often ask me, "Is my dog intelligent?" If you take the first definition of intelligence, "capacity to acquire and apply knowledge," all dogs certainly do have this ability. Owners can help their pets develop and better utilize their natural intelligence.

Dogs use their senses to acquire knowledge, and you can make up some simple games to help hone your dog's level of intelligence. For instance, show the dog a biscuit in the palm of your hand. Close both hands and put them behind your back and pass the biscuit from one hand to another. Then ask your dog to find the biscuit. Invariably, after one or two tries, a dog will learn how to locate the biscuit by using its keen sense of Smell (see box, SMELL, DOGS' KEENEST SENSE, p. 268). Other games involve hiding a dog's favorite toy in another room and asking the dog to find it, or teaching it to identify and fetch an object by shape.

Many of these "tests" of intelligence are actually exercises that are found in various levels of field trials and competitions. If you really want to help your dog develop its intelligence to the highest possible level, you can work with it and train it in obedience and advanced obedience, and enter it in competitions and field trails.

See also box, GAMES TO PLAY WITH DOGS, p. 134; box, OBEDIENCE TRAINING, p. 218.

INTER-DOG AGGRESSION (See also box, AGGRESSIVE BEHAVIOR IN DOGS, p. 7; box, DOMINANT BEHAVIOR, p. 98; INTERMALE AGGRESSION; JEALOUSY: JEALOUSY OF ANOTHER PET; box, PACK BEHAVIOR, p. 230; box, SUBMISSIVE BEHAVIOR, p. 276.)

Problem: The Ryans were having a terrible time with their Skye terriers, Sue and May. Sisters, the two dogs had always gotten on well. When May developed an ear infection she required twice-daily medication. Every morning and evening Mr. Ryan held May on his lap while his wife put drops in the dog's ears. He continued to hold May for five minutes to be sure she didn't shake out the drops, while he petted her to keep her still. Each time, Sue watched the entire process with great interest.

Shortly after the treatments began, Sue started to pick on May. Now she won't let her sister near the food bowl they'd always shared, but snarls and drives her away. When it's bedtime, Sue runs in, jumps up on her owners' bed, and growls ferociously at May when she tries to join her.

DIAGNOSIS

Whenever two dogs of any sex live in the same household they form a "pack" in which one animal is dominant over the other. Often this relationship isn't evident to owners.

Sometimes when dogs in the same household suddenly change from a friendly to a hostile relationship, it may be because something has happened to upset the dominance hierarchy between them. An illness, a stay in a kennel, or a change in family makeup, for instance, may cause the formerly dominant animal to feel its position is threatened.

The case above is a classic example of what happens when a dominance hierarchy goes awry. From the dominant dog's viewpoint the only way to set things right seems to be to strike out aggressively to regain the dominant role.

The formerly dominant terrier sees her position threatened by all of the extra attention her sister is getting. At the same time, the owners are unwittingly building confidence in the less dominant dog, with the result that it feels confident to challenge the other's leadership.

TREATMENT

There are a couple of ways to overcome a dog's sudden aggression toward a canine housemate. To do this, you must help the dogs reestablish a workable "pecking order," or dominance hierarchy.

■ When the reason for sudden inter-dog aggression is clear-cut, it may help to simply pay an equal amount of extra attention to the dog that feels left out so it doesn't need to vie for affection.

■ In any case of inter-dog aggression, the use of a Crate can be very effective. If each animal is placed in its own Crate whenever you are not at home it will prevent them from continuously fighting, jockeying for position. They will calm down, be under control, and be in balance with each other. You can also stop the dogs if fighting becomes too violent by putting them both back into their Crates.

■ When you are at home you can help dogs resolve their hierarchy problem. First, you must make it clear to the dogs that you are the leader of both of them—you have the Alpha Position.

■ As long as a question remains about which animal is the leader, the dogs will continue to fight. You can encourage one of them to become the leader by allowing it to dominate the other. Decide which dog will have the leadership position and then step in and encourage it to have the last word in any confrontation between the two animals. If the other dog continues to fuss or fight, stop it immediately.

■ After a while when the dogs see you clearly as the Alpha they will understand they have to fall in place under your leadership and will stop challenging each other continually. With your help they will be able to develop a peaceful relationship.

INTERMALE AGGRESSSION (See also box, AGGRESSIVE BEHAVIOR IN DOGS, p. 7; box, DOMINANT BEHAVIOR, p. 98; INTER-DOG AGGRESSION; JEALOUSY: JEALOUSY OF ANOTHER PET; box, PACK BEHAVIOR, p. 230.)

Problem: Ted's five-year-old boxer, Eddie, has always been nice as pie to other dogs in the park, so Ted thought he'd enjoy the companionship of another dog. All was well with the new shorthaired pointer puppy at first, but as soon as the pup began to mature, Eddie began to attack him. Ted scolded and scolded Eddie, but the dog seemed hardly to hear him, and the fighting is becoming worse and worse. Now the pointer has started to attack Eddie!

DIAGNOSIS

This is a classic case of intermale aggression. In a pack there is only one dominant adult male leader, and in the absence of a dominance hierarchy and clear-cut leader, two male dogs will continue to fight it out until one beats the other. In the wild, the loser would then leave the pack, but as this isn't possible in a home situation, the fighting will probably continue even after one dog is clearly the winner.

TREATMENT

To prevent a constant struggle for dominance between two male dogs, the owner must help the dogs establish a workable dominance hierarchy. (*See also* INTER-DOG AG-GRESSION.)

- First, to separate the dogs and avoid bloodshed, provide each animal with his own Crate. Because they're both being treated the same, this will also help establish balance in their relationship.
- Observe the dogs carefully to see which one is naturally the dominant animal. Once you've determined this, you will have to help that dog establish its position. In most cases the older, original dog will become the leader.
- Because dominance-related fighting between males is controlled by male hormones, one or both dogs should be neutered (*see box*, CASTRATION OF MALE DOGS—FACTS & MYTHS, p. 57; *box*, MALE DOGS' BEHAVIORAL CHARAC-TERISTICS, p. 198). This will automatically reduce their strong intermale reactions to each other. If the original dog is old and you don't want it to have surgery, neu-

tering the new, younger animal will usually help a great deal.

- Each dog has to be obedience-trained so it is completely under your control.
- Once all of these steps have been taken, the dogs can be gradually introduced to each other. If the dog you have decided will have the submissive role shows signs of aggression toward the other animal, say "NO," and bring the dog under leash control.
- Don't leave the dogs alone together until you're sure they've settled into their appropriate roles.

IRRITABILITY *See box,* BEHAVIOR CHANGES, **p. 33;** OLDER DOG PROBLEMS; PAIN-INDUCED AGGRESSION; QUARRELSOMENESS.

J

JEALOUSY IN DOGS—FACTS & MYTHS

Dog owners often consider jealousy to be the root of canine behavior problems that suddenly surface when a previously unknown person or animal comes to live in the home.

In fact, jealousy is a human, not canine, emotion and isn't what causes a dog to misbehave under these circumstances. Instead, the "bad" behavior is usually a perfectly normal canine reaction that stems from competition. When a dog's territory is invaded by a stranger who seems to threaten its position in the family, or pack, the animal naturally becomes upset and may act out its confusion and frustration in many different ways.

See also box, ANTHROPOMORPHISM, p. 13; *box,* PACK BEHAVIOR, p. 230; TERRITORIAL AGGRESSION; *box,* TERRITORIAL BEHAVIOR, p. 289.

JEALOUSY *(See also box, JEALOUSY IN DOGS—FACTS & MYTHS, p. 164.)*

JEALOUSY OF ANOTHER PET *(See also CHEWING PROBLEMS; DESTRUCTIVE BEHAVIOR; INTER-DOG AGGRESSION; INTERMALE AGGRESSION; box, PACK BEHAVIOR, p. 230; TERRITORIAL AGGRESSION; URINE MARKING.)*

Problem 1—a New Dog: Pierre, a standard poodle, was always tolerant of dogs visiting his home, but suddenly he's acting very "jealous" of the three-month-old puppy his owners brought home a few weeks ago. Pierre growls at the puppy whenever it comes near him, and has begun to raise his leg and urinate on the furniture whenever his owners are out.

Problem 2—a New Kitten: When Mary went back to work she decided to get a companion for her dog, Patty, a mixed-breed shepherd. She didn't have time to raise a puppy, so decided a kitten would be good company for Patty—the dog had always been friendly toward cats. Rather than being delighted with her new "friend," Patty completely ignores the kitten and has taken to chewing on everything in sight as if to say, "Pay attention to me!" Mary is very upset at this obvious display of "jealousy" and wants to stop it right away.

Problem 3—a Bird: John inherited his dad's parrot, Sam—a very talkative old bird. He brought Sam home to live with him and his German shorthaired pointer, Fritz, and set up the bird's perch in a corner of the living room. The dog watched silently as John fussed over the parrot and gave it food and water. Several times after that, John found Fritz staring fixedly at the bird, barking, while the parrot yelled at him. John dismissed this as "jealousy" and assumed the dog would soon get over it. But about a week later, John came home from work and was horrified to find a defiant dog standing in the middle of the room with Sam flapping in his mouth, squawking loudly. John quickly removed Sam from Fritz's grip and saw to his relief that he was unhurt, thanks to the bird dog's naturally "soft" mouth. The muttering, indignant parrot was returned to his perch, where he sat preening himself calmly, while John struggled to regain his own composure and wondered what he was going to do about the situation.

DIAGNOSIS

In each of these cases the dog feels threatened and is defending its place in the pack (*see box*, PACK BEHAVIOR, p. 230) by means of various undesirable actions.

TREATMENT

It's important to reinforce the proper pack order. Make it clear to the original dog that it's still leader of the animals, despite the new arrival, but you are the overall leader of the entire pack. (*See box*, ALPHA POSITION, p. 12.)

The same treatments apply to all three problems.

- The new animal should be confined initially so the first animal doesn't feel so threatened. Introduce the two gradually, but always when you are around to supervise.
- Don't allow the new pet to bother the other one unduly. Separate them if it seems to become annoying.
- Give the first animal a great deal of individual attention to reassure it of its firm position in your affections and your home. Take it for walks and play with it alone to reinforce your bonding and your clear leadership role. If the dog has been obedience-trained, give it a brief refresher course for the same reason.
- If the first animal persists in Urine Marking or other Destructive Behavior when you are not home, you'll have to confine it when you're not around so the behavior doesn't become a habit.
- Whatever sex it is, neutering an older dog will eventually cut back on its territoriality and aggression. If your new pet is a puppy it should also be neutered at the appropriate age by Castration or Spaying.

JEALOUSY OF AN ADULT PERSON (*See also* ONE-MAN DOGS; TERRITORIAL AGGRESSION.)

Problem: For four years, Fred has lived alone with his pug. The dog slept on his bed and stayed right by his side whenever he was home. The little dog was always very friendly with visitors, but the first time Fred's girlfriend, Tricia, went into the bedroom the dog flew into a rage. She barked and growled at Tricia and even tried to bite her on the ankle. Fred doesn't know what to do. He loves the dog, but he's also very fond of Tricia and doesn't want to lose her because of the animal's "jealous" behavior.

DIAGNOSIS

The dog's aggression is rooted in Pack Behavior. A dog that's extremely close to its owner (pack leader) may feel it needs to protect him from the "threat" of a new person in the home.

TREATMENT

You must help a dog understand the newcomer poses no threat to you but is, in fact, another pack member. The dog has to learn to respect and look up to any new human member of the household.

- Talk softly and soothingly to the dog at the same time the newcomer pats and strokes it. Many dogs will respond to this and soon adopt the newcomer as another family member.
- If the dog persists in its aggression, an immediate solution is to squirt some water into its mouth as soon as it begins to bark. This will startle the animal and focus its attention onto you. Then say "NO," and pet the dog when it calms down.
- In cases when a dog continues to rage and even tries to bite, the quickest and safest action is to confine it immediately in a Crate, behind a Gate, or behind a closed door. You can also leash the dog and attach the leash to a doorknob so the animal can't get at the visitor to bite.

- A longer-term cure in a difficult case is to have the newcomer gradually make friends with the dog by feeding it, walking it on a leash, playing with it, grooming it, and performing other everyday chores until the dog accepts him or her.
- In extreme cases a dog may need to be desensitized by a professional trainer. For an explanation of this, *see box*, DEPROGRAMMING AND DESENSITIZATION, p. 88.

JEALOUSY OF A NEW BABY *(See also* CHILDREN AND DOGS; *box*, DOMINANT BEHAVIOR, p. 98, *box*, PACK BEHAVIOR, p. 230; *box*, SUBMISSIVE BEHAVIOR, p. 276; TERRITORIAL AGGRESSION; *box*, TERRITORIAL BEHAVIOR, p. 289.)

Problem: A married couple has had a wheaten terrier that has been their constant companion for five years. They take him everywhere with them—away on weekends in the country, to the beach for the day, and so forth. In fact, they've treated him just like a child. Now they're going to have their first baby and are concerned about the dog's reaction. They want to make sure he doesn't become "jealous" of the baby.

DIAGNOSIS

A dog may see its position in the pack threatened by the competition of a baby and feel overwhelmed and displaced in the family. At the same time the owners may unwittingly give the dog Mixed Messages if they turn it into an outcast by closing it out of their lives (and rooms), at the same time requiring it to be obedient, docile, and loving to the baby. In this case a dog may become confused, and overly territorial, and may try to regain its position by dominating the baby.

TREATMENT

This is a complex problem that requires a two-step solution: socializing the dog to children in general before the birth, and then teaching it to accept the newborn baby into its home.

- First, introduce the dog to children and babies so it becomes used to their smells, sounds, and actions.
- After the baby is born, avoid giving Mixed Messages to the dog by acting fearful when it's around the baby, or the dog won't know how to behave and may feel you expect or want it to dominate the child.
- Be calm and affectionate with the dog and let it know you still love it and expect *it* to act calm, behave well, and be affectionate with the new baby.
- Be sure *you* are the focus of the dog's attention, not the baby, by talking soothingly to the dog and telling it how good it is while you attend to the child.

Before the Baby Is Born:

- Have the dog neutered if it has not been, by Castration or Spaying. At the same time, be sure it has no medical problems that might make it cranky.
- If the dog hasn't been obedience-trained, take this important step now so the animal is under complete control at all times. If it has previously been trained, now is the time to review and refresh the training. *(See box,* OBEDIENCE TRAINING, p. 218.)
- Introduce the dog to as many children and babies as possible, in the park or on the street, so it will begin to learn a baby is actually a small human. It's especially effective if friends can bring their babies to your home so the dog can get to know them (under full leash control) and become used to their smells, sounds, and sudden movements.

After the Baby Is Born:

- Before the baby comes home from the hospital, bring home a soiled diaper and a blanket or some clothing the baby has worn and allow the dog to sniff them so it will become used to your baby's own smell.
- Start off on the right foot. If the mother has been the dog's primary caretaker up until now, the dog will be very excited when she comes home and will rush to

greet her. Let someone else hold the baby when the mother enters the house so she can greet the dog enthusiastically and affectionately with a hug and a pat.

- With the dog under leash control, in Down/Stay or Go to Your Place, allow it to be with you when you feed and hold the baby. Most important, have the dog in the room when you're changing diapers. This will make it clear to the dog that this is a young animal—a baby—and will bring out its basic pack-oriented behavior of nurturing and protecting young.

- Never hold a baby high above a dog's head away from your body. A dog will assume you're inviting it to jump up to investigate or play and may grab at the infant.

- Whenever possible, give your dog extra attention and love so it won't feel closed out of your life.

- Until you're absolutely sure the dog can be trusted, don't ever leave it alone with the baby. Keep a pressure Gate on the door of the nursery even if you're just in the next room.

- Even after you're perfectly sure your dog fully accepts the baby, don't ever put the baby on the floor in the same room with the dog. The dog may perceive this as a submissive act on the baby's part and act dominant or aggressive toward it.

- If the dog seems at all fearful of the baby, you will have to move slowly and introduce them very gradually.

- Should the dog growl or seem at all aggressive, correct it immediately and let it know this is not acceptable behavior. If this happens, seek professional help right away.

See also CHILDREN AND DOGS.

JOGGING WITH A DOG

Problem: Jane has decided she would like to take her five-year-old Rhodesian ridgeback with her when she begins a new activity—jogging in the park. The first time she tried it, however, the dog didn't seem to know what to do and kept pulling her this way and that as she tried to keep up an even pace.

DIAGNOSIS

According to a study conducted by the American Animal Hospital Association (AAHA), 44 percent of dog owners like to take their dogs with them when they jog. Other owners have their dogs run alongside as they ride bicycles.

These are welcome and much-enjoyed activities for most dogs. But you can't expect a dog to know what's expected of it when you take it to a strange place and begin to indulge in an activity it's never taken part in before. In addition, it's important to condition your pet ahead of time so it can withstand the rigors of strenuous activity.

TREATMENT

Use your common sense if you're anticipating an exercise program with your dog.

- Take your dog's age, size, personality, and breed into consideration. Most dogs will try their best to keep up with you, no matter how tired or sore they may be. It's up to you to judge how much your own pet can comfortably do. Obviously, a small, short-legged animal won't be able to run as far or as fast as a large, long-legged dog can.
- Before you begin, take your pet to the veterinarian and explain what you have in mind. The doctor should check the animal's heart, be absolutely certain it doesn't have heartworms, and assess its circulatory system and joints to be sure there's no problem that could be exacerbated by running.
- If your pet's a young animal, ask the doctor when it's safe for it to begin to undertake a serious running program. Large and giant dog breeds, for instance, take longer to mature than small dogs, and their bones, muscles, and joints may not be strong enough to withstand prolonged, strenuous exercise until they're at least a year old.

- Safety first. Always have your dog on leash when you run or bicycle with it. This will not only keep your dog from harm, but enable you to control the speed of its gait and to shorten the lead and avoid a confrontation when you see approaching dogs, runners, cyclists, and so forth.
- Whatever age it is, any animal that hasn't previously participated in this type of exercise will require gradual conditioning before it's ready to run for extended periods of time. No matter how much running around the yard a dog may have done, this alone won't build up heart, lung, and muscle capacity capable of withstanding a serious running program. Begin with short five-to-ten-minute fast walking or slow jogging, and work up to longer and faster sessions until your dog is capable of running for twenty minutes or more without tiring.
- Don't forget to check your dog's feet. If an animal isn't used to running on hard surfaces, its foot pads may require some initial toughening up so they won't get red and sore.
- Before you begin any exercise session, walk your dog and allow it to relieve itself.
- Be aware of weather conditions. In hot, humid weather it's a good idea to exercise in the evening or early morning.
- Keep a close eye on your pet. If the animal begins to lag, froth at the mouth, or pant rapidly, it could be a sign of heatstroke. Stop running or cycling immediately, find a shady area if possible, and apply cool compresses to the dog's body and head. If the dog loses consciousness, take it to the veterinarian immediately. It may require intravenous fluids and/or other treatments to prevent brain damage.
- If an exercise session lasts longer than twenty minutes, offer your dog a small amount of water from time to time. Also offer some water or ice cubes immediately after exercising. Don't let an overheated dog drink too much too fast, or it will throw up (*see* DRINKING PROBLEMS: DRINKING EXCESSIVELY/TOO FAST; VOMITING).

JUMPING PROBLEMS

JUMPING ON THE BED

Problem: Every time Millie and her husband settle down to read in bed, Jake, their Labrador, jumps up on them. They push him down and say "NO," but he keeps jumping up. They have small children and don't want to close the bedroom door, and they do want Jake to have the run of the house at night for protection, but he's really too big to make a good bedmate.

DIAGNOSIS

Because of their pack origins *(see box,* PACK BEHAVIOR, p. 230), dogs are very social animals and love to be with their people. Most dogs need little if any encouragement to jump up to be near them.

TREATMENT

With a highly social, friendly dog the solution to too much togetherness is to shock the animal out of the undesirable behavior.

- Have a full water pistol or spray bottle handy, and the minute the dog starts to jump up, squirt it in the mouth or face and say "NO!" When it settles back down on the floor, you can pet and praise the dog, but in case it thinks this is encouragement to jump up again, keep the water pistol handy to spray immediately if the animal makes a move.
- Another way to shock a dog is to have a large cooking pot and spoon handy. The minute it starts to jump, bang the pot with the spoon and say "NO." The dog will soon realize this is not a positive experience.
- Alternatively, if you don't care about your dog having the run of the house but still want it in your bedroom at night, leash the dog and hold the end of the dog's leash. As soon as it begins to jump, correct it with a snap and say "NO." For how to do this, *see box,* LEASH CORRECTIONS, p. 192.

- A long-term solution is to train your dog to Go to Your Place. Then it will stay quietly all night in its own bed or place.

JUMPING ON CHAIRS OR COUCHES (See also box, A BED FOR A DOG, p. 31.)

Problem: Every time Mary comes home she finds her Belgian sheepdog, Annie, stretched out on the brand-new living-room couch, where she leaves a lot of her beautiful, long fur on the velveteen upholstery. Covers don't do much good, as Annie seems to be able to pull them off. Mary wants to break her dog of the habit of jumping on the couch.

DIAGNOSIS

Dogs and their ancestors the wolves always like to create a nest for themselves. A dog naturally finds a couch or chair more comfortable than the floor for its nest. In addition, the scent its owners leave on the furniture makes it an even more appealing nesting place for a dog.

TREATMENT

The best way to break a dog of this habit is to make the act uncomfortable in some way so it becomes pleasanter for the dog to sleep on the floor.

- You can use a Setup. Put a bunch of balloons on the couch. Then, with the dog on a leash, walk over to the couch, point at it, and say "NO." When you're right next to the couch, pick up a balloon and pop it right in the dog's face. Then walk a short distance away with the dog still on leash. Remove the leash and go into another room. If the dog wasn't sufficiently startled by the popped balloon and is still brave enough to jump on the couch, the remaining balloons will pop and frighten it into getting right down.
- With a very strong-willed, powerful dog such as an Akita, a popping balloon may not be deterrent enough. You may need to use a stronger Setup. Place a number

of set mousetraps on the furniture with a light sheet on top (the sheet will protect the dog from being hurt by the traps). If the dog jumps up, the traps will snap and startle the animal enough to make it give up the couch as a bed.

- Another form of Setup requires you to be at home. Leave the dog alone in the room with its favorite couch. After a few minutes, rush back in, and if the dog is on the couch, go into a hysterical act, screaming, banging pots and pans, and shouting "NO!" at the top of your lungs. At the same time, grab the dog by the scruff of the neck and pull it off the furniture. After one or two times, most dogs will decide it's not worth it to go through that again and will find another place to sleep.

- Finally, provide the dog with a bed of its own to nest in—a cushion, blanket, towel, or old sweater will do. Your scent on whatever bedding you provide will make it more attractive to the animal.

JUMPING ON THE KITCHEN COUNTER OR DINING TABLE (See also EXPLORATORY BEHAVIOR; GARBAGE STEALING/ DUMPING; GULPING FOOD.)

Problem: Sometimes very agile, strong little dogs— terriers and spaniels, for instance—are able to jump right up onto a kitchen counter or dining table to get at food. Some are brazen enough to jump right up onto the counter next to their owner as she's preparing something especially aromatic and delicious, such as a roast. Others will wait until a meal is finished and the people get up from the table and will then jump directly onto the table to lick the plates.

DIAGNOSIS

In the wild, wolves eat as much as they possibly can at one time because they don't know when they'll get another meal. In general, dogs do the same and often look for leftovers to finish up. You encourage this behavior if you regularly feed your pet table scraps; the dog will naturally figure it's all right to help itself when you're not around. It's also natural for a dog to explore and want to know what's up on a counter or tabletop.

TREATMENT
You need to make the experience of jumping on the counter or table negative. Instead of getting a tasty morsel the dog will have an unpleasant experience.

- Just as described in Jumping on Chairs or Couches, you can set a dog up with a booby trap. Put a particularly desirable morsel of food on the counter or table with a row of set mousetraps in front of it, covered with a dish towel. As soon as the dog jumps up, the traps will go off and startle it. This is usually sufficient to prevent any dog from trying to jump up again.
- You can also set a dog up by leaving the room when food is on the counter or table and bursting back in as described under Jumping on Chairs or Couches.
- If a dog persists in jumping on the counter or table, or if neither of the above solutions appeal to you, you can use an Elizabethan Collar. The Collar will block a dog's peripheral vision sufficiently so the animal won't be able to judge distance and will be afraid to try to jump up.

As soon as a dog begins to jump up on you in greeting, say
"NO" in a loud voice and raise your knee so it hits the dog in
the chest. Here, Kelly, a standard poodle, gets the knee treatment. (Bruce Plotkin)

JUMPING ON PEOPLE IN THE HOME IN GREETING
(See *also* FACE RUBBING; SNIFFING PEOPLE AND OTHER DOGS IN
GREETING.)

Problem: Mac is a lovable, galumphing Irish setter who
adores everyone. The trouble is that as soon as anyone,
family member or visitor, walks into Mac's house, he
jumps up on them with his front paws and practically
knocks them down. As a matter of fact, he did knock

down a four-year-old recently, and his owners want to break him of this bad habit.

DIAGNOSIS

Jumping up on people in greeting is rooted in pack ritual. When wolves meet, they make body contact and sniff and lick each other—a subordinate animal often licks a more dominant one. One of the nicest things about dogs is that they're always so happy to see people and rush to greet them. In an effort to make body contact and get their faces as close to a person's face as possible, many dogs will jump up.

TREATMENT

You don't want to make a dog miserable by not allowing it to greet people at all. The trick is to show it how to greet people in an acceptable way.

- You can avoid the problem altogether and prevent any size dog from jumping up if you immediately squat down to its level when you enter the house. Then you can greet each other enthusiastically without danger of your being knocked over or having your clothes torn.
- If this isn't comfortable for you or for older visitors who may not want to squat down, you can modify the dog's behavior in two ways. As soon as it begins to jump up, say "NO" in a loud voice and raise your knee so it hits the dog in the chest, while at the same time giving a hand signal: both hands raised, palms facing the dog's face. When the dog stays on the floor, lean down and pat and praise it. After one or two times most dogs will respond to the hand signal and vocal command alone.
- For a stubborn or very large and heavy dog such as a Saint Bernard, you may need to use a Setup. When a guest arrives at the door, put a leash on the dog and take it to answer the door with you. Watch closely, and the second the dog begins to jump, jerk the leash and say "NO." If you can get your guest to cooperate, have him knee the dog at the same time. Immediately

after jerking the leash, give the hand signal. Again, praise the dog when it responds. The aim is to have the dog learn to respond to the hand signal alone.

- A very good alternative solution for small and medium-sized dogs is to establish an acceptable place for the animal to jump up onto so it will be closer to a person's chest level. Examples are a hall bench, chair, or part-way up the staircase. The first time the dog starts to jump up on you or a visitor in greeting, say "NO," lift it up to the place you've selected, and then greet it. After one or two times, the dog will hop right up to its "place" to be greeted the minute you or anyone else walks in the door.

JUMPING ON PEOPLE OR OTHER DOGS WALKING ALONG THE STREET (See also box, DOMINANT BEHAVIOR, p. 98; MOUNTING BEHAVIOR.)

Problem: Some dogs will watch a person walking toward them on the street or standing quietly waiting for a traffic light to change, and if the stranger catches the dog's eye, the dog will immediately jump up on him. Other dogs will try to jump on any dog they pass while walking along.

DIAGNOSIS
These actions are based on the ritualized greeting behavior of the pack. When wolves meet, one will often jump on another in an effort to dominate it. Dogs have inherited this trait.

TREATMENT
This is a problem you have to cure right away, because most people don't take too kindly to having themselves or their pets "attacked" by a strange dog.

- If your dog shows a tendency to jump on people or other dogs on the street, learn to watch carefully so you can judge when it's about to "greet" a stranger. *Before* the dog begins to jump, jerk the leash or rattle a key ring to get its attention. Make the animal Focus on you, and let it know you're aware of its intention to jump. Say "NO," and Praise your dog lavishly when it remains by your side.

- If your dog is very "hyper" it can be difficult to keep it from jumping on every other dog it meets. For dogs such as this I recommend using a High Collar when walking so you always have full control over your pet.

JUMPING OVER FENCES (See also BOREDOM; CHASING PROBLEMS; EXPLORATORY BEHAVIOR; box, MALE DOGS' BEHAVIORAL CHARACTERISTICS, p. 198; box, PACK BEHAVIOR, p. 230; box, TERRITORIAL BEHAVIOR, p. 289.)

Problem: Lewis, a large Akita, has a nice big yard to stay in during the day when his owners are at work. But Lewis often gets it in his head that he'd like to explore the outside world and regularly jumps the six-foot fence around his yard. The neighbors are getting very tired of picking up dumped garbage cans and shooing him out of their vegetable gardens. So far Lewis has been picked up by the animal control unit six times, and his owners have had to pay increasingly large fines to get him back. In addition, they worry that Lewis might be hit by a car. It's against the village code to have a higher fence, and Lewis's owners don't want to have to keep him indoors all day.

DIAGNOSIS

There can be several reasons why dogs become "escape artists." Usually the root of this behavior lies in pack orientation. A strong sense of pack bonding may cause a dog to escape in order to go find its owners. If roaming dogs pass by, it may also want to join up with them or perhaps protect its territory by chasing them away. If there's a female in heat somewhere in the county, an unaltered male will almost always do his best to find her. Sometimes, however, a high-energy dog simply gets bored and wants to explore.

TREATMENT
Your aim is to stop the behavior quickly, before it becomes a deeply ingrained habit.

- To avoid Boredom, be sure the dog has plenty of exercise, and don't leave it out in the yard alone for more than about eight hours at a time.
- The safest and quickest immediate cure for fence-jumping is to put an Elizabethan Collar on the dog.
- As long as the dog is fenced in, safe from attack from roaming dogs, a trolley is another solution. This consists of a long lead attached to a pulley strung on a line stretched between two trees or the house and a tree or pole. The lead should be long enough so the dog can run around the yard safely, get in the shade and lie down, etc., but not so long it can jump the fence.
- You can discourage a dog from trying to jump over a fence by attaching an obstacle or obstacles to the inside top of the fence itself. A row of balloons or a foot or two of chicken wire, for instance, will make it difficult for the dog to judge the fence's height and width.
- Have your male dog castrated if he hasn't been. This will eventually cure him of his desire to go in search of females. *(See box,* CASTRATION OF MALE DOGS—FACTS & MYTHS, p. 57.)

K

KENNEL SHYNESS (See also box, ANXIETY IN DOGS, p. 14; FEARFULNESS.)

Problem: Jim Baxter had just arranged to buy a lovely little basenji puppy when his company told him he was being sent to England for six months. Jim didn't want to subject his new pet to England's mandatory quarantine, so he arranged with the breeders to keep the pup until he returned.

Six months later he picked up his new dog. When he got home, the half-grown puppy ran to its cage, and he decided to leave her alone to settle down. Much to his dismay, she wouldn't come out of the cage when he went to see her later. Jim tried to coax her with food, but she just cowered in the corner of the cage. She acted fearful of everything and whimpered and trembled when he came close. If he lifted her out of the cage to go outdoors, she seemed terrified, lay flat on the ground, and ran right back into the cage the minute the door was opened.

DIAGNOSIS

A dog that has been isolated and sheltered from Socialization and stimulation because it has remained in a cage at a breeder's kennel or pet shop for too long and hasn't been exposed to many people often develops a syndrome called "kennel shyness." Although it may seem friendly toward people when it's safely in its own Crate, a dog such as this hasn't become used to normal day-to-day activities or interactions with humans. It doesn't know what's expected of it and becomes extremely fearful, confused, nervous, and disoriented when it's exposed to the world outside its cage.

TREATMENT

No matter how old a kennel-shy dog is, it's a young puppy in terms of experience and must be patiently and calmly desensitized and introduced to the world around it.

- The first step is to obedience-train a kennel-shy dog. Not only will training provide the animal with a sense of structure, but the training process itself will help it form a bond with you and teach it to understand you will protect it and lead it.
- A dog that's spent all of its life in a small area should be introduced to your home very gradually. At first, confine the animal to one room until it becomes relaxed and calm. With the dog leashed by your side, you can then take it into another room and allow it to explore. Do this one room at a time until the dog has an opportunity to familiarize itself with the entire house.
- Keep the dog under leash control whenever new people come into the household and let it become acquainted at its own pace.
- An extremely kennel-shy dog can be very difficult to train or teach because it may be spooked by simple reprimands. If this is the case, you'll have to be especially patient, and it may require professional help to cure your pet of its problem.

KENNELING A DOG See box, BOARDING A DOG, p. 38. (This is a phrase used when an owner puts a dog in a cage or Crate.)

KILLING OTHER ANIMALS See box, CHASE BEHAVIOR, p. 58; PREDATORY AGGRESSION.

KISSING *(See also* LICKING PROBLEMS: LICKING PEOPLE/
OBJECTS.)

Problem: Carolyn was horrified when she saw her ten-
year-old daughter kissing their dog, Freddie, directly on
the lips. "Don't do that," she said. "You don't realize
what dogs put their noses into!"

DIAGNOSIS

Many dog owners kiss their pets, and vice versa. Wolves
and dogs not only sniff each other's bodies all over, but
often lick and "kiss" on the nose and mouth. This is a
form of greeting, affection, and bonding and can also help
pack members recognize the scent of prey on an individual's breath.

In general, kissing a dog should pose no problems as
long as the animal is in good health, but a parent may un-
derstandably object when a child continually kisses a dog
on the lips.

TREATMENT

Just like any other behavior, excessive "kissing" can be
modified in a dog, but in this case the easiest and best solution is to prevent or avoid the problem.

- You may want to suggest to a child that a pat, hug,
  or even a kiss on the top of the animal's head is just
  as good a sign of affection as a mouth-to-mouth
  kiss.
- If a dog persists in putting its nose directly in your face
  you can fend it off easily with a "NO" at the same time
  you blow directly into its face. Most dogs don't like
  this and will back right off.
- Another way to prevent a dog from "kissing" or licking
  your face is to use something such as after-shave or cologne. Dogs don't like the smell or taste of anything
  with alcohol in it. *(See box,* Liquids as Aids in Behavior Modification, p. 196.)

KITTENS AND DOGS *See box,* CHASE BEHAVIOR, p. 58; JEALOUSY: JEALOUSY OF ANOTHER PET; PREDATORY AGGRESSION.

KNOCKING INTO PEOPLE *See* HERDING BEHAVIOR PROBLEMS; LEANING ON PEOPLE.

L

LAMENESS, SYMPATHY

Problem: When Missy was a little puppy her mistress accidentally stepped on her front paw. The puppy yelped and held her paw up in the air as she limped around the room. Her mistress felt terrible and made a big fuss over her. Now Missy is an adult dog, but every time her mistress looks crossly at her or gives her a mild reprimand the dog lifts her paw up as if it's hurt and limps off into another room.

DIAGNOSIS

This is a case of what we call "sympathy lameness," in which a dog that's not badly hurt or not hurt at all acts as if it can't put its weight on a foot or leg.

Other examples of the syndrome are a dog that jumps off a bed or couch, lands hard, and then limps as if it's badly injured; or a dog that doesn't like to walk on snow and ice and feigns lameness in order to be picked up. Sometimes a dog that has suffered from a previous leg or foot injury also lapses into limping from time to time.

"Lameness" that can be turned on by a dog at will is clearly a bid for sympathy, attention, or perhaps "forgiveness" for a transgression, and is usually exacerbated by an owner who responds just the way the dog wants.

TREATMENT

- If a dog exhibits lameness or soreness in a foot or leg and it's not an obvious bid for attention, be sure to examine the limb in question and get a veterinary assessment if you have any questions about the cause of the problem.
- If a half-grown, large-breed puppy limps first on one foot and then on another, or exhibits intermittent lameness, it may be suffering from what's sometimes referred to as "growing pains." This condition can occur when a big puppy is allowed to become overweight, putting a strain on developing joints. It can also be the result of a dietary imbalance because of oversupplementation with vitamins and minerals. Young large-breed animals that develop a limping problem should immediately be seen by a veterinarian to prevent further joint damage. In the meanwhile they should not be allowed to exercise.

  Although there are steps that can be taken to deprogram a dog that exhibits sympathy lameness, most owners don't consider this a serious enough problem to merit elaborate steps to correct.
- The most effective treatment for sympathy lameness is to refocus the dog's attention. Toss a favorite Toy or Bone across the room and the dog will usually forget the lameness as if by magic. For some dogs the offer of a walk or romp in the yard will prove healing.
- If the lameness occurs only when you're walking outdoors, consider the possibility that you may be asking your dog to walk too far, or that your pet's feet are really sore. Sometimes chemicals used for ice and snow removal can irritate a dog's foot pads, for example. If your dog's feet look inflamed, apply a mild healing ointment and then rinse the feet off in warm water each time you come home from a walk.

It can be annoying when a large dog like Kelly leans on you while you're trying to read. (Bruce Plotkin)

Kelly is being given a sideways knee nudge to stop him from Leaning against his owner's leg while he's walked on a leash. (Bruce Plotkin)

LEANING ON PEOPLE (See also HERDING BEHAVIOR PROBLEMS.)

Problem: Audrey's Great Dane has a very annoying habit. Every time she sits down in a chair to read or watch TV the big dog sits right beside her on the floor and leans against her, practically pushing her out of the chair. She pushes him away, but moments later he's back, leaning on her. Sometimes he also puts his massive head in her lap as he pushes his whole body against her.

DIAGNOSIS

Leaning behavior is very common among wolves and meets several needs. Wolves lean on each other out of affection and for warmth and body contact. Pack members often close ranks and lean against each other for reassurance when they're in a difficult or dangerous situation such as defending their territory against an intruder.

Leaning against a person is also a dog's way of making contact and getting reassurance. Large and giant dogs are especially apt to lean on people, probably because they've grown too big to be picked up and sit in their owners' laps as they could when they were puppies.

Although an owner may find it nice that a dog is so affectionate, most people find it annoying to be leaned on, especially when the dog is large. Leaning behavior sometimes becomes so habitual a dog will lean against anyone who sits down in the house, strangers and visitors as well as family members.

Leaners often develop a further habit. They push and rub and lean against their owners when walking outdoors on leash.

Leaning can be a problem if you want your dog to enter competitions. Leaning makes a dog look awkward and off-balance and will usually cause judges to deduct points.

TREATMENT

A dog that leans on people excessively needs to be redirected to act in a different manner.

- If you want to keep your dog with you, but not on you, teach it to Go to Your Place. Locate the place the dog will go somewhere close to your favorite chair, or develop a place for the dog in each room you're apt to be in frequently. This system is especially useful if you often have visitors who don't enjoy close contact with a dog.
- If you don't want to have a specific place for the dog to go, teach it Down/Stay. It will then lie calmly at your feet or by your side wherever you happen to be sitting.
- When a dog leans and rubs against you as you're walking it on leash or in the show ring, modify the action by giving a sharp Leash Correction and saying "NO"

each time the dog begins to lean. Or use your knee in a sideways motion to bump the dog away as you're walking along at the same time you say "NO."

LEARNED AGGRESSION

Problem: Fred had a very valuable coin collection and decided to get a dog to protect it. He adopted a dog the local shelter said was "half shepherd, half Doberman." Then he bought a lot of dog-training books and read about how to make a dog become an aggressive watch-dog. He began to train the dog and encourage it to growl and snarl. Soon the dog learned it was all right to snarl at his owner.

In the meantime, Fred was having moderate success house-training the dog. One day Fred came home to discover the dog had soiled a costly handwoven hall rug. Grabbing the animal by the scruff of the neck, Fred led him over to the "mistake" and began to shake and scold him. At that moment the dog turned around, snarled, and bit Fred on the wrist.

DIAGNOSIS

All dogs have latent aggressive tendencies stemming from the need for self-preservation. Puppies and wolf cubs learn about aggression while they're still in the litter play-fighting. They also learn the limits of aggression from their littermates: if a pup bites its brother or sister too hard, it will be bitten back hard.

It's very dangerous to try to train a dog to be a serious guard dog yourself, because if you use incorrect methods you'll teach the dog to respond in an aggressive way and it will soon become disrespectful and aggressive toward you. You will have created a dog with a multitude of aggressions.

TREATMENT

- If you feel you really want a guard dog, get professional help from a trainer who's experienced in this

type of work so you can control the aggression with the trainer's assistance. With the trainer's guidance you will become the dog's dominant leader, organizer, and stabilizer—pack leader—all in one. *(See box,* ALPHA PO-SITION, p. 12; *box,* PACK BEHAVIOR, p. 230.)

- It *is* possible in some cases to deprogram a dog that has been taught to be aggressive toward people, but again, only with professional help. A skilled trainer can re-structure a dog's responses and teach it to consider you its leader so it won't be aggressive toward you.
- Once the training or retraining is completed, the trainer can advise you whether or not the dog can ever be trusted around strangers, especially children.

LEASH CORRECTIONS

A leash correction is designed to startle a dog and instantly stop it when it's about to do something un-desirable. It is not meant to hurt the dog, but make it stop, Focus on you, and then be ready to receive your instructions.

A leash correction can be given properly only if a dog is wearing a Training Collar. When the dog is walking along by your side, the collar will be slack around its neck. When you need to give a leash cor-rection, jerk the leash quickly and firmly with your right hand and then relax. This action tightens the collar around the dog's neck for just a brief instant, brings the animal up short, and allows you to then direct its actions. If the correction is accompanied by a sharply toned "NO!" the dog immediately knows it should stop whatever it's doing.

LEASH PROBLEMS

LEASH-BITING/GRABBING

Problem: Marsha has a terrible time walking her Airedale, Tom. Every time they go for a walk, Tom continuously grabs the leash in his mouth, making it impossible
for them to continue walking along in a straight line. Not
only is his behavior annoying, but after a while he de-
stroys the leash with his constant biting on it.

DIAGNOSIS

Leash-biting or grabbing usually stems from a combination of play activity and rebelliousness. It's a bad habit
many dogs are allowed to develop because their owners
don't stop it when it begins. When a young puppy is
learning to walk on a leash, an owner may think its grabbing the leash or biting it playfully is cute. Sometimes a
puppy grabs and holds a leash in its mouth to prevent its
owner from being able to give a Leash Correction, or because it wants to go in the direction it chooses. Other
puppies put a front paw on top of the leash for the same
reason.

TREATMENT

- To prevent leash-biting/grabbing from developing,
  don't allow a puppy to play with its leash, even for a
  moment When the leash isn't in use, put it away in a
  place where the puppy can't get it.
- Sometimes owners like to teach a dog to fetch its leash
  when it's walk time. This is fine, as long as the dog
  doesn't then chew on the leash or decide to play tug-of-
  war with you when you try to take the leash away from
  it. If these behaviors begin to develop, it's best not to
  allow the dog to fetch its own leash.
- To stop the annoying leash-biting/grabbing habit, you
  have to teach yourself to anticipate your dog's actions.
  As you are walking, watch your pet carefully. The instant it begins to turn its head as if to grab the leash in

its mouth, give a firm Leash Correction and say "NO!" Do this each time your dog acts as if it's about to bite the leash.

- If the dog does succeed in getting the leash in its mouth, stop walking, make the dog sit, and give the Drop It! command. Don't engage in a tugging match with the dog, but insist that it let you take the leash out of its mouth. As soon as you've succeeded, begin to walk again and watch the dog more carefully so you can correct it before it grabs the leash.
- If you have a retriever or other breed of dog that loves to carry things in its mouth, you can redirect its leash-grabbing by giving it a favorite object to carry while you walk—a ball, Frisbee, or dumbbell, for instance.

LEASH-PULLING See PULLING ON A LEASH.

LETHARGY See ABNORMAL ACTIVITY LEVELS: LOW ACTIVITY LEVEL; OBESITY.

LICKING PROBLEMS

LICKING PEOPLE/OBJECTS (See also CHEWING PROBLEMS; EXPLORATORY BEHAVIOR; KISSING; MOUTHING; box, SUBMISSIVE BEHAVIOR, p. 276.)

Problem: Every time Nate comes home after jogging, his terrier licks and licks his legs. At first Nate thought it was cute, but now he's begun to dislike the constant licking every morning.

DIAGNOSIS

Just like kissing, licking can be a sign of affection and respect for a dog. In a wolf pack, a submissive animal will show deference for a more dominant one by licking its face and body. Very submissive dogs often lick people's faces, hands, and other exposed skin areas for the same reason.

But when a dog is not especially submissive, the reason for licking is usually less complex. Dogs like the taste of the salt that's left on people's skin when they perspire, and may actually have a need for this and other minerals they can get from licking human skin.

Puppies lick objects for the same reason. They often chew on rocks and sticks to obtain calcium and other minerals and will usually lick the objects preparatory to chewing them

TREATMENT
There is really no treatment necessary when a dog licks you after you've perspired except to wash the salt off your body without delay.

- If you really don't like to be licked, use some perfume, after-shave, or other alcohol-based lotion or scent. Most dogs can't stand the taste of anything with alcohol in it. (*See box,* LIQUIDS AS AIDS IN BEHAVIOR MODIFICATION, p. 196.)
- Provide your pet with a good supply of Bones or Chew Toys. These will give the animal plenty of appropriate things to lick as well as chew.
- If your dog or puppy seems to lick excessively, suspect a dietary lack. Talk to your veterinarian about changing diets, or adding mineral supplements to your pet's rations. Don't add any supplements without a veterinarian's approval. Over-supplementation can lead to nutritional imbalance and may have serious medical repercussions.

LICKING SELF *See box,* ACRAL LICK DERMATITIS/GRANULOMA, p. 4; *box,* FLANK SUCKING, p. 125; SCRATCHING PROBLEMS: SCRATCHING SELF.

LIQUIDS AS AIDS IN BEHAVIOR MODIFICATION

Liquids of various kinds are extremely useful aids when you want to modify a dog's behavior. They can be used in different ways to set a dog up, either sprayed, rubbed, or made into a paste and wiped onto a surface. When a dog engages in an unwanted action, the surprise of water in the face or a mouthful of horrid taste will soon cause it to stop the behavior.

Plain water in a child's water pistol or plastic plant spray bottle, squirted directly in the face, will stop most dogs in their tracks.

Dogs don't like the taste of anything with alcohol in it. So if you want to stop a puppy or dog from Chewing, Licking, or Mouthing your fingers or any other part of your body, spray or rub them with a little after-shave, cologne, or perfume.

A bitter-tasting liquid placed on an object will usually deter a puppy or dog from chewing or grabbing it. There are bitter-tasting liquids made just for pets, or you can use a product designed to prevent children from biting their nails.

When you have a problem with a seriously destructive dog you can make your own highly potent "potion." Mix equal parts of lemon juice and rubbing alcohol with a dash or two of Tabasco. Either spray the mixture on the object you want to protect or make a paste by mixing the liquid with some flour. The paste works especially well in preventing wood-chewing and can be smeared or wiped directly onto any upright surface.

See also box, BEHAVIOR MODIFICATION, p. 34; *box,* WATER BALLOONS AS TRAINING TOOLS, p. 320.

LISTENING PROBLEMS See DEAFNESS, SIGNS OF; *box*, FOCUSING, p. 128; *box*, HEARING: PROBLEM-SOLVING USING A DOG'S KEEN SENSE OF HEARING, p. 147.

M

MALE DOGS' BEHAVIORAL CHARACTERISTICS

In a wolf pack, a male is always the most dominant animal, and most mature, unneutered (intact) male domestic dogs are also dominating and highly protective of their territories. Just like their wild cousins, male dogs continually indulge in marking behavior, leaving their scent wherever they go.

Because of the natural instinct to reproduce, intact male dogs have females on their minds almost all of the time. This leads to Jumping over Fences, roaming, and all types of aggression directed toward other males. Unneutered male dogs also often develop the habit of Mounting.

If a male dog is not going to be involved in a serious breeding program, I strongly advise Castration at an early age to prevent potential Aggressive Behavior. Just as with females, early neutering will offset sexually related behavior problems. Castration later in life will diminish these problems or in many cases eliminate them completely.

See also box, DOMINANT BEHAVIOR, p. 98; INTERMALE AGGRESSION; *box,* SCENT MARKING, p. 256; *box,* TERRITORIAL BEHAVIOR, p. 289; URINE MARKING.

MAKING A BED See DIGGING: DIGGING INDOORS/MAKING A NEST.

MALE-TO-MALE AGGRESSION See INTERMALE AGGRESSION.

MARKING BEHAVIOR See *box*, SCENT MARKING, p. 256; *box*, TERRITORIAL BEHAVIOR, p. 289; URINE MARKING.

MASSAGE FOR DOGS

Massage is a wonderful way to relax and calm your dog. It relieves tension and stress and provides an opportunity to bond with your pet in a quiet, enjoyable way. It stimulates the skin and also enables you to check the animal all over for external problems such as pain, injury, parasites, skin problems, and growths. An important side effect of all-over massage is that it accustoms a dog to having its body touched everywhere. A dog that's regularly massaged from puppyhood will have no difficulty accepting grooming, Nail Clipping, medical treatments, or handling by a show judge. Many handlers massage their dogs regularly before they enter the show ring to relax them and capture their full attention.

If an adult dog has never been massaged before, start slowly and don't force it. Begin by stroking and rubbing the body parts the dog likes to have touched as you speak to it softly. After a few sessions, move on to gently handling the areas the dog doesn't especially like to have touched. Gradually work over the dog's entire body, inside the ears, around the eyes and nose, inside the mouth. A dog that gets used to being touched in these areas won't object to having its ears or teeth cleaned or to being medicated. Pay particular attention to the dog's feet. These are very sensitive, and many dogs don't like them touched.

Work your fingers between the foot pads and around the toes. Then grasp each foot and hold it firmly for a few moments. This should teach a dog to allow you to hold its feet while you do chores such as Nail Clipping.

Dogs and wolves often nudge each other gently in the groin area, just in front of the genitals. Experienced dog owners and handlers know that stroking an animal gently in this area will reassure and calm it.

Once you've accustomed your dog to regular all-over massaging, make this part of your regular care routine for your pet.

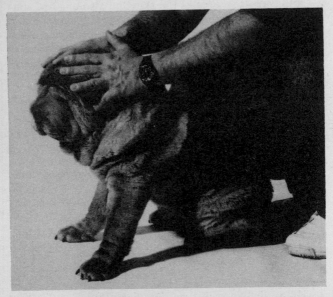

A Shar Pei puppy enjoys a Massage. When a puppy is massaged regularly, it will have no difficulty accepting grooming and handling. (Bruce Plotkin)

MATERNAL AGGRESSION

Problem: Nora, the McKees' sweet golden retriever, has just had puppies and Joel McKee, age eight, wants his friend Steve to see them. Even though Joel's parents have told him not to go near Nora and the pups without them, he doesn't think it will do any harm to just *look* at them. So after school he leads Steve down the back steps into the basement, where Nora and her pups are in a big box Joel's father built for them. The little puppies are all sleeping curled up between their mother's legs while she lies on her side dozing. Steve, all excited, leans over the low side of the box and tries to touch a puppy before Joel can stop him. Instantly, Nora is on her feet, hackles raised, growling deep in her throat. "Your dog tried to bite me," Steve shouts to Joel's mother as he pounds up the stairs into the kitchen.

DIAGNOSIS

Wolf mothers have to protect their cubs from danger in order for the species to survive, and it's also a very strong natural instinct for a mother dog to protect her young from danger. Any sudden moves by a stranger or attempts to touch her puppies can be perceived as "danger" to a dam with puppies.

TREATMENT

- It's very important to teach children not to go near a mother dog with puppies unless an adult is around to supervise.
- When you know your pet is about to give birth, select a comfortable spot nearby and sit with her. If there are children in the family, include them in the birthing process, too. Your pet dog will then regard you as friendly members of the Pack and won't feel the need to guard her puppies from you. Most dogs appreciate the company of their human family when they give birth.

- Nonfamily members, adults and children alike, should always be accompanied by a family member when they go to see the puppies.
- There is no treatment necessary for this type of aggression. It will disappear once the pups are weaned and out on their own.

MEDICATING A DOG See EAR CARE; EYE CARE; PILL-GIVING PROBLEMS.

MIND READING See *box*, ESP—DO DOGS HAVE IT? p. III.

MIXED MESSAGES

A "mixed message" is a message composed of two or more different, conflicting components. When you give a mixed message to a dog you confuse it because it doesn't have a clear idea what it is you want it to do or how you want it to behave.

One type of mixed message is when you say one thing to a dog while at the same time you contradict what you say by your actions. For example, if your dog barks aggressively at a visitor and you say "No!" to it, you're telling it, "I don't want you to do that." But if you pat your dog reassuringly on the side at the same time, you seem to the dog to be praising it for barking aggressively and telling it, "It's all right to do that." The poor dog doesn't know what you mean!

A different type of mixed message occurs when an owner allows a dog to do something at some times but not others. This assumes a dog has the reasoning power to recognize the difference in circumstances. For instance, an owner may regularly invite a dog to jump up on the couch and sit beside him while he's reading, but then scold it severely if it jumps on the couch by itself. The dog will be completely confused. Is it or is it not all right to jump on the couch? The same thing happens when owners allow their pets to beg when they're alone but not when company comes, or let it jump up on them but not on anyone else. A dog has no way of figuring out when it's all right to do something and when it's not.

Try to put yourself in your dog's place. Think about what you're communicating to your pet and be sure you're giving it the message you want, not a confusing mixed message.

See also box, TALKING TO YOUR DOG, p. 282.

MOTEL, STAYING IN See CAR PROBLEMS: CAR TRAVEL.

MOUNTING BEHAVIOR (*See also box,* DOMINANT BEHAVIOR, p. 98; JUMPING PROBLEMS: JUMPING ON PEOPLE OR OTHER DOGS WALKING ALONG THE STREET; *box,* MALE DOGS' BEHAVIORAL CHARACTERISTICS, p. 198; PLAY PROBLEMS: TOO-ROUGH PLAY.)

Problem 1: Twelve-year-old Ginny was walking home from school when the neighbors' Saint Bernard, Bernie, ran out to greet her. She stopped and patted the big dog for a moment. Suddenly Bernie stood up, put his front feet on her shoulders, pushed her to the ground, and began to move sexually against her. Amazed and frightened, Ginny shouted loudly until Bernie's owner came out and pulled him away.

Problem 2: Fritzie, a two-year-old miniature dachschund, has a very embarrassing habit. No sooner does a visitor to the house sit down than he immediately runs over, wraps his front legs around the person's legs, and proceeds to "hump." He even "attacked" the plumber as the poor man was squatting on the floor leaning underneath the kitchen sink. Fritzie's owners are really annoyed—no amount of scolding seems to break the dog of his sexy behavior.

DIAGNOSIS

Mounting behavior is primarily sexual in origin, but it is interconnected with dominance. Within a wolf pack hierarchy, wolves continually mount each other to establish dominance levels. Both male and female dogs sometimes mount other household pets or even babies and small children to establish their dominance over them. When puppies are growing up in a litter, mounting behavior is part of their everyday give-and-take play interaction. As a puppy grows up in a home it may even take to mounting inanimate objects such as pillows or blankets.

In a mature adult dog, mounting is usually sexual and may be stimulated by a nearby female dog in heat, or even by a girl or woman who is menstruating. Large and giant dogs often don't exhibit mounting behavior until they are four or five years old and reach sexual maturity. Some dogs, often those that are very aggressive, seem to have an especially high sexual drive.

An owner may unconsciously encourage mounting behavior or excite a dog sexually with body-to-body roughhousing or play that involves close contact with the dog standing on its hind legs, paws on the owner's shoulders or chest.

Although mounting behavior can be annoying in a dog of any size, it can be downright dangerous when a large dog mounts a human.

TREATMENT

- Early Castration will usually eliminate mounting behavior entirely.
- When a dog has not been castrated as a puppy, the behavior may become ingrained, but if the operation is performed on an adult dog, mounting will usually diminish after a while when all the testosterone has left the animal's body. This can take six to eight weeks. Your veterinarian can tell you more about this.
- Avoid close body contact or rough play with the dog if it excites him.
- If a young puppy exhibits mounting behavior, stop it immediately with a hand clap or Noisemaker and sharp "NO!" Remove the puppy from the object of its mounting behavior and redirect its attention to a Chew Toy or Bone. Do this every time the pup begins to mount.
- You can also use a Setup to recondition a dog that mounts. With the dog on leash, re-create the conditions in which it usually mounts. Have someone sit down and cross his legs, for instance. As soon as the dog approaches the person and begins to mount, give a sharp Leash Correction and say "NO!" Alternatively, you can arm the "victim" with a water pistol to shoot in the dog's face as soon as it begins to mount.
- After several corrections, a word should do the trick. Praise your pet when it responds to your "No."
- A very dominant or aggressive dog will benefit from early Obedience Training to control all of its dominance tendencies.

MOUTH CARE See TOOTH CARE PROBLEMS.

MOUTHING (See also EXPLORATORY BEHAVIOR; KISSING; LICKING PROBLEMS; NIPPING; box, TEETHING BEHAVIOR, p. 283.)

Problem: The Tibetan terrier is about six and a half months old and is doing very well. Her owners are delighted with her sweet nature and very pleased with how well she's responding to house-training. The only problem is that whenever they pick her up to pat her and praise her, she immediately takes their fingers in her mouth. She doesn't nip or bite, but sort of sucks on their fingers and covers them with saliva, which is annoying.

DIAGNOSIS
Mouthing behavior is a form of affection and often surfaces when a puppy is teething. Puppies usually mouth people's fingers, but some animals also mouth socks, shoes, and so forth.

Adult dogs sometimes exhibit mouthing behavior in the show ring. A dog that wants to please its owner by carrying something in its mouth may mouth its owner's hand in an effort to get attention.

Owners may unconsciously encourage mouthing behavior when they allow a dog to mouth their hands affectionately.

TREATMENT
When a puppy is mouthing excessively, the treatments are similar to those used for Licking and Nipping.

- Grasp the puppy's muzzle, but instead of giving it the strong squeeze you'd use to stop it from nipping, squeeze its muzzle closed gently while you say "No."
- To discourage a puppy from mouthing, put some of the bitter-tasting liquid that's designed to discourage nail-biting on your hands. *(See box,* LIQUIDS AS AIDS IN BEHAVIOR MODIFICATION, p. 196.)
- Give a quick Leash Correction if a dog mouths your hand during show competition to let it know you're not pleased with its behavior.

MUZZLES FOR DOGS

Muzzles are used on dogs for a variety of reasons. They provide temporary control and prevent biting when you have to treat an injured animal or perform a medical or grooming procedure the dog doesn't like. A muzzle will prevent a dog from barking or biting, and one with a short lead attached, called a headcollar or control halter, is sometimes used to handle an extremely strong or aggressive dog.

A muzzle should never be considered a solution to a behavior problem, but can be useful during training or if an unpredictable dog has to go out in public. A dog with a muzzle on its nose can neither eat nor drink, and therefore a muzzle should never be left on for any length of time.

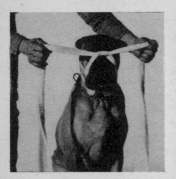

If you have to treat an injured animal or perform a medical procedure a dog doesn't like, make a temporary Muzzle from a gauze strip. Wrinkles serves as a model. (Bruce Plotkin)

N

NAIL-CLIPPING PROBLEMS/TECHNIQUES

Problem: When Bob took his year-old greyhound to the veterinarian for a checkup, the doctor told him the dog should have her nails clipped every few months. Because she spent most of her time in a grassy yard, her toenails were becoming overgrown and would eventually cause foot problems. The veterinarian showed Bob how to clip them and told him what type of clippers to buy. But when Bob tried to clip his pet's nails she became very upset, wouldn't let him hold her paw, and tried to pull away. Because he couldn't get her to stay still, Bob was afraid he'd hurt her or cut too far into her nails. He felt very foolish and annoyed with himself, but finally gave up and took her to a groomer to have her nails clipped.

DIAGNOSIS
Dogs' feet contain many nerves and are often very sensitive. Some dogs, like wolves, can actually feel the warmth of a nearby small animal when they dig *(see box,* TOUCH—THE TACTILE SENSE IN DOGS, p. 297). Most dogs have a strong aversion to having their feet touched or held and will struggle wildly to get loose.

A dog that doesn't like having its feet handled may nip when you attempt to clip its nails. To avoid a problem, use a muzzle, as we have with Goldie, a Chihuahua. (Bruce Plotkin)

TREATMENT

- To prevent this problem, make a point of touching and holding a puppy's paws and legs on a regular basis. If the puppy struggles or pulls away, stroke it gently with one hand while you hold and manipulate its foot pads with the other. Never scold a puppy with sensitive feet or grab its feet tightly, but gradually get it to realize you won't hurt it when you hold its feet. Some puppies may never learn to enjoy foot touching, but they should be able to develop a tolerance for it. For more about this, *see box,* MASSAGE FOR DOGS, p. 200.
- When an older dog already has a severe foot-sensitivity problem, you need to take measures to desensitize it.

Before you attempt to clip its toenails, try to indulge in the same type of activity described above. Some dogs will quickly realize you won't hurt them when you touch their feet and you'll be able to proceed with nail-clipping right away.

■ To make a dog's nails easier to clip, soak its feet in warm soapy or salty water for a few minutes before you begin. This will soften the nails and will also act to desensitize the animal's feet.

■ If your pet remains very touchy about allowing you to handle its feet, enlist the aid of a helper in order to clip its nails. If you have no helper, put a temporary Muzzle on the dog. Otherwise you'll run the risk of hurting the animal as it struggles and making matters a lot worse. Put the dog up on a table or countertop where you can work comfortably; a very small dog may be more secure in your lap. Have the helper hold the animal tightly against his chest, one hand under the dog's chin. Then quickly and firmly grasp each front paw and clip the nails, being careful not to cut into the quick. Praise the dog all the while you're working. Usually the back paws are less sensitive and easier to work on. Once the job is finished, give the dog a treat and praise it lavishly. Have a styptic pencil or other blood coagulator at hand in case you cut too far. This will stanch the bleeding quickly. Try not to become too upset it you cut the dog. Stay calm, and probably your dog will, too.

■ A very small dog may do better in your lap, especially if you have no helper. Hold the dog so its rear end is pressed against your body.

■ Some dogs are frightened by the sight of the metal clippers, especially if they've been severely restrained and worked on by a rough professional groomer. To offset this, put the clippers down on the floor and allow your dog to sniff them and get used to them before you approach with the clippers in your hand.

NAME, NOT RESPONDING TO (See also box, TALKING TO YOUR DOG, p. 282.)

Problem: The O'Hara family heeded the advice they'd read to name their new puppy right away so it would quickly learn its name. They dubbed their new sheltie "Mr. Macdonald." Ten-year-old Colleen O'Hara called him "Mr. Mac," little Sean liked "Mackie," and Mr. and Mrs. O'Hara regularly referred to the dog as "Macdonald." As time went on, however, they became more and more frustrated. The dog just didn't seem to be learning his name and never came when they called him.

DIAGNOSIS

Puppies are anxious to please their owners and, barring a hearing problem, usually learn quickly to respond to their names. But a puppy will naturally become very confused if it's addressed by a different-sounding name each time it's called. To a dog, there is no relationship between the sounds of a two-beat name such as "Mr. Mac" and a nickname like "Mackie." This puppy simply doesn't know what its name is.

It is important for a puppy or dog to learn to respond to its name immediately, for safety reasons and as a first step toward future training.

TREATMENT

With a little bit of common sense, you can easily help a puppy learn its name. Follow these steps:

- You can name your dog anything at all, but for the purpose of teaching a puppy its name, family members must agree on what they will call it and remain consistent.
- A simple one-or-two syllable name is easiest for a puppy to learn to recognize quickly. Also, a word with a strong initial consonant is easier for a dog to identify than a softer-sounding word. Thus "Becky" would be preferable to "Ellen" as far as ease of learning for a

dog. To avoid confusion, reject a name that's similar in sound to that of a human in the household.

- Whatever name you choose, use it constantly so your pet associates pleasant activities with its name. When you feed your puppy, say "Here's your dinner, Bo." As you groom your pet, pat it, and play with it, always refer to it by name. Most puppies eagerly follow their owners around. As yours does, speak to it by name.

- Crouch down on the floor and call your puppy by name. Most puppies will run to you eagerly. When yours does, praise it lavishly. If your puppy is distracted or doesn't seem to understand what you want, clap your hands, make kissing and clicking sounds with your mouth, or wiggle a favorite toy or food treat so it will run to you. Again, praise it as soon as it comes, using its name when you speak to it.

- Soon your puppy will learn to run to you whenever you call its name. When it does, pet it underneath the chin so it looks up at you, and praise it. (See boxes, PATTING A DOG, p. 235; and PRAISE TO MODIFY A DOG'S BEHAVIOR, p. 244.)

NEGATIVE REINFORCEMENT

There is often some confusion about the meaning of the term "negative reinforcement." To a psychologist, negative reinforcement means "the reinforcement of a behavior by the removal of an averse stimulus." Negative reinforcement is *not* the same thing as punishment.

Perhaps the best way to explain it is by example. A dog starts to bolt as you're walking it on a leash. You give a firm Leash Correction and say "No" (negative reinforcement). The dog settles down and again walks calmly at your side. The dog has responded to the "averse stimulus" of the leash correction, and in order to avoid a further correction (remove the averse stimulus), it changes, or modifies, its improper behavior. Another example occurs when an invisible fence gives a dog an electric shock if it tries to cross it. The shock is a negative reinforcer the dog quickly learns to avoid (remove) by staying away from the fence.

When used hand in hand with plenty of Praise, negative reinforcement is an important tool in programming a dog to behave in an appropriate way.

See also box, BEHAVIOR MODIFICATION, p. 34.

NESTING BEHAVIOR See DIGGING: DIGGING INDOORS/ MAKING A NEST; *box,* FEMALE DOGS' BEHAVIORAL CHARACTERISTICS, p. 122.

NEUTERING See *box,* CASTRATION OF MALE DOGS—FACTS & MYTHS, p. 57; *box,* SPAYING OF FEMALE DOGS—FACTS & MYTHS, p. 272.

NIPPING *(See also* BITING PEOPLE; CHEWING PROBLEMS; EXPLORATORY BEHAVIOR; HERDING BEHAVIOR PROBLEMS; LICKING PROBLEMS; MOUTHING; PLAY PROBLEMS: TOO-ROUGH PLAY; *box,* TEETHING BEHAVIOR, p. 283.)

Problem: Julia's German shorthaired pointer puppy is adorable and has always been very well behaved. But lately he's taken to continuous nipping. He runs around the apartment, nipping her daughter as she plays or sits quietly watching TV, and nipping Julia's hand every time she tries to pet him or pick him up. She tells him "No!" but it doesn't do much good. He stops, but then nips her again a while later. She's distressed. What happened to her lovable little baby dog, and what should she do?

DIAGNOSIS

Nipping usually occurs for the first time when a puppy is teething. Like Chewing, nipping helps relieve the soreness and itching of teeth and gums, and some teething puppies seem to get into a really intense nipping phase.

Nipping is also a form of testing and exploration almost all puppies indulge in. It can precede Chewing, but is often simply a sign of affection or an invitation to play. Some puppies seem to treat their human families as if they were other pups and will run and nip people on the leg or buttocks to initiate play, especially outdoors. It will exacerbate a nipping problem if you indulge in excessively rough play with a puppy or allow it to become too excited.

Owners sometimes think a puppy will "outgrow" a tendency to nip. Even though intense nipping is usually just a stage in a puppy's development, it should be stopped before it becomes a bad habit.

TREATMENT

- An old-fashioned remedy for nipping was to tap the puppy on the nose with a finger. This doesn't work. It just causes a puppy to try to bite the tapping finger, increases nipping behavior, and, more important, will make a puppy become hand-shy. Don't put your fingers near a puppy's mouth or in it unless you're examining it or giving medication.

- One way to stop a puppy from nipping is to give it a quick tap underneath its chin the minute it begins to open its mouth. Because your hand is turned upward when you do this and you're not aiming your tap directly at the puppy's face, this type of correction won't create Hand-Shyness.

- The most positive correction is to do what a mother wolf or dog would to stop a pup from nipping. Grasp the pup firmly around its muzzle with your hand (the mother wolf or dog uses her own mouth to grasp a youngster's muzzle) and firmly squeeze its mouth closed at the same time you say "NO!" Do this every single time the puppy begins to nip. Then release the puppy and hand it an appropriate Chew Toy. Praise the puppy when it chews its toy.

- Keep an overexcited puppy on leash. Don't allow it to run around outdoors or in the house heedlessly, nipping as it goes. The minute it begins to act wild and tries to nip, snap on the leash and say "No."

- When your puppy regularly runs up to you from behind, nips you, and runs away, you can deprogram this activity with a Setup. Stand quietly, your back to the dog, with another family member facing the animal. The minute the other person warns you the dog has started to race up to you, wait a beat, then whirl around, and put your hands palm down, and say "NO!" in your harshest tone. Try to time this action so you turn around at the moment the dog reaches you and is all set to nip.

- Alternatively, you can startle a puppy into stopping its nipping with a Noisemaker, Throw Chain, or Water Balloon, or squirt some water in its face at the same time you say "NO!" Then redirect the puppy's attention to a Chew Toy or Bone.

- Provide a teething puppy with plenty of appropriate items to chew.

- If you suspect your pup is suffering from severe teething discomfort, give it some ice cubes to chew on to soothe its gums.

NOISEMAKERS

I often recommend using your voice, clapping your hands, whistling, or making a mouth noise to make a dog stop what it's doing and focus on you. But noisemakers are also extremely effective, especially when there are a lot of distractions around or when you're some distance from your pet.

A noisemaker should be small and light enough to be tossed some distance. A large key ring works very well and is usually immediately available. A shake can is easy to make and also does the trick. Simply fill an empty tin can with small stones or marbles and tape the top closed.

Whatever noisemaker you opt for, the trick is to toss it at the dog the minute it begins to do something you don't want it to—root around in some spilled garbage, for instance. This will startle it so it will stop and look at you. At this point you can give the dog whatever instructions you want. After several experiences with a noisemaker, many dogs learn to stop whatever they're doing the minute an owner rattles the can or shakes the keys.

See also box, FOCUSING, p. 128; *box,* THROW CHAIN, p. 290.

NOISES, FEAR OF See FEARFULNESS.

NUDGING See AFFECTION, EXCESSIVE/DEMANDING; HERDING BEHAVIOR PROBLEMS; LEANING ON PEOPLE.

NUZZLING See KISSING; LICKING PROBLEMS; MOUTHING.

0

OBEDIENCE TRAINING

People often question the need for obedience training when a dog is intended to be a pet and is not going to compete in shows or obedience trials. In my opinion, obedience training is essential for *every dog,* for the following reasons:

Obedience training is the foundation of all of your communications and interactions with your dog. Because dogs are strongly influenced by pack mentality, they need the order and structure in their lives obedience training will give them. Not only does obedience training help your dog learn what it is you want it to do, it teaches *you* how to communicate with your dog effectively.

Obedience training enables you to program good behavior in your pet and eliminate undesirable behavior. For instance, it will help a shy dog become more confident, because it will learn to look up to you as its leader and know what's expected of it in every situation. It will also teach an aggressive dog to look up to you for guidance and redirect its aggressions in appropriate channels.

A dog that's been obedience-trained will always trust you, look up to you, and know what's expected of it in any situation.
See box, PACK BEHAVIOR, p. 230.

OBESITY (See *also* ABNORMAL ACTIVITY LEVELS: LOW ACTIVITY LEVEL; APPETITE PROBLEMS: EXCESSIVE APPETITE.)

Problem: Tess is worried about her spaniel. He never seems to want to move anymore and sleeps all of the time. The veterinarian insists the dog weighs too much and points out that the poor animal's stomach almost hits the floor when he walks. Tess can't understand how her dog can be overweight. She feeds him only one meal a day.

DIAGNOSIS

Even though obesity is a physical, not behavioral, problem, it can cause behavior changes. A severely overweight dog will find it uncomfortable to move and walk, let alone play or romp with its owners. Although obesity can be caused by an underlying medical disorder, most often it's simply the result of overfeeding. Frequency of feeding has nothing to do with whether a dog is eating too much for its own good. One meal of 2,000 calories is too much for a dog that requires only about 1,000 calories a day to stay in shape.

Some owners don't even realize how many between-meal bites and treats they give their dogs. Others, who equate food with love, purposely feed dozens of biscuits and other tidbits to their dogs to show the animals how much they care for them. They take great pleasure in watching their dogs scoff up biscuit after biscuit.

Obesity is a life-threatening condition, however, and should be taken seriously. Excess weight puts a tremendous strain on a dog's heart, circulatory system, and joints, just as it does in humans.

TREATMENT

- Your veterinarian will be able to suggest an appropriate weight-loss diet for your dog.
- With your veterinarian's approval, gradually increase the amount of exercise the dog gets. If it's hard for you to spend the required amount of time outdoors walking your dog, you might want to consider getting a Treadmill and teaching your dog how to use it.

OBJECT-GUARDING AGGRESSION (See also FOOD-GUARDING AGGRESSION; GROWLING; TERRITORIAL AGGRESSION.)

Problem 1: A woman brought home a three-month-old briard puppy to keep her older briard company. The first day the puppy was in the apartment, he grabbed all of the dog toys and bones that were lying around, put them in a big pile in the middle of the living-room floor, and lay down on top of them. If the woman or the other dog came near, the puppy growled menacingly at them and continued to lie on the pile of toys all day.

Problem 2: Rex is a Norfolk terrier who has a very bad habit. Every time his owners sit down at the table to eat, he grabs the paper napkins off their laps, runs under the bed with them, and snaps and growls if anyone tries to get the napkins away from him.

DIAGNOSIS

This is classic canine behavior and is closely related to territoriality and possessiveness. It is similar to food-guarding but has a different motivation. Young wolf cubs often become possessive of objects such as old bones or sticks, will run away with them, hide them, and chase off any littermates that try to take the object away. Puppies also do this.

Sometimes people think it's funny when a pup grabs something and runs away and they make a "game" out of chasing it. But more often it's the natural reaction of an especially territorial puppy.

In the case of an older dog, object-guarding may be a

learned behavior. If a dog has been allowed to act possessive toward things over a period of time, it will have gotten the message that this behavior is all right.

Object-guarding happens only when there is a person
or another dog around, and when it occurs in the home it
won't happen outdoors (e.g., if you offer the napkin-
grabbing terrier a paper napkin out in the yard, he'll probably ignore it.)

TREATMENT

The treatments for these problems are aimed at preventing the aggressive behavior.

- Place the object or objects the dog always guards in the
  center of a room on the floor. With the dog on leash, let
  it pick up the object.
- While holding the leash, approach the dog. If the dog
  begins to growl, snap the leash and say "NO" in a
  strong voice. Continue to approach and to give the
  Leash Correction every time the dog growls.
- When you are next to the dog, give it the Drop It! command. If the dog drops the object with no protest,
  praise the dog. If, on the other hand, the dog growls
  again as you reach for the object, repeat the correction
  and verbal reprimand.
- Continue this routine until the dog regularly either
  drops the object or allows you to take it out of its
  mouth.
- If the dog is in the habit of running off and hiding with
  the object, keep it on leash but allow it to run off to its
  usual place and go with it. Proceed to follow the same
  steps outlined above.

OBSESSIVE-COMPULSIVE BEHAVIOR IN DOGS

Obsessive-compulsive behavior is behavior caused by a fixed idea or emotion. It occurs regularly, repeatedly, and seems to have no useful motivation. As a matter of fact, it is usually destructive in some way.

Acral Lick Dermatitis, Flank Sucking, and other forms of self-mutilation fall into the category of obsessive-compulsive canine activities. So do Pica, wind-sucking, and incessant seemingly motiveless Vocalizing. Circling and pacing can also be described as obsessive-compulsive actions.

The initial causes of these behaviors are usually difficult to ascertain, but they may be a form of Displacement. Obsessive-compulsive behavior may be helped by redirection.

See also CHEWING PROBLEMS; DIGGING; DESTRUCTIVE BEHAVIOR; SEPARATION ANXIETY; TAIL CHASING/ BITING.

OLDER DOG PROBLEMS

ADOPTING AN OLDER DOG

Problem: After her dog died, Fran decided to get another, but she didn't want the trouble and care of raising a new puppy. She went to a local animal shelter and picked out a big Labrador-shepherd neutered male named Elmer. The shelter people said he was about four years old, had been a family pet, and was given up when his owners moved. He seemed friendly, affectionate, and well behaved. But the minute Fran took him into her house he began to raise his leg on the furniture. She quickly took him into the kitchen, where she planned to have him sleep, and before she could stop him, he knocked over the garbage can and began rooting around in it. Now she wonders if it wouldn't have been a better idea to get a puppy after all.

DIAGNOSIS

When you adopt a previously owned dog, you should expect it to take time and a lot of work to mold that animal into a pet you can live with. You can't expect a dog that's lived with another family in a different house to walk into your home and immediately know what the rules are.

A dog that's spent all of its life outdoors, for instance, may never have been properly house-trained or taught not to dump over the garbage. By the same token, an animal that's lived in a two-room apartment will be initially overwhelmed in a ten-room house. Remember, a "second-hand" dog may have been taught a completely different set of behaviors from those you want it to have.

TREATMENT

In a case such as this you must try to put yourself in your new dog's place and patiently teach it to conform to your life-style.

- To prevent accidents and confusion, keep the dog in a confined area. A Crate or small gated room will work well. (*See box,* GATES TO CONFINE DOGS, p. 138.)
- Stick to a regular Schedule with a new dog, just as you would for a puppy. An adult dog will quickly learn when to expect to be fed, walked, played with, etc.
- Other family members need to realize it will take a while for an older dog to get to know them. Don't allow children to overwhelm a newly adopted older dog. At first, restrict wild play, running, and shouting around the dog until it becomes used to normal activity in your house.
- Introduce your new dog to the rest of the house gradually, a room at a time. With the dog on leash, walk it to each room, let it explore, and at the same time let it know if there are areas where you don't want it to go. If you don't want it to get up on the upholstered furni-

ture, for instance, lead it over to the couch, point to the couch and say, "Elmer, NO!"

- Keep the dog confined, or with you, until you're sure it's learned what it should and shouldn't do. Most adult dogs will be completely acclimated to a new home in about a week, but if problems persist you'll have to keep your pet confined until they're solved.
- Obedience Training is very important for a newly adopted older dog. It will provide the animal with structure while at the same time showing it you are its leader and protector.

BEHAVIOR CHANGES IN OLDER DOGS (See also box, ANXIETY IN DOGS, p. 14; box, BEHAVIOR CHANGES, p. 33; BLINDNESS, SIGNS OF; DEAFNESS, SIGNS OF; PANTING, EXCESSIVE; URINE LEAKING/DRIBBLING.)

Problem: The Knights have had their dog, Josie, for fourteen years. They got her when they were first married and moved to the suburbs. She helped them raise their two children, and the whole family is devoted to the dog. But they've begun to notice she sleeps almost all of the time, doesn't want to play, and seems anxious when they go out. Lately she's also had a couple of urine-leaking accidents. They want to know what they can do to keep Josie happy and well now that she's getting old.

DIAGNOSIS

Just as people do, dogs age at different rates. Some dog breeds are still young-acting into their teens. Giant and very large breeds, however, have shorter life expectancies and therefore seem old at an earlier age. Big dogs often lose the use of their hind legs when they're old. As they age, all dogs go through a number of physical changes that may cause them to behave differently than they did when younger.

Old dogs' vision and hearing often begin to fail, and they may suffer from pain and stiffness because of arthritic joints. This may lead to crankiness and restlessness, and may also make it difficult for an old dog to go up and down stairs or jump up on a favorite chair or couch. Hearing and vision loss can contribute to nervousness and anxiety and cause a dog to pant excessively. Old dogs also sleep a lot, very deeply, and may become testy when suddenly awakened. In fact, an older dog that is startled out of sleep may even nip or bite.

Urinary incontinence and even a complete break of house-training are not uncommon in older dogs. In addition, old dogs dislike change of any sort and often become more dependent on owners, causing them to suffer from Separation Anxiety when left alone. The death of other household pets may contribute to an old dog's anxiety and loneliness.

TREATMENT
An older dog requires special consideration and care from its owners.

- Be sure to have your older dog checked over by the veterinarian on a regular basis. Many physical problems of older dogs can be eased if they're caught early. Any sudden or serious behavior changes call for an immediate veterinary assessment.

- Ask your veterinarian about your older dog's diet. As the animal becomes less active and its metabolism slows, it requires fewer calories per day. A too-rich diet can cause an older dog to become overweight, a condition that will put extra stress on aging organs and joints. In addition, it may cause Diarrhea, which of course will lead to accidents in the house. Old dogs often fare better with two small meals a day rather than one large dinner.

- If your dog develops urinary incontinence it may be due to a physical condition that can be helped with appropriate medication. If there is no underlying physical cause, ask your veterinarian about limiting your dog's water intake. You may need to change your schedule so you can walk your pet or let it out more frequently. A well-trained older dog will be upset enough about accidents—don't make it worse by scolding.

- House-training accidents may also occur when a dog finds it painful or difficult to negotiate steps. If this seems to be a problem for your pet, you can make it a ramp out of a sturdy board. Alternatively, provide your old dog with an Indoor Comfort Station, or retrain it to use papers or absorbent pads.
- Sometimes an older dog becomes confused when it goes outdoors, forgetting why it's there. It may stand in the yard for a few minutes and then come in, never having voided or defecated. If this becomes a problem, go outside with the dog and use whatever verbal command it's been taught to respond to, such as "Go, Bitsy," or "Be a good dog." For a pet that doesn't respond to a verbal command you may have to stroke its abdomen or use a suppository inducer to encourage it to evacuate outdoors.
- Stick to a well-established Schedule with an older dog.
- Provide your old pet with a safe place to go to sleep and "get away from it all." If the dog is used to a Crate, this is ideal. But if the dog has always slept in your bedroom, for instance, give it a bed there. An older dog that's always slept up off the floor on a couch or bed may be distressed when it can't jump up anymore. To help it out, place a low chair, hassock, or makeshift ramp next to the favorite couch or bed to serve as a "step" so the dog can get up.
- Teach children in particular not to disturb the dog when it's sleeping.
- If your dog seems inattentive or confused, it's probably losing its hearing or eyesight. If this is so, be careful not to startle your pet.
- When an old dog develops severe Separation Anxiety you may want to go through steps to recondition it to accepting your absence. For many owners of old dogs, however, the most logical solution is to reorganize their lives or hire walker-companions so the dog isn't left alone for long periods of time.
- An old dog may become very upset and confused if you have to take it into a strange place, especially if any of its senses have failed. If you must take it to a

new place, keep your pet on leash, by your side, and touch it or speak to it frequently to reassure it. If you have to move or take your dog to a hotel, for instance, allow it to explore the entire area while safely leashed (*see* EXPLORATORY BEHAVIOR). Confine the dog until you're sure it won't become mixed up and "lost." Always bring along a familiar bed or blanket to help the dog feel secure in a new place.

OFF-LEASH OBEDIENCE TRAINING

Off-leash obedience training follows on-leash obedience training and is designed to give you complete control of your dog without using a leash, both indoors and outside.

A dog that's been given off-leash training can safely walk unleashed in the park or the country with its owner, and is also perfectly behaved in the house, no matter what happens or who visits. Following off-leash training, many dog owners opt to work further with their pets and go on to obedience trials.

ON-LEASH OBEDIENCE TRAINING

On-leash obedience training consists of a well-defined, step-by-step training program in which a dog learns to respond to its owner's wishes while wearing a Training Collar and Leash. Owners learn to communicate with their dogs using body language, Leash Corrections, Praise, and vocal commands.

ONE-MAN DOGS *(See also* JEALOUSY: JEALOUSY OF AN ADULT PERSON; TERRITORIAL AGGRESSION.*)*

Problem: Ralph lived alone, and because he worked nights he rarely had any guests in his apartment. His chow, Pete, was his constant companion when he was home and never left his side. A problem arose when Ralph changed jobs and decided to move to a larger place. Now that Ralph could entertain, Pete was terrible. The dog wouldn't let anyone come in the apartment, but stood guard in the hallway whenever the doorbell rang. "I guess he's just a one-man dog," said Ralph apologetically as he led Pete to the bedroom and closed the door.

DIAGNOSIS
Some dog breeds are apt to become highly protective of one person, or of an entire family. A dog such as this that's never been socialized to anyone except its owner is bound to become what's commonly called a "one-man dog." It will feel the need to protect its owner from all newcomers.

TREATMENT
An antisocial dog must be reprogrammed to accept other friendly people.

- With the dog on leash, ask one person to come and ring the doorbell. Holding the dog next to you, go answer the door and invite the visitor in. Keep the dog on leash, by your side, as you go about taking the visitor's coat and sitting down in the living room.
- Keep the dog on leash while you talk to the visitor for a few minutes. Then ask the visitor to offer a treat to the dog. If the treat is accepted, have the visitor pet the dog gently underneath the chin. Tell the dog how good it is when it acts calm and friendly.
- If the dog reacts aggressively, give it a Leash Correction and say "NO!"
- Once the dog is able to tolerate one person in the house and realizes this person is a friend and poses no threat

to you, ask the first visitor to bring someone else along and go through the same routine. Praise the dog when it acts in a friendly way.

OVEREXCITABILITY See ABNORMAL ACTIVITY LEVELS: HYPERACTIVITY.

OVERPROTECTIVENESS   See   FOOD-GUARDING AGGRESSION; OBJECT-GUARDING AGGRESSION; ONE-MAN DOGS; TERRITORIAL AGGRESSION.

P

PACK BEHAVIOR

As descendants of wolves, all dogs are naturally pack animals, and much of their behavior can be directly traced to pack orientation.

A wolf pack is a hierarchy, within which there are many levels of dominance. The leaders, or Alpha pair, are dominant over all other individuals in descending order. However, an Alpha animal can be challenged and overthrown at any time. Because of this possibility, all wolves and dogs are either leaders (dominant animals) or followers (subordinate animals) all of their lives. An animal in the middle range of a pack can be both dominant over those below it and submissive toward (subordinate to) those above it. A pet dog, too, may be both dominant and submissive. For example, it may be submissive to its owners at the same time it's dominant over the family cat or a new puppy.

Pack social order leads to strong bonding between individual animals. Domestic dogs are also bonding social animals and often suffer from Anxiety, confusion, and loneliness when their owners leave them alone. Much of what owners perceive as "bad" behavior is rooted in what we call Separation Anxiety.

Because of dogs' inherent pack instincts, it's very important for an owner to immediately establish himself as the leader, or Alpha animal, in the dog's world. Not only does a dog need guidance and leadership, but if an owner doesn't assume the role of leader, the dog will constantly try to dominate him.

See also box, ALPHA POSITION, p. 12; *box,* DOMINANT BEHAVIOR, p. 98; *box,* SUBMISSIVE BEHAVIOR, p. 276.

PAIN-INDUCED AGGRESSION *(See also* INJURED BEHAVIOR.*)*

Problem: Frankie was a usually cheerful dachshund who was especially fond of his mistress's brother, Tom. Whenever Tom came to town on business he stayed at Frankie's house. The little dog always greeted him with great joy, and Tom always took him for extra-long walks in the park. So it was a terrible surprise and shock to Tom when he arrived at the apartment one day and squatted down and fondled Frankie behind the ears, and the dog bit him on the wrist! When Tom jumped back with an "Ouch!" Frankie went up and nuzzled him as if to say he was sorry. "What in the world is going on here?" Tom wondered.

DIAGNOSIS

Once Tom's sister arrived home, the mystery was solved. It seems Frankie had been going through a terrible time with an ear-canal infection. It hadn't occurred to her to warn Tom the dog's ears were extremely sore—so sore they even had to be extremely careful when they put his collar on. When Tom unknowingly grabbed Frankie's ears and neck tight and began to rub them hard the pain was just too much and Frankie struck out blindly.

This type of aggression can occur with any dog, especially if it's already in pain and is startled or grabbed suddenly.

TREATMENT

- Obviously, this wasn't a case of "aggression," and no treatment is needed. Once the dog's ear infection is cured, all will be back to normal. In the meantime, if a dog has any kind of painful physical problem it behooves the owner to warn dog-walkers, visitors, and so forth.
- Children in particular must be told never to grab a dog they don't know and never to go near an injured dog.

PAIN—HOW DOGS SHOW IT

Owners often ask me how they can tell if a dog is in pain. It can sometimes be difficult to know when a dog is hurting, because, just as with humans, some individuals are more tolerant of pain than others. While one dog with a minor bump may act as if it's in terrible pain *(see* LAMENESS, SYMPATHY*)*, another may be stoical in the face of great discomfort.

In general, a dog suffering from slight pain after minor surgery, for instance, will want to be left alone. It will go off somewhere quiet to sleep and won't be interested in food or attention. This type of pain should last no longer than twenty-four hours.

More severe pain may be the result of a chronic condition such as arthritis, or it can follow a fracture or major surgery. A dog that hurts badly will find it difficult to move, may groan or whine when it moves, and will usually lose its appetite. Sometimes dogs with chronic pain seek reassurance from their owners and become very demanding of affection. Other dogs may want to be left alone. You should take your cue from your own pet. Don't force attention on it, but do give it plenty of love if it asks for it.

Sudden, severe pain from a serious injury such as a ruptured spinal disk, fall, or accident with a car will cause a dog to cry out, moan, and even collapse. A badly hurt dog will pant rapidly, may try to hide, and will often growl or snap if approached in Pain-Induced Aggression.

A dog's owner is the best judge of whether or not an animal is in pain. If you suspect your pet is hurting badly or if pain-related behavior lasts for more than a day, consult your veterinarian, who can determine the cause and give your dog pain-relieving medication.

See also INJURED BEHAVIOR.

PANTING, EXCESSIVE *(See also box,* ANXIETY IN DOGS, **p.** 14; BALL-PLAYING FETISH; INJURED BEHAVIOR; OLDER DOG PROBLEMS; *box,* PAIN—HOW DOGS SHOW IT, **p.** 233.)

Problem: Timmy can't figure out what's going on with his five-year-old English sheepdog. The dog has taken to panting continuously, no matter what the temperature. Her constant panting is beginning to get on Timmy's nerves; it's not only noisy, but the dog dribbles onto the floor all the time.

DIAGNOSIS
Panting is a normal activity of dogs when they're too hot. When the moisture evaporates from a dog's tongue it lowers the animal's body temperature.

Excessive rapid panting even when it's not hot may be a sign of pain, poisoning, heart trouble, or severe Anxiety. A well-trained older dog may become very anxious if its bladder is full or it needs to defecate.

Excessive panting can also occur when a dog becomes overexcited or hyperkinetic and gets itself into a frenzy, usually when playing *(see* PLAY PROBLEMS: EXCESSIVE PLAY).

TREATMENT
If your dog's panting seems excessive, it's important to determine the cause.

- First, have the dog checked over by a veterinarian.
- When there doesn't seem to be a physical cause for the panting, suspect Anxiety. Make sure an older dog has ample opportunity to relieve itself so it doesn't become anxious that it might make a mistake.
- If something about the household has changed recently, go out of your way to reassure an older dog that everything's all right and that you are still there to take care of it.
- In a case where a dog becomes frenzied during exercise or play, make the animal stop and lie down quietly. (If your dog has had Obedience Training, put it in a

Down/Stay.) Force it to focus on you and stroke it gently to calm it down and relieve its anxiety.

PAPER-TRAINING PROBLEMS See CRATE PROBLEMS: CRATE SOILING; HOUSE-TRAINING PROBLEMS.

PATTING A DOG

Dog owners pat their pets all the time. Gentle patting is a form of contact, and a scratch behind the ears or stroke underneath a dog's chin conveys support and reassurance to the animal.

Sometimes people mistakenly or absentmindedly turn a pat into a negative message. It probably seems more like punishment than praise to a dog when its head is driven downward as you slap or pound it repeatedly on the top of the head, and a hard blow on the rump may seem more like a reprimand than a sign of affection. Gear your patting to your own pet's size and hardiness.

A scratch behind a dog's ears may also inadvertently cause pain if the animal has an ear problem. (*See* PAIN-INDUCED AGGRESSION.)

If you remain "tuned in" to your dog you'll quickly learn what type of patting it responds to best.

See also box, MASSAGE FOR DOGS, p. 200; *box,* TOUCH—THE TACTILE SENSE IN DOGS, p. 297.

PAWING BEHAVIOR See AFFECTION, EXCESSIVE/DEMANDING.

PERSON PREFERENCE See ATTENTION PROBLEMS: PAYING MORE ATTENTION TO ONE PERSON THAN ANOTHER; ONE-MAN DOGS.

PHOBIAS See FEARFULNESS.

PICA (Eating Nonfoods) *(See also* CHEWING PROBLEMS; COPROPHAGIA.)

Problem: Esther's Lhasa apso has just come home from the veterinary hospital. He had eaten six of the small stones that line the flower pots on the patio and had to be treated for an intestinal obstruction. Esther can't figure out what's wrong with him. As soon as she lets him out the dog just won't let the stones alone. The veterinarian says he's ruining his teeth as well as his insides.

DIAGNOSIS

Pica, the deliberate ingestion of inedible objects, is closely related to Coprophagia. In most cases it has nutritional, not behavioral, origins.

Although Chewing is a perfectly normal dog behavior, the actual swallowing of objects such as stones, earth, paper, and cloth is not. Even when a puppy chews things, it rarely actually eats them.

As seen in the problem above, severe pica is very dangerous for a dog, and may even lead to death from intestinal obstruction if it's not treated immediately.

TREATMENT

To treat pica, *see* COPROPHAGIA, treatment steps.

PILL-GIVING PROBLEMS

Problem: It seemed easy when the veterinarian showed Mel how to give his Akita, Angel, a pill. The next morning, Mel gave her her pill and Angel acted as if she'd swallowed it. But half an hour later, as she lay nearby chewing on her bone, Mel suddenly saw the pill lying on the floor near her head. He pried the dog's mouth open and again put the pill on the back of her tongue. Again, Angel made swallowing motions with her throat, and again, out came the pill some time later. Mel is upset and annoyed. How come it seemed so easy in the doctor's office?

DIAGNOSIS

A dog has no idea it's to its advantage to swallow a pill. On top of that, the majority of medications for dogs taste and smell so terrible it's no wonder a dog spits them out if possible.

TREATMENT

- The simplest and easiest way to give a pill to a dog that's eating well is to camouflage the medicine. Roll the pill up in a small ball of cheese, bread, or meat and toss it to the dog.
- Sometimes a dog becomes suspicious after several pills have been disguised and begins to take apart the food ball before swallowing it. You can fool even the most wary animal by giving it several food balls with no pill inside first. After a while, the dog will tire of dissecting the balls and will gulp down the medicated one.
- Don't make the mistake of mixing medication of any kind in a large bowl of food. The dog may discern the smell and taste and not eat at all, or it may only eat part of the meal, leaving you to guess how much medicine it actually ingested.
- If a dog is not eating well and won't accept a food ball, you'll have to give the pill directly. Grease the pill or capsule with some butter or cooking oil. Grasp the dog's muzzle from the top and point its nose up toward the ceiling. With the other hand, force the dog's jaw open and place the pill or capsule as far back as you can, in the middle of the dog's tongue. Close the dog's mouth, hold it closed, and stroke its throat until it swallows. If your dog is skittish or difficult to handle, enlist the aid of a helper to hold the dog while you medicate it. For how to do this, *see* EAR CARE.

PLANE TRAVEL See AIRPLANE TRAVEL.

PLANT-CHEWING (See also CHEWING PROBLEMS; GRASS-EATING.)

Problem: The Defemios were really upset when they came home. They thought their half-grown puppy was well behaved enough to be given the run of the house. But there on the sunporch floor were torn and chewed bits of the orchid plants they'd so painstakingly grown!

DIAGNOSIS

A puppy or dog that's developed a Chewing habit will often chew plants as well as other things in the house. Plants are soft and easy to chew, and they usually smell good to a dog. In addition to its destructive aspects, plant-chewing can be a dangerous habit for a dog. Some plants have sap that will irritate the insides of a dog's mouth and/or make it vomit. Others can cause an animal's throat to close up and, if enough is ingested, may even result in death.

TREATMENT

- Most puppies and dogs can be taught to leave house-plants completely alone by following the steps to control Chewing.
- Nasty-tasting liquid sprayed on a plant will usually discourage a dog from chewing it. (*See box,* LIQUIDS AS AIDS IN BEHAVIOR MODIFICATION, p. 196.)
- In the meantime, to be on the safe side, if your pet is an avid plant-chewer put plants temporarily out of reach.

PLAY PROBLEMS

EXCESSIVE PLAY (See also ABNORMAL ACTIVITY LEVELS: HYPERACTIVITY, PROBLEM 1; BALL-PLAYING FETISH; *box,* GAMES TO PLAY WITH DOGS, p. 134; TOYS FOR DOGS.)
Problem: Roscoe, the Scotts' Alaskan malamute, doesn't seem to know when to stop. He wants to play all the time

and will pester and pester whoever's around, jumping, barking, running around wildly, and bringing toys to be tossed. The only time he's quiet is when he's asleep. The constant demands to play are exhausting all the human members of the family.

DIAGNOSIS

Play activity is an important part of every dog's growing up. Wolf cubs and puppies play with each other constantly, and play provides very important lessons by honing a young animal's senses and abilities. Creeping, pouncing, chasing—these "play" activities are forerunners of behavior needed in adult life. Play also teaches the limits of Aggressive Behavior. If a young cub or pup goes too far and hurts a littermate in play, there will be swift retaliation! Vigorous play also provides needed exercise and stimulation and prevents Boredom.

Regular play helps bond a dog to its owner and makes the animal feel content and relaxed.

A very active young dog may need to play and/or exercise a lot. If the only time you pay attention to a dog is at playtime, the animal may feel the need to insist on playing all of the time as an attention-getting maneuver.

TREATMENT

- Be sure an active dog gets enough exercise.
- Provide your dog with an ample supply of toys.
- With a little encouragement, most dogs can "invent" games to play by themselves. A rolling ball, for instance, can entertain a dog for hours.
- Limit your playtime to one or two hours a day, and try to stick to a regular playtime routine so the dog knows what to expect.
- Never indulge in strenuous play with a dog right after mealtime. There is evidence that vigorous play after eating is one cause of bloat (gastric dilatation/torsion), especially in large dogs.
- For steps to stop a dog from continually pestering you to play, *see* AFFECTION, EXCESSIVE/DEMANDING.

TOO-ROUGH PLAY (See also BITING PEOPLE; JUMPING PROBLEMS; MOUNTING BEHAVIOR; NIPPING; PAIN-INDUCED AGGRESSION; TUG-OF-WAR.)

Problem: Danny is a big twelve-year-old who's developed a liking for football. When he's at home, he regularly takes the family's Norwegian elkhound, Bozo, out in the backyard to play. He tackles the dog, knocks him over, races around with Bozo chasing him, and then indulges in a wrestling match with the dog. Danny's mother doesn't think this kind of play is a good idea, but his father feels it's just fine, so the boy continues. Then one day when the boy has roughly thrown the dog on the ground and is holding him down, Bozo nips Danny on the hand.

DIAGNOSIS

Adolescent and preadolescent boys often feel a need to let off steam, and they usually don't know their own strength. To them, the family dog may seem to be the perfect "playmate," because it will accept any roughness without complaint.

But too-rough play with a dog almost always leads to problems. In the wild, when play between two animals becomes too rough it escalates into a fight. What's more, when a dog is allowed, or taught, that it's all right to indulge in aggressive play with a person, it should be no surprise if a self-defensive bite or nip ensues.

Close, rough body contact will probably also lead to Mounting Behavior in an unneutered male, and will certainly give a dog the message that jumping up on and knocking into people is acceptable.

TREATMENT

- Although it's never acceptable for a dog to nip or bite anyone, owners should realize that excessively rough treatment may cause a dog to bite in self-defense.
- Children of all ages should be taught from the very be-

ginning to treat a dog with respect and never force it into rough play.

■ There are active games a child can play with a dog that don't entail close body contact. Fetching games provide good exercise for both child and dog and teach the dog to drop an object in order to continue playing. Frisbee-catching is another excellent high-activity game that won't lead to aggression.

■ When a child acts aggressively with a dog it can help prevent problems if the child goes along with you to obedience class. The child can become the dog's trainer and will learn how to control his pet without force or aggressive actions.

PLAY-BOWING (See also AFFECTION, EXCESSIVE/DEMANDING; BARKING PROBLEMS: EXCESSIVE BARKING; PLAY PROBLEMS.)

Problem: The Marianos can't figure out what's going on with their half-grown Sheltie. She continuously runs up to one of them or to their old shepherd, plops down with her front legs out and her rear end wiggling up in the air, and then runs away. They wonder what she wants them to do.

DIAGNOSIS

Bowing with the front part of the body down, rear up in the air, is a natural action of herding dogs. A herding dog will go in front of a sheep, for instance, bow down to block it from moving ahead, and then bow down again to keep it from going in the other direction.

When a pet performs a bowing action in front of a person or other animal and then runs off merrily, it's called a "play-bow." Play-bowing means "Come chase me," or "Come and play with me." Wolves often play-bow to encourage each other to run and give chase in the hunt.

TREATMENT

Normal play-bowing requires no treatment. It's essentially a lighthearted behavior that most owners enjoy, and is usually outgrown.

If play-bowing becomes annoying or is accompanied by excessive Barking, it should be moderated.

- Whether you're outdoors or inside, leash your dog and have it sit or lie down quietly. If it begins to get up, give a Leash Correction.
- If the dog continues to be overexcited and you're outdoors, walk with it in proper heel position, by your left side, until it calms down.
- Indoors, give your pet the Go to Your Place command if it's learned it.

PLAY-GROWLING (See also GROWLING.)

Problem: Mildred has a Finnish spitz named Inga. The dog has an odd habit. She'll bring a toy to Mildred and toss it in the air repeatedly in what seems an obvious invitation to play. But as soon as Mildred tries to pick the toy up, Inga wags her tail furiously, grabs the toy, and growls deep in her throat. Mildred's confused. Is her dog being playful or aggressive?

DIAGNOSIS

When an obviously happy dog growls, it's called a "play-growl." Play-growling, like Play-Bowing, is an invitation to play and is completely different from angry growling in origin and connotations. It's based on happiness and excitement. A dog that's play-growling has its ears and tail perked up while its tail or entire rear end is wagging with anticipation and pleasure. (An angry dog, on the other hand, growls with its ears flattened against its head, tail down, and hackles up. *See* HOW TO INTERPRET YOUR DOG'S BODY LANGUAGE, FACIAL EXPRESSIONS, AND VOCALIZATIONS p. xi, for more about how to determine a dog's mood from its body position.) A dog that's play-growling will stop from time to time and wait to see what's coming next.

Play-growling is regularly indulged in by friendly adult dogs and by puppies and wolf cubs as they play-fight. A mother wolf or dog will often play-growl or huff-growl when she wants to encourage her young to play. An owner, too, can encourage a dog to play by using a combination of Play-Bowing and play-growling.

TREATMENT
Like Play-Bowing, play-growling is tolerated and enjoyed by most dog owners as long as it doesn't become excessive.

- If play-growling becomes annoying or escalates to the point where it's intimidating, stop playing, take away the toy, say "No," and do what a mother wolf or dog would do if a puppy got out of line. Grasp the dog by the loose skin on the back of its neck and give it a Scruff-Shake (see Punishment).

POSSESSIVENESS See FOOD-GUARDING AGGRESSION; JEALOUSY; OBJECT-GUARDING AGGRESSION; TERRITORIAL AGGRESSION.

PRAISE TO MODIFY A DOG'S BEHAVIOR

Throughout this book I continually tell you to praise your dog. Praise is probably the single most effective tool in dog training when given correctly. Unfortunately, it's often overlooked by many dog owners.

Because your dog is a pack animal, it looks up to you, its leader, and wants to please you. Praise in the form of a "Good dog" or a pat under the chin will immediately make a dog realize it's doing the right thing.

Praise should be confined to times when a dog has done something well. If you continuously tell your pet it's a good dog when all it's doing is sitting quietly beside you, its effectiveness will be lessened.

See also box, BEHAVIOR MODIFICATION, p. 34; *box,* PATTING A DOG, p. 235; *box,* REINFORCEMENT— REPETITION AND REWARD IN TRAINING, p. 253; *box,* TALKING TO YOUR DOG, p. 282; *box,* TIMING—IT'S IMPORTANCE IN ALL ASPECTS OF DOG TRAINING, p. 292.

PREDATORY AGGRESSION *(See also box,* CHASE BEHAVIOR, p. 58.)

Problem: Sean and Colleen are going to get married. The problem is, Colleen has a beautiful blue-gray British shorthair cat and Sean has a Kerry blue terrier that "hates" cats and all other small animals. It's so bad Sean doesn't dare walk his dog without a tight hold on the leash or the terrier will take off after every squirrel, pigeon, cat, or even small dog he sees. They both love their pets and want to keep them after they're married but know they have to do something so the dog won't kill Colleen's cat.

DIAGNOSIS

Some dogs have a highly developed predatory instinct. They see every small animal as a potential hunting victim. This instinct originated with wolves, which must chase game in order to survive. Kerry blues are terriers that were bred over generations to be ratters, and naturally they chase and try to kill all small prey.

TREATMENT

Ideally, if you want to have a cat and a prey-chasing dog in the same household, you should introduce them to each other when they are both young so they grow up together. When this isn't possible, the dog must have its behavior modified so it no longer views the cat as prey. *(See box,* BEHAVIOR MODIFICATION, p. 34.) These steps will only serve to protect the cat while it's indoors. The dog's strong Chase instinct is apt to be strongly triggered if it sees the cat running around outdoors.

- First, the dog must be Obedience-Trained so you can control it by voice.
- Then train the dog not to chase the cat by keeping the dog leashed at all times and correcting it whenever it even shows a sign of going after the cat.
- The best way to accustom the animals to each other and teach the dog not to view the cat as prey is to Crate both animals in the same room every time you go out. This will prevent anything untoward from happening in your absence. What's more, the cat won't be able to run and trigger the dog's chase instinct; at the same time they will get used to each other's presence in the house.
- These steps—leash and verbal correction of the dog, and crating of both animals when you're not home— should be followed until you're absolutely certain the dog won't go after the cat in your presence. Don't allow them to be alone together in the house, however, until you *know* there won't be a problem when you're not around to supervise.

PROGRAMMING A DOG See *box*, BEHAVIOR MODIFICATION, p. 34.

PROTECTIVENESS See FOOD-GUARDING AGGRESSION; JEALOUSY; OBJECT-GUARDING AGGRESSION; ONE-MAN DOGS; TERRITORIAL AGGRESSION.

PULLING ON A LEASH (See *also* EXPLORATORY BEHAVIOR; ZIGZAG BEHAVIOR.)

Problem: Whenever Linda walks her weimaraner she wishes she had a smaller dog. The dog pulls and pulls on the leash so hard it feels as if her shoulder is going to come out of its socket. Linda pulls back, but the dog continues to drag her along, oblivious to her complaints.

DIAGNOSIS

Just as a wolf will do when faced with new territory, a very curious, active dog naturally wants to run ahead quickly to see what's around the corner or behind a tree. Everything outdoors is exciting to a dog such as this, and it thinks you should also be eager to forge ahead and explore.

At the opposite end of the spectrum, some dogs don't want to walk at all, stay behind their owners, and pull backward.

TREATMENT

A dog that pulls on its leash must be reconditioned to walk correctly by using Leash Corrections.

- If you haven't already done so, take the dog to obedience class. Once the dog learns to Heel correctly there should be no leash-pulling problems.

PUNISHMENT

Punishment is defined as "a penalty for misbehavior." It shouldn't be confused with Correcting, in which you stop a dog from indulging in an unwanted action and then show it what you want it to do. Physical punishment does nothing to teach a dog to behave, particularly if it's after the fact. Reacting in anger by yelling, shouting, or threatening a dog only confuses it. Calling a dog to you to be scolded or punished will make the dog become fearful and distrustful of you. Hitting a dog or raising your hand as if to hit it will cause a dog to become hand-shy, fearful, and aggressive. *Never hit a dog!*

However, there are some times when a dog's persistent misbehavior calls for strong measures. The best type of punishment is the kind a dog brings on itself in a Setup situation. For example, if a dog chews on something that's been treated with a foul-tasting liquid, the dog will punish itself, in effect, and quickly learn not to chew on that type of object again.

The only type of physical punishment I feel is appropriate is to do what a mother dog or wolf would do to stop a recalcitrant cub or pup. If you catch a puppy or dog in the act of misbehaving, grasp it with one hand by the loose skin on the back of its neck (scruff) and shake it once or twice. (The mother animal would use her mouth to grab her youngster.) This is sometimes referred to as a "scruff-shake," and will make the animal stop what it's doing right away and wait to see what you want it to do.

See also box, CORRECTING A DOG, p. 76; *box,* LIQUIDS AS AIDS IN BEHAVIOR MODIFICATION, p. 196; *box,* TIMING—ITS IMPORTANCE IN ALL ASPECTS OF DOG TRAINING, p. 292.

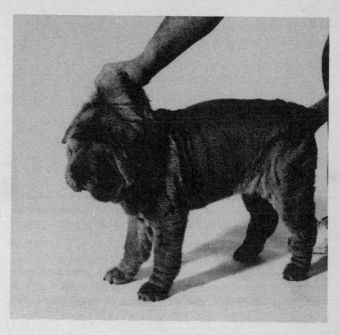

A scruff-shake is an appropriate form of physical Punishment because it mirrors the actions of a mother dog. (Bruce Plotkin)

PUPPY-GUARDING See MATERNAL AGGRESSION.

Q

QUARRELSOMENESS *(See also* INTER-DOG AGGRES-
SION; *box,* PACK BEHAVIOR, p. 230; *box,* TERRITORIAL BEHAVIOR,
p. 289; *box,* VOCALIZING BEHAVIOR, p. 318; YAPPING/YIPPING
BEHAVIOR.)

Problem: Despite the fact they grew up together, the two
little Pekingese continuously bicker and quarrel with each
other, yapping, growling, and barking day and night. It
seems they never rest, and their constant quarreling is beginning to wear on their owners' nerves.

DIAGNOSIS
Some dog breeds are especially vocal. At the same time
they may be especially possessive and territorial. A dog
such as this will always be "on guard" and anxious, lest
any dog or person encroach on what he considers his
space or property. This can lead to what seem to be
never-ending noisy quarrels with housemates.

TREATMENT

- Owners must be careful not to allow or encourage a
  naturally vocal dog to bark and yap. Don't reward a
  dog such as this for vocalizing, but immediately make
  it stop its noise. For how to do this, *see* BARKING PROB-
  LEMS: EXCESSIVE BARKING.
- Although the problem above differs from that in Inter-

Dog Aggression, the treatments are the same. A proper pack hierarchy has to be established and the dogs stopped from bickering or the quarreling will become worse and worse.

R

RAGE SYNDROME

The word "rage" signifies violent, intense anger. When a dog exhibits sudden, aggressive, tantrum-like behavior for no apparent underlying reason and with no warning it is often diagnosed as suffering from "rage syndrome." Some breeds of dogs have been suspected of having genetic predispositions toward this behavior.

True rage in dogs occurs rarely. It is thought to be caused by an unknown genetic malfunction and is almost impossible to treat successfully. A dog suffering from genuine rage syndrome is a dangerous animal and is usually destroyed.

Most canine aggression is not caused by rage but has a logical cause and is treatable. The problem is that the term "rage syndrome" has become a popular catchall phrase for veterinarians and dog trainers who are either unable or unwilling to get at the root of a dog's aggression. If your dog is diagnosed as having rage syndrome, please get a second opinion before you have it put to sleep.

See also AGGRESSION; *box,* AGGRESSIVE BEHAVIOR IN DOGS, p. 7; BITING PEOPLE; *box,* BRAIN DISORDERS, p. 47; IDIOPATHIC AGGRESSION.

RAMBUNCTIOUSNESS See ABNORMAL ACTIVITY LEVELS: HYPERACTIVITY; PLAY PROBLEMS.

RAWHIDE CHEW TOYS See *box*, CHEW TOYS FOR DOGS, p. 61.

REACTIVE AGGRESSION See *box*, DISPLACEMENT—WHAT DOES IT MEAN? p. 95; FEAR-INDUCED AGGRESSION.

RECONDITIONING See *box*, BEHAVIOR MODIFICATION, p. 34; *box*, DEPROGRAMMING AND DESENSITIZATION, p. 88.

REDIRECTED AGGRESSION See *box*, DISPLACEMENT—WHAT DOES IT MEAN? p. 95.

REFLEXIVE BEHAVIOR See AUTOMATIC BEHAVIOR.

REINFORCEMENT—REPETITION AND REWARD IN TRAINING

When you reinforce something you make it stronger. When we speak of reinforcement in dog training, we are usually referring to making a lesson stronger by means of repetition and reward in the form of Praise.

If a dog is to learn a lesson or command thoroughly, it must be repeated many times for reinforcement. Because a dog wants to please its owner it should be rewarded with praise every time it performs correctly. This will further reinforce the lesson. Then the dog will be able to understand what pleases you and what you want it to do.

See also box, FOOD REWARDS AS TRAINING TOOLS, p. 132; *box*, PRAISE TO MODIFY A DOG'S BEHAVIOR, p. 244; *box*, TALKING TO YOUR DOG, p. 282; *box*, TIMING—ITS IMPORTANCE IN ALL ASPECTS OF DOG TRAINING, p. 292.

REPROGRAMMING See *box*, BEHAVIOR MODIFICATION, p. 34; *box*, DEPROGRAMMING AND DESENSITIZATION, p. 88.

RESERVED BEHAVIOR See ALOOFNESS.

ROAMING See BOLTING: BOLTING FROM THE HOUSE; *box*, CHASE BEHAVIOR, p. 58; *box*, FLIGHT BEHAVIOR, p. 126; JUMPING PROBLEMS: JUMPING OVER FENCES; *box*, MALE DOGS' BEHAVIORAL CHARACTERISTICS, p. 198.

ROLLING BEHAVIOR

ROLLING IN BAD-SMELLING THINGS

Problem: Just as the Thompsons sat down on the terrace for lunch with their guests, Mark, their basset hound, came wandering up the lawn from the lakeside, wagging his tail furiously and smelling like a badly rotted fish. As the guests held napkins up to their noses, Mr. Thompson grabbed the dog by the collar and quickly led him away to the garage. Mrs. Thompson apologized to her guests. "We just can't keep him from rolling in horrible things," she explained.

DIAGNOSIS

A wolf that's hunting prey will often roll on a dead animal to mask its own scent. For instance, if a wolf's stalking a herd of Roosevelt elk and comes across the carcass of an elk, it will roll around on the body. Then when it nears the elk herd, the hunted animals won't be able to detect the smell of wolf. All they'll smell is another elk.

Dogs share this instinctive habit of rolling in bad-smelling things whenever they have the opportunity; decomposing, rotten fish or small animal carcasses are the usual choice—whatever happens to be available in the area.

TREATMENT

A dog with this habit can have its behavior modified so it will think twice before rolling in smelly things.

- Set the dog up *(see box,* SETUPS, p. 264). Take it on leash with you to an area where there are likely to be some smelly things it would like to roll in. Any beach, lakeshore, or path in the woods is apt to have at least one such object. As soon as the dog approaches the object, give a quick Leash Correction and say "No." Repeat this over and over until the dog learns to walk right by the smelly objects without so much as a sniff.
- If your dog normally runs loose, you can modify its behavior in much the same way by following it and using a Throw Chain or Water Balloon to startle it into stopping before rolling. Or put a leash on the dog and let it hang loose so you can grab it and give a Leash Correction. In either case, repeat the lesson a number of times until the dog learns to associate an unpleasant experience with rolling in things and decides not to risk it.

ROLLING ONTO BACK See *box,* SUBMISSIVE BEHAVIOR, p. 276.

ROUTINE See *box,* SCHEDULES FOR PUPPIES AND OLDER DOGS, p. 257.

RUNNING AWAY See BOLTING: BOLTING FROM THE HOUSE; *box,* CHASE BEHAVIOR, p. 58; *box,* FLIGHT BEHAVIOR, p. 126; JUMPING PROBLEMS: JUMPING OVER FENCES; *box,* MALE DOGS' BEHAVIORAL CHARACTERISTICS, p. 198.

RUNNING WITH A DOG: See JOGGING WITH A DOG.

S

SCENT MARKING

Scent marking is a device used by wolves and dogs (and many other animals) to mark off, or define, the boundaries of their territories. Other animals that come across the scent know they must stay clear or face a fight with the resident animal or family.

Male dogs scent-mark with urine, feces, and the discharge from scent glands. Female dogs also mark, but don't indulge in scent-marking behavior as frequently as males do. Anal glands, located on either side of a dog's rectum, add to the odor when a dog defecates. Wolves and wild dogs can discharge the foul-smelling substance in these glands at will; domestic dogs rarely do, and the glands can become impacted (*see* SCOOTING BEHAVIOR). There are also scent glands between dogs' foot pads. That's why you often see a dog dig up the earth after urinating or defecating.

Scent-marking behavior can lead to house-training problems, especially in uncastrated male dogs.

See also DIGGING: DIGGING OUTDOORS; *box,* TERRITORIAL BEHAVIOR, p. 289; URINE MARKING.

SCHEDULES FOR PUPPIES AND OLDER DOGS

A schedule, or regular routine, is important whenever a puppy or older dog first comes to live with you.

A schedule is like an outline. It helps you clarify your responsibilities to your dog and fit them into your life and at the same time makes it clear to your pet that its own biological and social needs will be met on a regular basis.

The beginning of your ownership of a puppy or dog is a crucial programming period during which your future relationship is established. During this time it's particularly important to adhere to a fairly rigid schedule. This is especially true while you're house-training a puppy. But after a while it's usually possible to compromise a bit to meet both of your needs. For instance, you'll probably be able to leave your dog alone for longer periods of time with no ill effect. If problems arise, however, you'll need to return to a strict schedule for a while in order to iron them out.

See also box, TIME — DO DOGS HAVE A SENSE OF IT? p. 291.

SCOOTING BEHAVIOR

Problem: Sid doesn't know what his mixed-breed puppy is trying to do. All of a sudden the animal jumps up and scoots along the floor, dragging his rear end on the carpet. Sometimes the puppy makes a moaning noise as he does this. Then he stops and acts perfectly normal.

DIAGNOSIS

Although it seems like a behavior problem, scooting always has a medical cause. A puppy or dog scoots along on a rug or carpet to relieve the terrible itching in its rectum. The itching may be caused by intestinal parasites or impacted anal glands.

TREATMENT

- A puppy or dog that is exhibiting scooting behavior needs prompt veterinary care. If it has worms the doctor can give medication to get rid of them. If the problem is impacted anal glands, they, too, can easily be treated.
- Some individual dogs have a tendency to chronic anal gland impaction. If your dog has this problem, have the glands emptied on a regular basis by a groomer or veterinarian or learn how to perform the procedure yourself.

SCRATCHING PROBLEMS

SCRATCHING FLOORS, FURNITURE, WALLS See
DESTRUCTIVE BEHAVIOR; DIGGING; SEPARATION ANXIETY.

SCRATCHING SELF

Problem: The Norfolk terrier scratched and scratched herself so badly she'd worn a bare spot on her rump. Her constant thump-thumping on the floor as she scratched was also driving her mistress up the wall.

DIAGNOSIS

Although it manifests itself as a behavior problem, constant scratching usually has a medical basis in dogs and can be caused by parasites or allergies.

Allergies in dogs don't cause sneezing or runny noses, but itchiness. Canine allergies can be caused by fleas, inhaled allergens, regular physical contact with something allergenic, or food. Food allergies are nonseasonal, while many environmental allergies only appear seasonally. Allergies can suddenly surface at any time in a dog's life, and allergic dogs usually become itchier as they age.

Excessive scratching can also be a form of Displacement, or Obsessive-Compulsive Behavior, similar to Acral Lick Dermatitis Granuloma or Flank Sucking.

TREATMENT

- A dog that scratches excessively should have a thorough veterinary exam to check for parasites or an allergic reaction to something in the environment. Environmental allergies in dogs can be very difficult to solve, and it usually takes serious detective work on the part of the owner to figure out what the cause is. Dietary allergies are generally easier to solve with a veterinarian's help.
- While a scratching problem is being treated it can help to have the dog professionally bathed with a soothing shampoo.
- An Elizabethan Collar will prevent a dog from continuing to scratch itself and allow the skin to heal.
- You can help redirect scratching behavior if you give the dog something especially desirable to chew on such as a fresh Bone or new rawhide Toy.

SCREEN-RIPPING See DESTRUCTIVE BEHAVIOR; SEPARATION ANXIETY.

SCRUFF-SHAKING See box, PUNISHMENT, p. 247.

SEIZURES IN DOGS

It can be extremely alarming to a dog owner to see a pet in the midst of a seizure. Dogs can suffer from seizures (convulsions, fits) for a number of reasons. If a dog's brain function is disturbed because of a systemic disease, hypoglycemia (low blood sugar), or severe overheating, the animal may suffer from a seizure. In cases such as this the incidence of seizures will diminish once the cause is remedied.

Frequently, however, seizure disorders are idiopathic (of unknown cause) and recur regularly. This type of seizure disorder is called epilepsy, or primary epilepsy, and is thought to occur more often in some dog breeds.

Seizures differ in severity. A small (petit mal) seizure usually lasts only a few seconds and may not even be noticed by a dog owner. The animal may simply stand still and tremble, or it may snap at imaginary objects in the air, or stare blankly into space.

A generalized grand mal seizure cannot be ignored and may be extremely frightening to an owner the first time it occurs. Grand mal seizures often appear in clusters, with several occurring in a twenty-four-hour period. A grand mal seizure is characterized by collapse, loss of consciousness, the stiffening of muscles, twitching, leg-paddling, and jaw snapping. Sometimes urinary and fecal incontinence accompanies these other symptoms. The actual collapse usually lasts no longer than a few minutes, but to a concerned owner it may seem like hours. After this stage the dog may be disoriented, confused, and sleepy, and may even suffer from temporary blindness. It can take hours, even days, for a dog to return to normal after a grand mal seizure.

There is nothing an owner can or should do during an actual seizure except leave the dog alone. Contrary to myth, no animal will swallow its tongue during a fit, and putting your hands in its mouth may result in an involuntary bite. Once the dog is in a post-fit (postictus) stage, it should be kept warm and quiet and given a lot of reassurance and love.

If your dog has a seizure, try to keep track of the duration of each stage of the incident. This will help the veterinarian determine the cause, if any, and the proper treatment. Individualized symptomatic therapy can be successful in treating canine seizures, but each animal varies, and owner involvement is vital to success.

SELF-MUTILATION See *box*, ACRAL LICK DERMATITIS/ GRANULOMA, p. 4; *box*, FLANK SUCKING, p. 125; *box*, OBSESSIVE-COMPULSIVE BEHAVIOR IN DOGS, p. 222; TAIL CHASING/BITING.

SEPARATION ANXIETY (*See also box*, ANXIETY IN DOGS, p. 14; BOREDOM; DESTRUCTIVE BEHAVIOR; OLDER DOG PROBLEMS; *box*, PACK BEHAVIOR, p. 230; *box*, VOCALIZING BEHAVIOR, p. 318; WHINING.)

Problem 1: Ellen and Keith are teachers. They purposely got their springer spaniel puppy in June, so they'd be home all summer to raise him. For almost three months one or the other of them was home with the puppy almost every hour of the day and evening, walking him, playing with him, training him, and keeping him company. When they went back to work in the fall the puppy was almost half-grown and well on his way to becoming an extremely well-behaved animal.

What a surprise they had when they came home after their first full day at work! The puppy had made a complete mess of the front hall. He'd apparently scratched at the floor so hard he'd worn the surface down to the bare wood. To make matters worse, he'd had Diarrhea all over.

Problem 2: Hildie was going to drive out West to visit her sister. The drive would take about three days. Because her three-year-old rottweiler, Henry, was always so well behaved, Hildie decided to bring him with her. Even though he'd never been away from home before, Henry seemed to enjoy the first day's drive, and after he'd had his dinner and a long walk, Hildie left him quietly sleeping in the motel room while she went out to eat.

As she walked back to her room later, she was surprised to hear Henry barking frantically. Quickly opening the door, she couldn't believe what she saw in the room. Henry had torn the place apart—bedding was on the floor, the TV was knocked over, and all of her clothing was strewn around. Luckily it was still early, so his noise hadn't kept anyone up, but as she began to straighten up the room she wondered what had happened to her well-behaved dog.

Problem 3: Nancy had always had boxers. When she decided to get another dog she didn't feel she had time to raise a puppy, because she was very busy with her career. So she went to a breeder who found her a previously owned four-year-old female boxer, named Maude. Nancy knew Maude needed time to adjust to her new home, so she took several weeks off work to orient the dog and establish a good Schedule for both of them.

After a couple of weeks everything was going smoothly and Nancy went back to work. When she came home the first day she was horrified to find Maude had urinated and defecated all over and torn the apartment apart. She immediately called the breeder to see if he had any explanation for the dog's behavior. He told her Maude had lived in a big household where someone was home all the time. Now Nancy knew that Maude suffered from separation anxiety when she was left alone.

DIAGNOSIS

Just like wolves, all dogs are social pack animals. In the absence of an actual pack, a domestic dog relies on its owners for companionship and social contact.

When a puppy or dog that's used to company is suddenly left alone at home, or when a dog is left alone in a strange place, it may feel abandoned, be frightened, and suffer from a syndrome we call "separation anxiety." It becomes nervous and anxious. In an effort to bring you back it may vocalize loudly and incessantly. Or it may frantically try to get out to find you, scratching at doors, screens, windows, and even walls. Some dogs will chew on their owner's clothing for security. Others chew furniture and rugs, knock things over, and engage in other types of Destructive Behavior in their distress. If a dog becomes completely hysterical it may vomit, urinate, and have diarrhea.

With young dogs, separation anxiety usually surfaces at the stage when they're almost grown and no longer require their owners' constant care. It can also occur when an adult dog is left by itself in a strange place. In the case of a dog that's used to constant company the syndrome may crop up the first time the animal's left alone.

TREATMENT

- Separation anxiety can be prevented if you socialize a puppy or dog to tolerate your absence from the very start. Gradually get your pet used to staying quietly by itself in the house as soon as it's old enough to be left for a few hours at a time.
- If you plan to take your dog with you to motels or hotels, take it to a friend's house and leave it alone there a couple of times so it learns you'll return and get it after a while. Instruct your friend to keep the dog on a leash and correct it if it begins to become frenzied or act up.
- A puppy or dog that's accustomed to sleeping in a Crate will usually feel calm and unafraid in your absence as long as it has the security of its crate. This will also prevent it from indulging in Destructive Behavior.
- As difficult as it may be, don't scold or punish a dog that's misbehaved in your absence because of separation anxiety. If you act angry it will only confirm the dog's belief that bad things happen when you go out.
- To desensitize a dog with separation anxiety, you'll need to gradually get it used to your absence by leaving it for progressively longer periods of time until it is accustomed to remaining quietly and calmly alone. One way to do this is to use a Crate. Have the dog sleep in its crate in your bedroom for a few nights. Then move the crate to a different room for the night. The dog will know you're in the house but it won't be near you. Gradually move the crate farther away until the dog learns to separate from you and can stay quietly in the crate even when you're not in the house. A pressure Gate can work the same way, helping the dog learn to remain calm, in its own room, until you return.
- When a dog has already developed severe separation

anxiety and indulges in Barking, Chewing, or other Destructive Behavior, you'll have to treat each of these problems separately.

SETUPS

When you use a "setup" to deprogram a dog, you manage things so the animal brings a prearranged punishment on itself when it indulges in an undesirable action. It will prevent a dog from doing a particular thing and eventually modify the dog's behavior.

Let's say your dog regularly pulls over the kitchen trash can every time you go out, scattering papers and rubbish all over the floor. To set the dog up, leave the trash can in its usual place but spray the contents with a bitter, foul-tasting liquid (*see box*, LIQUIDS AS AIDS IN BEHAVIOR MODIFICATION, p. 196) before you go out. When the dog pulls the can over and begins to scatter the contents, it will be surprised and shocked at the horrible taste in its mouth and will quickly run off and leave the rubbish alone. The next day the dog probably won't even try to pull the can over, but if it does it will be greeted by the same horrid taste. It usually won't take more than two days of this for a dog to learn to stay completely away from the trash can.

What you have done is effectively break a dog's bad habit by seeing to it that it brings a Punishment on itself. It's learned its actions will result in an unpleasant experience. In technical language this is referred to as behavioral engineering—you engineer all of the factors in a way to reprogram the dog away from the undesired action.

See also box, BEHAVIOR MODIFICATION, p. 34; *box*, DEPROGRAMMING AND DESENSITIZATION, p. 88.

SEXUAL BEHAVIOR See *box*, FEMALE DOGS' BEHAVIORAL CHARACTERISTICS, p. 122; *box*, MALE DOGS' BEHAVIORAL CHARACTERISTICS, p. 198.

SHAKE CAN: See *box*, NOISEMAKERS, p. 217.

SHEDDING PROBLEMS (See *also* SCRATCHING PROBLEMS: SCRATCHING SELF.)

Problem: Sheila was disgusted. Every day she swept and vacuumed, but she simply couldn't keep up with the balls and balls of fur from her Siberian husky's shedding. She'd wanted a long-haired dog, but this was ridiculous! She was beginning to feel as if the dog were losing hair just to annoy her.

DIAGNOSIS

Although shedding is not a behavioral problem, owners often come to resent heavy shedding so much they feel as if it is.

All dogs shed all year long; it's the normal hair-replacement cycle. Differences in degrees of shedding have to do with the length and thickness of the coat and the hair itself. When a dog is under stress it will always shed excessively, and some systemic diseases may cause extensive hair loss. Excessive shedding can also be exacerbated in any dog by a poor diet or an overheated environment.

TREATMENT

- If your dog's shedding seems really excessive, have it checked over by the veterinarian for possible internal sources of the problem.
- Heavy shedding can be greatly reduced by daily grooming at home and regular professional bathing and grooming. Dogs with especially heavy, thick coats often benefit from having their fur stripped, thinned, or clipped once or twice a year.

- If your dog's coat and skin seem too dry, ask your veterinarian about adding some vegetable oil to its diet.
- A brisk daily run outdoors will help remove a lot of loose hairs from your dog's coat in addition to adding to the animal's general good health.

SHYNESS See FEARFULNESS.

SINGING BEHAVIOR (See also box, VOCALIZING BEHAVIOR, p. 318.)

Problem: Every time Nellie sits down at the piano, her cocker spaniel sits right beside her on the floor. As she begins to play, he tilts his head back and makes noises in his throat. Even though she knows it's not possible, Nellie could swear he's actually singing!

DIAGNOSIS

Some dogs always react to music by vocalizing. Although we really don't know why this happens, it undoubtedly has to do with their keen sense of Hearing. A dog that "sings" probably hears overtones in the music that human ears can't detect. These tones strike a responsive chord in the animal, making it want to join in with the music.

TREATMENT

- There is, of course, no "treatment" necessary for a singing dog. Some owners, however, have turned their dogs' propensity to "sing" into a trick. "Singing" dogs have even appeared on the "Tonight Show"!

SLEEPING WITH PEOPLE See JUMPING PROBLEMS: JUMPING ON THE BED.

SLOW RESPONSE TO COMMANDS See DEAFNESS, SIGNS OF; box, DEFIANCE—FACTS & MYTHS, p. 87; STUBBORNNESS.

SMILING BEHAVIOR

Problem: When Grace comes home from work every day, her Yorkshire terrier, Leo, runs out into the hall wriggling all over and smiling at her. The problem is, Grace can't get anyone to believe he actually smiles, because he won't do it any other time.

DIAGNOSIS

Like many other traits and actions we ascribe to our dogs, "smiling" is really not a canine response to happiness. But many dogs do pull their lips back from their teeth and seem to smile when they're excited and joyful.

TREATMENT

- Just as for Singing Behavior, there is no "treatment" for smiling. Some dogs can be taught to smile, or show teeth, on command for a photograph.

SMELL, DOGS' KEENEST SENSE

Dogs rely on their sense of smell more than on any other of their keen senses. Their natural scenting abilities are inherited from their wolf ancestors. Wolves require a highly developed sense of smell in order to locate prey and detect enemies; they use scent to identify pack members and to mark and determine territorial boundaries. Without a well-defined, discriminatory sense of smell, a wolf wouldn't last long in the wild.

Domestic dogs don't require a sense of smell to survive, but they do utilize their scenting ability to recognize friend and foe. Scent-hunting dogs have especially well-developed olfactory sensibilities, as do guide dogs, Search-and-Rescue dogs, and dogs that help detect smugglers at airports. Dogs use their sense of smell in all of their everyday activities, and a keen sense of smell helps even a totally blind or deaf dog get around well.

See also box, SCENT MARKING, p. 256; SNIFFING PEOPLE AND OTHER DOGS IN GREETING.

SNAPPISHNESS See NIPPING; QUARRELSOMENESS.

SNARLING See GROWLING.

SNIFFING PEOPLE AND OTHER DOGS IN GREETING (See *also* FACE-RUBBING; see *box,* SMELL, DOGS' KEENEST SENSE, above.)

Problem: Gloria is constantly embarrassed by her pointer, Fred. Every time people come in the house, he runs over to them and proceeds to sniff them in the crotch area. As if this weren't bad enough, he sniffs every dog he meets in the rectum and "private parts"! No matter how many times she tells him "No" and pulls him away, Fred persists in this disgusting habit. Gloria's beginning to think the dog is perverted.

DIAGNOSIS

Dogs use their keen sense of smell to identify individuals. What to humans may seem a "disgusting" habit of sniffing the crotches of other dogs and humans is simply a dog's natural way of identifying them.

TREATMENT

- There's no need to prevent a dog from sniffing other dogs in greeting. Remind yourself that this is a normal canine activity and you will probably be able to get rid of your embarrassment when your dog engages in public sniffing of other dogs.
- When a dog persists in greeting people with excessive sniffing, use Leash Corrections and other steps to modify its behavior; see JUMPING PROBLEMS: JUMPING ON PEOPLE IN THE HOME IN GREETING.
- If your dog has had Obedience Training, have it sit whenever visitors arrive at your home. Then, if the visitor is so inclined, he can offer his palm to the dog to sniff. This will usually satisfy a dog's curiosity.

SNORING

Problem: No sooner does Lenny go to sleep than his Boston terrier, Barney, begins to snore loudly, waking him up. Lenny gets angry, jumps up, and yells at the dog to wake *him* up. But as soon as he gets back to sleep, the dog snores again. Lenny loves Barney, but he's beginning to get really annoyed at the dog for constantly interrupting his sleep. He finds he constantly snaps at the animal for no good reason.

DIAGNOSIS

This is another problem with a physical cause that's often perceived by owners to be behavioral in origin. A dog has no control over snoring. Dogs with flat, pushed-in faces (brachycephalic breeds) have a natural tendency to breathe loudly, snort, and snore. They can also suffer from genetic respiratory-system disorders, such as an overlong soft palate. This condition can cause excessive noisy respiration and snoring.

TREATMENT

- If a dog seems to be snoring excessively, have it examined by a veterinarian.
- An extremely overlong soft palate can be shortened surgically, but this is usually not done unless the problem is severe.
- To avoid being kept awake by a serious snorer, close the dog in a room as far away from your bedroom as possible.

SOCIALIZATION, THE KEY TO A
WELL ADJUSTED DOG

Many behavior problems that surface in a dog's life can be avoided completely by early socialization. Just what is socialization, and how is it done?

Socialization consists of introducing a puppy to as many different people and experiences as possible so it becomes accustomed to them and learns to adapt to a variety of situations and events with equanimity. A well-socialized dog will be able to accept strangers, can go into a crowded place without apprehension, won't be fearful in a car or at the groomer's, and in general will be a well-adjusted individual.

Although it's highly preferable to socialize a dog to all kinds of experiences when it's a young puppy, it is possible to socialize an older animal. It will simply take a lot more time and patience on the owner's part and may even require help from a professional trainer. *(See also* OLDER DOG PROBLEMS, ADOPTING AN OLDER DOG.)

Among other problems that an unsocialized dog may develop are Fearfulness and Kennel Shyness.

SOILING See CRATE PROBLEMS: CRATE SOILING; DIARRHEA; HOUSE-TRAINING PROBLEMS.

SOUND STIMULANTS See *box,* NOISEMAKERS, **p. 217;** *box,* THROW CHAIN, **p. 290.**

SPAYING OF FEMALE DOGS—FACTS & MYTHS

It's a widely accepted practice to spay—or more correctly, perform an ovariohysterectomy (OHE) on—most pet female dogs. The benefits of this operation have been recognized far longer than those of Castration of males.

This is primarily true because of the obvious advantages for pet owners: the elimination of unwanted "heat" periods and prevention of pregnancy. But other medical benefits also provide compelling reasons for having a pet female dog spayed. Early spaying reduces or virtually eliminates the chances of a dog's developing mammary gland cancer, mastitis, uterine infections, tumors of the reproductive tract, and many other diseases and disorders to which unspayed (intact) female dogs are highly susceptible.

Although spaying doesn't have the wide spectrum of behavioral advantages for females that Castration has for male dogs, it does result in a calmer, less anxious, more responsive pet. And, contrary to popular belief, the operation does not cause a dog to become fat. Overfeeding and a lack of sufficient exercise are the only things that put excess weight on any dog.

Ideally, the operation is performed before the dog's first heat, when she's around six to eight months of age. The old myth that a female dog should be allowed to have one litter so her behavior is "settled" before spaying is simply not true. Waiting produces no behavioral benefits and may put a dog's future health at risk.

See also box, FEMALE DOGS' BEHAVIORAL CHARACTERISTICS, p. 122.

STOOL-EATING   273

SPITE—FACTS & MYTHS

Owners often think a dog has misbehaved out of "spite." They reason that the dog, miffed at being left alone, has engaged in Destructive Behavior to "get even" with them for abandoning it.

Just like Defiance and Guilt, spite is an anthropomorphic term. A dog doesn't have the ability to think in terms of "getting even," or of punishing you for leaving it alone.

When a dog misbehaves in your absence, it may be due to Separation Anxiety, loneliness, or simply Boredom, but not spitefulness!

See also box, ANTHROPOMORPHISM, p. 13; DISPLACEMENT—WHAT DOES IT MEAN? p. 95.

SPOILED BEHAVIOR See AFFECTION, EXCESSIVE/DEMANDING; BARKING PROBLEMS: EXCESSIVE BARKING; BEGGING; PLAY PROBLEMS; WHINING; YAPPING/YIPPING BEHAVIOR.

SPRAYS See *box,* LIQUIDS AS AIDS IN BEHAVIOR MODIFICATION, p. 196.

STARING AT PEOPLE See EYE CONTACT.

STEALING FOOD See GARBAGE STEALING/DUMPING; GULPING FOOD; JUMPING PROBLEMS: JUMPING ON THE KITCHEN COUNTER OR DINING TABLE.

STAY See *box,* DOWN/STAY, p. 99.

STOOL-EATING See COPROPHAGIA.

STRANGERS, FEAR OF See FEARFULNESS; JEALOUSY: JEALOUSY OF AN ADULT PERSON; ONE-MAN DOGS.

STUBBORNNESS (See *also box*, CORRECTING A DOG, p. 76; *box*, DEFIANCE—FACTS AND MYTHS, p. 87; *box*, TIMING—ITS IMPORTANCE IN ALL ASPECTS OF DOG TRAINING, p. 292.)

Problem: Francis is disturbed at the way his Scottie, Andy, is behaving. The dog had gone through Obedience Training with no problem, seeming to understand every command and exercise with ease. But now Andy stubbornly refuses to obey some of Francis's commands. When his master calls him to come, for instance, Andy just looks at him and continues to sit still. After a while, the dog may deign to obey, but Francis is concerned that Andy's stubbornness may get worse with time.

DIAGNOSIS

Some dog breeds are naturally more apt to be stubborn than others. Stubborn behavior in a dog is a form of Dominant Behavior; it's a way of challenging your authority. Just like a bratty child, a dog that's acting stubborn is saying, in effect, "Make me." Sometimes a dog begins by being just a bit stubborn. It waits for several beats before it finally obeys a command, testing you and pushing its advantage to the limit. When a previously well-trained dog that clearly understands what's wanted is allowed to get away with acting stubborn the problem will eventually escalate to the point where the animal will refuse to obey you at all.

When a dog that hasn't been obedience-trained seems to act stubborn, it may be because it doesn't understand what you want it to do. (*See box*, TALKING TO YOUR DOG, p. 282.)

TREATMENT

- If your dog hasn't been obedience-trained, be sure it knows what you want before you label it as acting stubborn. Go back to the beginning and clearly show it what you want it to do.

- The minute a previously well-trained dog appears to be acting stubborn, snap a leash on the dog and go through all of the steps of the obedience routine.
- Give a well-timed Leash Correction every time the dog delays for an instant or refuses to obey a command. Don't allow a dog such as this to get away with challenging your leadership, but consistently correct it firmly and calmly.
- A dog that's stubborn and dominant by nature may continue to act stubborn from time to time, just to see if it can get away with it. Be prepared for this, and don't let it.

SUBMISSIVE BEHAVIOR

As I pointed out elsewhere (*see box*, DOMINANT BE-HAVIOR, p. 98; *box*, PACK BEHAVIOR, p. 230), every wolf in a pack except the Alpha pair of animals is subordinate to all those individuals above it in the pack hierarchy. Subordinate animals always act in a submissive manner to those above them. Among domestic dogs as well, some animals are naturally more dominant or submissive than others. During the first weeks with the litter, every puppy assumes its place in the dominance hierarchy and its tendency to be either a dominant or subordinate animal becomes part of its basic nature.

In the presence of a more dominant animal a submissive animal lowers its head, tail, and entire body. It may even roll over onto its back, exposing its belly and genital area to show it's no threat, at which point the dominant animal often belly-licks it for reassurance. At the same time a submissive animal will often lick the dominant one's face and dribble some urine. When two equally dominant animals fight, the loser signals defeat by adopting an "I give up" submissive pose.

A naturally submissive puppy can become a fearful dog if it's not socialized very carefully by its owners.

See also FEAR-INDUCED AGGRESSION; HOW TO INTERPRET YOUR DOG'S BODY LANGUAGE, FACIAL EXPRESSIONS, AND VOCALIZATIONS, p. xi; URINE LEAKING/DRIBBLING.

SUBMISSIVE URINATION See URINE LEAKING/DRIBBLING.

SWALLOWING NONFOODS See COPROPHAGIA; PICA.

SWIMMING PROBLEMS (See also BOATS, BEHAVIOR ON.)

Problem: Lydia had always understood all dogs were born knowing how to swim. She was very surprised when her half-grown poodle fell off a dock at the lake and thrashed around, seeming to almost drown until she pulled him out of the water. Now she wonders if it's safe to allow him near the water.

DIAGNOSIS

Although it's true that all dogs can swim, they sometimes need a bit of practice to perfect their skill. The first few times they're in the water, most dogs do what seems like a bad imitation of the "dog paddle," splashing and thrashing around in an awkward manner. After a while they become better at swimming, don't splash so much, and are able to control their speed and direction well. Many dogs learn to enjoy swimming and jump into the water whenever they have the opportunity.

Dogs sometimes jump into the water in an effort to reach their owners. They'll run around on a pool apron or the beach and finally, when they can stand the separation no longer, jump in and swim to their owners.

The only serious problem a swimming dog can have is an inability to get out of the water if there's a straight drop from the shore, a dock, a poolside, or a boat. A dog that has no way of getting out of the water could easily become exhausted and drown.

TREATMENT

- Let your dog become used to the water gradually, and don't force it to swim if it doesn't seem to like it much—some dogs don't.
- Be sure the dog knows how to get out of the water, es-

pecially if it's young, old, or overweight. It may require a hand from you to negotiate a slippery ladder or ramp.

- If you're going to take your dog out on a boat or live by the shore and your dog is elderly, fat, or infirm or just doesn't like the water much, you may want to get it a life vest. Life vests for dogs are available from specialty pet stores and mail-order companies.
- If you're in the water with a dog that is just learning to swim well, be careful not to get scratched by the nails on its wildly flailing front feet.
- Be careful if your dog becomes excessively anxious when you're in the water. If it jumps in and swims to you, it may try to climb up on top of you while you're swimming. This can be very dangerous for both dog and human swimmer, especially if the swimmer happens to be a child.
- Don't allow a dog to become too waterlogged. Young dogs, like young children, tend to stay in the water too long sometimes, especially if there's a good game of fetch or keep-away in progress. If this appears to be a problem, call the dog out of the water and distract it with some other activity or put it indoors for a while.

SYMPATHY LAMENESS See LAMENESS, SYMPATHY.

T

TABLE SCRAPS, FEEDING *(See also* APPETITE PROBLEMS: EXCESSIVE APPETITE; BEGGING: BEGGING FOR FOOD; *box,* FOOD REWARDS AS TRAINING TOOLS, p. 132; OBESITY.*)*

Problem: Martha's sister keeps telling her she shouldn't feed her little schnauzer table scraps, but she doesn't see any harm in it as long as he gets regular dog food once a day. But now he's beginning to be a pest, constantly begging for a handout.

DIAGNOSIS

According to a recent survey made by the American Animal Hospital Association (AAHA), over half the pet owners in the United States feed their dogs table scraps occasionally. The majority of these owners report their pets are not overweight.

People feed their dogs table scraps for a number of reasons, but most often because the animal begs. The old "food is love" syndrome also enters in; owners feel a pet that is given treats in the form of table scraps will love them more and know how much it is loved.

Even when a dog isn't yet overweight, regular treats of table scraps can upset an otherwise well-balanced diet and will inevitably lead to weight gain. The fat and sugar found in much human food is difficult for dogs to digest and can lead to stomach upsets as well as Obesity. Finally, a dog may become so used to the taste of "people

food" it will become a finicky eater. (*See* APPETITE PROB-
LEMS: LOSS OF APPETITE/ACTING FINICKY.)

TREATMENT

- For steps to recondition a dog that continually begs for
  food, *see* BEGGING: BEGGING FOR FOOD.
- Substitute a dog biscuit for a table scrap when you feel
  it's appropriate to give your pet a food treat.

TAIL-CHASING/BITING

Problem: What Jamie considered cute and funny when
her English bull terrier was young has turned into a very
irritating habit. The dog continually chases his tail,
around and around like a whirling dervish. Sometimes he
even catches his tail and bites it until it bleeds. She wonders what to do to stop him from this ridiculous activity.

DIAGNOSIS

Although tail-chasing and biting can have medical causes,
such as itchy parasites or skin diseases, an anal sac impaction, or neurologic tail disorder, it is usually behavioral in origin. Diet doesn't seem to be a factor in
tail-chasing.

Excessive tail-chasing can be part of an especially
hyperactive dog's behavior. (*See* ABNORMAL ACTIVITY LEV-
ELS: HYPERACTIVITY PROBLEM 1.) But it's often a learned
attention-getting action. When owners laugh and encourage a puppy to chase its tail, they're giving it the message
that this activity will earn their attention. Later, when normal tail-chasing doesn't cause its owners to respond, the
dog goes into more and more frantic activity.

Tail-chasing is also believed to be a form of Displacement in some dogs, frustrated at too much confinement
for instance. Tail-biting is a form of self-mutilation that
falls under the heading of Obsessive-Compulsive Behavior.

TREATMENT

- First, have the dog examined by a veterinarian to be sure the tail-chasing isn't caused by an itch or pain.
- If there's no medical cause for the behavior and you believe it to be an attention-getting action, the best treatment is to ignore the animal. If it gets no response from you when it chases its tail, the fun will soon go out of the activity.
- When tail-chasing seems especially frantic, suspect it might be caused by frustration of some sort. Give the dog a lot of exercise and attention and perhaps the problem will go away by itself.
- To stop a dog from harming itself by biting its tail, you can use an Elizabethan Collar, wrap the tail with a gauze strip, or paint it with some foul-tasting liquid (*see box*, LIQUIDS AS AIDS IN BEHAVIOR MODIFICATION, p. 196). Ask your veterinarian for advice if these steps don't work.

TALKING TO YOUR DOG

Your voice is one of the most effective tools you have as you work with your dog and establish rapport with it. Dogs and wolves always vocalize to communicate with each other, and a dog's keen sense of hearing allows it to pick up even the slightest inflection in your voice and recognize what it means. When puppies and dogs are talked to all the time they become relaxed, alert, and closely "tuned in" to their owners. No matter how young, a puppy soon knows when you're pleased or displeased with it by listening to your tone of voice. Owners who are alone with their pets a lot often speak to them as if they were other human beings, sharing plans for the day and so forth. Dogs really learn to enjoy this kind of "conversation," and perk up and listen whenever they're spoken to.

Be very careful not to confuse your dog as you talk to it, especially when you're teaching it to respond to its name or to a command. I speak elsewhere of the confusion a puppy may feel when it's addressed by a number of different names (see NAME, NOT RESPONDING TO). The same confusion will occur if you use different words or phrases to give the same command. For instance, "Stop it!" "Quit it!" "Don't do that!" and "No!" may all mean the same thing to you, but a dog will have a hard time finding any relationship or common meaning between these different-sounding commands. As I often say, put yourself in your dog's place and be consistent and clear when you speak to it.

When you do this your puppy will quickly learn to recognize key words or phrases and be well on its way to becoming a responsive, well-behaved dog.

See also box, MIXED MESSAGES, p. 203; *box,* PRAISE TO MODIFY A DOG'S BEHAVIOR, p. 244; *box,* VOCALIZING BEHAVIOR, p. 318.

TEETHING BEHAVIOR

Puppies are born without teeth, but by around six
weeks of age a puppy will have a full complement of
twenty-eight baby, or "milk," teeth. When a puppy is
about three or four months old, its permanent teeth
begin to erupt, pushing out the baby teeth. It takes
two or three months for all of the permanent teeth
(forty-two in all) to come in, and during this entire
time a puppy is actively teething.

Like their human counterparts, some puppies have
more difficulty teething than others. They may suffer
from loss of appetite, nausea, Diarrhea, and fever. A
teething puppy that seems sick or unusually uncomfortable, rubs its face constantly, or drools excessively should be seen by a veterinarian.

Most puppies are simply mildly uncomfortable
from the itching, burning, and sometimes painful
gums that accompany the eruption of teeth. To ease
the discomfort, teething puppies usually engage in
seemingly frantic Chewing, Mouthing, and Nipping.
Everything has to go into their mouths! This is normal teething behavior and can be eased and tolerated
better by owners if plenty of appropriate chewing
material is provided.

Sometimes the baby teeth don't all fall out, teeth
come in crooked, or teeth are overcrowded in a dog's
mouth. The last problem is often seen in brachycephalic (short-faced) breeds. All of these problems
should be remedied by a veterinarian to prevent future tooth and gum problems.

See also TOOTH CARE PROBLEMS.

TELEPATHY *See box,* ESP—DO DOGS HAVE IT?, p. 111.

TEMPERAMENT, ASSESSING A DOG'S

Problem: Joe and Susanna want to get a dog, but they keep hearing about how important it is to choose a pet with a "good temperament," especially as they plan to have children. They're wondering what a dog's temperament actually is, and how they can be sure to pick intelligently.

DIAGNOSIS

When we speak of a dog's temperament we're referring to its basic nature: the way an individual animal reacts to stimuli; the way it thinks and behaves. Is it by nature dominant or submissive, social or aloof, stubborn or pliable, calm or excitable, brave or fearful? All of these traits, and others, are influenced by an animal's genetics to a large extent. A purebred dog's temperament is primarily determined by careful breeding over many generations in an effort to attain the ideal temperament for its breed. Thus, almost all chows are aloof, retrievers outgoing and affectionate, Akitas strong-willed and territorial, and so on.

But factors other than genetics shape an individual dog's temperament. Each animal inherits its own parents' behavioral as well as physical characteristics, and a puppy's early handling and Socialization or lack of it are also important influences on the temperament of the adult dog it will become.

Appropriate training and handling, geared to an individual dog's own temperament, will help that dog become a satisfactory pet.

TREATMENT

■ To choose a puppy with the kind of temperament you want, it's important to do a lot of research about dog breeds. Although a mixed-breed puppy can make a fine pet, it's difficult, if not impossible, to predict what its basic temperament will be. Read all you can about various breeds, but also go to dog shows and talk to as many knowledgeable people as you can. Consult with breeders, but, more important, talk to dog owners, who will usually give you a more unbiased opinion based on their experiences with a breed. Veterinarians and groomers are also good objective judges of the basic temperament of many dog breeds.

■ Once you make a decision to get a certain breed, or type, of dog, you have to find a source for your pet. I urge you not to purchase a purebred dog from a pet shop or backyard breeder if you want to be sure your pet has a particular temperament. If you don't know the temperaments of a puppy's parents and have no idea how it was previously handled, you'll be getting a dog with no predictable personality or nature. It's important to see a puppy's mother, and father if possible, and observe it interacting with its siblings in the litter. This way you can tell if the puppy you choose has a fundamentally dominant or submissive nature. There are temperament-judging tests you can perform on a puppy.

■ Remember, every dog is an individual with its own particular temperament. When you begin to train your new puppy, be sure to take its temperament into consideration. Too-harsh treatment of a basically sensitive dog will cause it to become fearful. On the other hand, if you give kid-glove treatment to a dog that's hardy and stubborn by nature it will end up an aggressive, badly trained dog that dominates you.

TERRITORIAL AGGRESSION (See also box, TERRITORIAL BEHAVIOR, p. 289.)

Problem 1: Mark is a gentle, sweet Westie. he's nice to everyone, except anyone who happens to come to the door of the house. As soon as the doorbell rings he becomes a snarling guided missile. His owners don't dare open the door to accept a package or let a visitor in without first catching Mark and closing him in the closet.

Problem 2: The Franklins' collie is a perfectly trained dog. She responds to all commands and has even learned

"Go to Your Place." Her "place" is a corner underneath the dining-room serving table where she always sleeps. The problem is, she won't let anyone near her corner. She begins to growl, snarl, and bark whenever anyone even walks into the room.

Problem 3: Fred is an Akita. He loves to sleep on the front steps of his house, where he stays quietly; he never roams. When anybody comes up the path he wags his tail happily. But if another dog walks by on the road or so much as sets a paw on the edge of the lawn, Fred attacks. His owners have had so many complaints and paid so many veterinarian bills for injured dogs they think they'll have to invest in a fence to keep Fred in.

DIAGNOSIS

Territorial guarding is a natural canine behavior originating in a wolf's need to protect its den, itself, its food, and its young. It's more highly developed in some breeds, such as terriers and dogs that have been bred over generations to be guarding or herding animals. Intact (uncastrated) males are apt to be more territorial than females. *(See box,* MALE DOGS' BEHAVIORAL CHARACTERISTICS, p. 198.) Territorial behavior in itself is generally not a problem, but it becomes one if it is allowed to escalate into full-blown aggression. This may occur if owners allow a dog to get away with mildly aggressive acts, or if they encourage a dog to be aggressive.

It's evident that territorial aggression is interconnected to all other types of aggression in dogs.

TREATMENT

In treating all kinds of territorial aggression, the most important first step is to give a dog Obedience Training so that it's always under control. It will also help if you neuter (castrate) a male dog.

Problem 1: A dog that attacks people who come to the door can simply be closed up when people arrive, but the real problem will remain.

- Instead of closing the dog up, have a leash handy in the hallway. As soon as the dog begins to go into its aggressive act, put the leash on and tell the dog, "Stay." Insist that it sit by your side and stay there.
- While you hold the dog on the leash, have someone else open the door. The minute the dog begins to attack the visitor, give an immediate Leash Correction and say "NO!" Make the dog stay quietly by your side. Correct it if it growls or is aggressive in any way.
- Perform these actions every time someone comes to the door. You can also help the dog get over its automatic aggressive behavior toward visitors if you pull a trick on it. Have its favorite family member come up to the front door and ring the bell. When the dog goes into its aggressive act, leash it as usual and then tell the family member to come in. The dog's aggression will immediately disappear. Praise it lavishly.
- With some dogs you will only need to keep this up for a week or so until they get the message and stop their aggressions. Others may require more time. Until you're absolutely sure the dog is over this form of aggression, continue to leash it whenever anyone comes to the door.

Problem 2: A dog that guards a particular place in the home is acting in much the same way as a dog that's guarding an object (*see* OBJECT-GUARDING AGGRESSION), except it's guarding a place rather than a thing. The best solution to this kind of aggression is to startle the dog when it acts aggressive and reprimand it sharply.

- As soon as the dog begins to growl and act aggressive when you come into the room, squirt it directly in the face with bitter-tasting liquid (*see box,* LIQUIDS AS AIDS IN BEHAVIOR MODIFICATION, p. 196).
- Alternatively, if you can't get close enough to the dog to squirt it, toss a Throw Chain or Noisemaker near it, or clap your hands loudly and shout to startle the animal and make it Focus on you. When you have its at-

tention, tell it "NO" in very firm tones and approach nearer. Each time you do this, go nearer the dog. Finally, when you're only a foot or so away from the dog's "place," call the dog to you. When it comes, pet it and Praise it.

Problem 3: The problem of a dog that attacks other dogs outside is a bit more difficult to treat because you can't be outdoors with the dog all day. For some suggestions besides those below, *see* INTER-DOG AGGRESSION; INTERMALE AGGRESSION.

- If you are at home you can utilize a Throw Chain or Noisemaker to startle the dog. The minute you hear it barking at another dog preparatory to attacking, rush out and scream "NO!" while you bang on a pot or toss a shake can or Throw Chain at your dog. Once you get it to Focus on you, tell it to stop and then call it to you. Have it sit and stay by you until the other dog goes away. Praise it.
- If you can work with the dog outdoors for a few hours each day, leash it and sit down by its side to wait. As soon as another dog appears and your dog begins to get up, say "NO, Stay." If your dog starts to go after the visiting animal, stop it with a snap of the leash. If it responds to your verbal command, praise it lavishly.
- If you are not home all day or are going to be out for even an hour, the only safe alternatives are to either fence the dog in or keep it indoors. Don't leash it outdoors, because other dogs could come and attack it and it would have no defense.

TERRITORIAL BEHAVIOR

In the wild, each wolf pack and each individual animal within the pack needs a well-defined territory, or area in which to live, hunt, and raise young. To delineate this territory and warn non–pack members off, the animals scent-mark the boundaries. If an intruder doesn't heed the warning and invades a pack's or individual animal's territory, it will be attacked and driven off if possible.

Dogs, too, are territorial by nature, some more so than others. When a dog is encouraged or allowed to become overterritorial, it will eventually become aggressive to protect its territory or even its belongings (*see* TERRITORIAL AGGRESSION; OBJECT-GUARDING AGGRESSION). When an intact (uncastrated) male reaches sexual maturity, he may define his territory by wider and wider boundaries, Scent-Marking the entire area and aggressively attacking all intruders, especially other males.

See box, MALE DOGS' BEHAVIORAL CHARACTERISTICS, p. 198; *box*, PACK BEHAVIOR, p. 230; *box*, SCENT MARKING, p. 256.

TERRITORIAL MARKING *See box*, PACK BEHAVIOR, p. 230; *box*, SCENT MARKING, p. 256; *box*, TERRITORIAL BEHAVIOR, above; URINE MARKING.

THIRST, EXCESSIVE *See* URINARY PROBLEMS: EXCESSIVE URINATION.

THROW CHAIN

A throw chain is simply a straight piece of metal chain links, usually a Training Collar with several knots in it, that you can toss at a dog to startle it, stop it from an undesirable action, and make it Focus on you. It makes a loud clunking noise when it's thrown and serves the same purpose as a Noise-maker, but it works better outdoors because it's easier to throw some distance. Just as with a Noise-maker, once a dog has been conditioned several times outdoors with a Throw Chain, a mere rattle of the chain, indoors or out, will make it stop in its tracks and look at you for instructions.

THUNDERSTORMS, FEAR OF See FEARFULNESS.

TIME—DO DOGS HAVE A SENSE OF IT?

Owners often ask me if their pets have a sense of time. Does a dog know the difference if you leave it for four hours or for eight, for instance? The answer is yes and no.

No, of course a dog can't read a clock and isn't really aware of the specific amount of time that passes, and a pet will usually greet you just as joyfully when you've gone out to the corner for a minute to mail a letter as when you come home from the movies. But yes, in the sense that a dog certainly *is* aware of the fact that after you've been gone all day it begins to get hungry, or bored, or its bladder becomes uncomfortably full. Its biological clock lets it know a long time has passed. However, a dog that's suffering from severe Separation Anxiety will begin to fret the minute you walk out the door—this has nothing to do with sense of time.

Once a dog's an adult animal, an owner needn't feel guilty or upset if he's out an hour longer than he intended to be. But he should be aware of the fact that if he's out several hours longer than usual his pet may become restless and uncomfortable. For instance, if your dog is accustomed to staying quietly alone for up to eight hours you should make arrangements for your pet to be fed and walked if you're going to be out much longer than this.

See also box, INDOOR COMFORT STATION, p. 157; *box,* SCHEDULES FOR PUPPIES AND OLDER DOGS, p. 257.

TIMING—ITS IMPORTANCE
IN ALL ASPECTS OF DOG TRAINING

In order to teach a dog anything at all you have to learn to time your responses to concur exactly with the action you want to praise or correct. You have to catch a dog *in the act* for your praise or correction to mean anything at all. A mistake should bring immediate punishment; a correct action, immediate praise.

If you scold or punish a dog after the fact—for instance, if you shout at a dog when you come home to find it's misbehaved in your absence—it will only confuse the animal and make the training process more difficult. A dog has absolutely no idea what you're reacting to if you wait even one or two beats before you say "Good dog" or "No!" By that time it's already gone on to another activity or is thinking about something else. If you can teach yourself to go a step further and anticipate your pet's actions by reading its body language *(see* HOW TO INTERPRET YOUR DOG'S BODY LANGUAGE, FACIAL EXPRESSIONS, AND VOCALIZATIONS, p. xi), you'll be able to correct it successfully *before* it reacts to a stimulus. This works especially well outdoors, for example when you spot something up ahead like a squirrel waiting to be chased.

Timing is also essential when you're giving a dog Obedience Training. If you tell a dog to do something and it doesn't react within three seconds, correct it immediately. *(See box,* CORRECTING A DOG, p. 76.) Otherwise the dog will get the idea it can obey your commands in its own sweet time instead of when you want it to and will never become properly trained.

See also box, PUNISHMENT, p. 247; STUBBORNNESS.

TODDLERS AND DOGS See CHILDREN AND DOGS.

TOILET-PAPER UNROLLING

Problem: The Fitzes are wondering what to do about their border collie's habit of going into the bathroom, grabbing the end of a roll of toilet tissue, and running all over the house with it. The result is somewhat amusing, but it's also embarrassing to come home with friends and find the house festooned with toilet paper, as if some Halloween pranksters had been at work.

DIAGNOSIS

Toilet-paper unrolling is a habit some high-spirited dogs develop. They obviously find it lots of fun to run around pulling out the paper until it's all over the house. With other dogs this an example of Exploratory Behavior. Curious, they grab hold of the end of a piece of paper and run with it, not realizing it's a long roll. Still other dogs want to capture your attention and make you chase them when they run around dragging paper behind them.

Many dog owners find toilet-paper unrolling harmlessly amusing, but if it becomes excessive the habit should be stopped.

TREATMENT

- Of course, closing the bathroom door will prevent the behavior, but many people don't want to do this.
- To modify a dog's persistent toilet-paper unrolling, set the dog up by treating one sheet of paper with a bitter-tasting liquid (*see box,* LIQUIDS AS AIDS IN BEHAVIOR MODIFICATION, p. 196) and placing it on top of the roll. When the dog grabs the paper it will get a nasty taste in its mouth. This will prevent most dogs from trying to grab the paper again.
- Another form of Setup is to stand by the toilet-paper roll with a blown-up balloon. Call the dog to you, and as it goes to grab the paper, pop the balloon near it to startle it. Just so the dog doesn't think the popping was

a one-time event, place another balloon on top of the roll of paper. Most dogs won't risk a second balloon-popping and will find something else to do.

- With a really determined, strong-willed dog you may have to go one step further. If your toilet-paper-roll holder is recessed, you can wedge a set mousetrap behind the roll of paper so it will snap when the paper is pulled. The noise of the springing trap will frighten most dogs enough so they'll stay away in the future. Be very careful to place the trap securely behind the roll so the dog's nose can't be hurt, and remember to warn family members about the Setup.

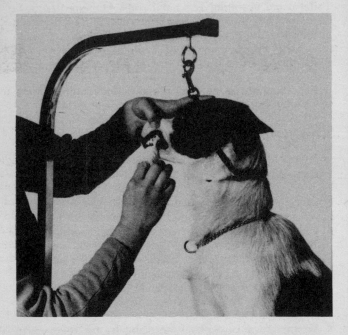

As an introduction to Tooth-Cleaning, Sally is having her gums rubbed with a moistened gauze square wrapped around a finger. (Bruce Plotkin)

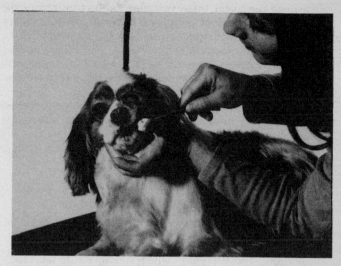

Harry, a cavalier King Charles spaniel, doesn't mind having his teeth brushed. (Bruce Plotkin)

TOOTH CARE PROBLEMS

Problem: Kenneth read it was important to brush a dog's teeth. This made sense to him, so he bought a child-size toothbrush and some toothpaste made for youngsters. Putting his pug, Poochie, up on the kitchen counter, he proceeded to try to brush her teeth. Poochie was calm until the toothbrush actually went inside her mouth. Then she reacted with horror, spit, foamed at the mouth, and almost killed herself trying to get away and down from the counter.

DIAGNOSIS

In recent years veterinarians have urged pet owners to take better care of their dogs' teeth. Veterinary science has lengthened the life expectancy of most animals, with the result that many dogs now live to a ripe old age. But often lack of tooth and gum care means these older animals spend their later years suffering from mouth pain or subjected to numerous tooth extractions. Small-breed dogs and those with pushed-in faces (brachycephalic breeds) are often especially long-lived, and at the same time are more prone to mouth and tooth problems. A sore mouth or an inability to eat comfortably will make a dog lose its appetite and become cranky.

What's more, a dog's tooth and gum problems inevitably lead to bad breath, a condition bound to diminish owner-pet interaction!

TREATMENT

- Before you attempt to brush your dog's teeth, consult with your veterinarian, who will show you how to proceed.
- To accustom your dog to having its mouth worked on, always open your pet's mouth, put your fingers inside, and gently rub the gums when you brush or massage your dog.
- Begin to get a dog used to toothbrushing by using a moistened terry-cloth washcloth or gauze square to rub its gums and teeth. When your dog is used to this, dab the moistened cloth with a bit of baking soda.
- A child's toothbrush, or one designed especially for dogs, comes next. Bristles work better than cloth, but if your dog balks at the sight of a brush, continue using terry cloth or gauze.
- Never use toothpaste designed for adults or children for dogs. It tastes too strong, foams too much, and will cause a dog to revolt. Use a toothpaste designed for dogs, available in pet-supply stores, or mix your own from one part salt and two parts baking soda.
- If you notice anything unusual in your dog's mouth— red or swollen gums, loose teeth, etc.—seek veterinary help. The better-cared-for your pet's teeth are when it's young, the better it will feel when it's an older animal.

TOOTH-SHOWING See SMILING BEHAVIOR.

TOUCH—THE TACTILE SENSE IN DOGS

Along with their other senses, dogs have a highly developed tactile sense, inherited from their ancestors the wolves. In close, socially oriented pack living, a touch serves many purposes for a wolf. It can be reassuring or threatening, sexual or playful, and can impart praise or reprobation. Wolves are able to feel vibrations in the ground that may signal the arrival of a herd of elk or moose, for instance, and their sensitive foot pads are able to detect the body heat given off by a small buried animal.

All puppies and dogs need a lot of touch contact with other living creatures. If a dog is deprived of this it will become withdrawn and antisocial, just as a person will. Regular everyday touch contact is important for your pet's well-being. A gentle pat or touch can give your dog more reassurance than a dozen kind words.

Dogs have inherited wolves' tactile sensitivity and are often able to "predict" natural disasters such as earthquakes, avalanches, volcanic eruptions, and floods by feeling earth vibrations long before people can. Some dogs have very excellent heat sensitivity in their feet. Search-and-Rescue dogs, for example, use this thermal sense to help locate buried disaster victims.

See also box, ESP—DO DOGS HAVE IT?, p. 111; *box,* MASSAGE FOR DOGS, p. 200; *box,* PATTING A DOG, p. 235.

TOUCHING A DOG See *box,* MASSAGE FOR DOGS, p. 200; *box,* PATTING A DOG, p. 235.

TOYS FOR DOGS *(See also box,* BONES FOR DOGS, p. 45; *box,* CHEW TOYS FOR DOGS, p. 61; *box,* GAMES TO PLAY WITH DOGS, p. 134.)

Problem: Whenever seven-year-old Katie talks her mother into buying her a toy, the child insists they then go to a pet store and get a toy for Renee, her Brussels griffon. Renee loves to get new toys, but after a while the dog tires of each thing and abandons it. The apartment is littered with dog toys, and Katie's father is getting tired of tripping over them. He finally says, "Enough! No more dog toys. Dogs don't need toys anyway."

DIAGNOSIS

In addition to appropriate Chew Toys and/ or Bones, many adult dogs as well as puppies do enjoy playing with toys. Some dogs only like balls, Frisbees, or other things to fetch; others like squeaky toys and squashy toys. Dogs often invent games of their own to play with toys. A favorite toy not only provides a dog with entertainment when it's alone, but may also prompt an owner to play and interact with it.

TREATMENT

- There are lots of inappropriate pet toys on the market, so shop wisely for safety's sake. If you want to buy your dog a toy, be sure the toy is strong enough not to be easily torn apart and has no small parts the animal might be able to remove and swallow. Get a toy intended for dogs, not one for cats or birds.
- Use your common sense. Don't buy a tiny toy for a big dog or a huge toy for a little one. Try to think like your dog and get a toy the *dog* will enjoy, not something that appeals to you.
- Unless you want to teach your dog to play with and chew your socks and shoes, don't give it an old sock, shoe, or slipper for a toy. There's no way it will be able to differentiate its "toy" from your best Ferragamos or

Guccis! *(See* CHEWING PROBLEMS: CHEWING OBJECTS/ CLOTHING.)

- Any puppy or dog will become confused when there are too many toys lying around, just as a child will. It won't know what to play with and consequently won't play with anything. To avoid this, create a toy box for your dog. Put an open-topped carton or basket in a corner with all of your dog's toys in it. Then, when you want to play, tell your pet, "Go get a toy." Show it what to do several times, and soon your dog will learn to fetch a toy when it wants to play with you. Some dogs can even be taught to put their toys away when they're finished with them!

TRAINING COLLARS

Training collars are straight with a large ring at each end. The most common kinds are plain metal links, but they also come in nylon or leather. Special fursaver training collars prevent a long-haired or soft-coated dog's neck hair from rubbing off or catching in the links; they have vinyl casing over the metal links, or are made of smooth, flat metal links. All types come in various lengths and weights to suit different-sized dogs. A training collar is used with a leash when a dog is obedience-trained.

Training collars are often called "choke" collars, and are thought of as cruel and inhumane by some people. In my opinion, this couldn't be further from the truth. In the first place, when used correctly a training collar will never choke a dog. What's more, it's a great deal more inhumane to neglect to train a dog properly and *then* need to use a training collar or other, harsher, method such as a spike collar or muzzle to restrain and control the animal.

To put a training collar on a dog, slip the entire length of collar through either one of the end rings to form a loop. Hold the loop with the long end hanging down on the left, so the collar forms a P. With the dog in front of you, facing you, slip the loop over its head. The long end, or running end, will be on the dog's right side. Snap the leash on the ring at this end. Be careful *not* to attach the leash to the ring through which you slipped the collar.

When put on correctly, a training collar enables you to perform a quick, sharp Leash Correction to make the dog stop what it's doing and focus on you. It then allows you to immediately release the pressure.

See also box, HARNESSES FOR DOGS, p. 146; *box*, OBEDIENCE TRAINING, p. 218.

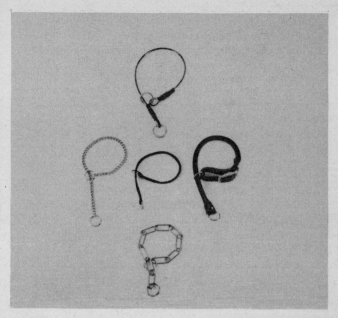

Five types of Training Collar. From the top, clockwise: a fur-saver of vinyl-coated metal links; a leather collar; a fur-saver of smooth flat links; a traditional metal link collar; in center: a lightweight nylon collar. All of the collars are in the correct "P" formation, ready to slip onto a dog's neck. (Bruce Plotkin)

Wrinkles demonstrates the correct position of a Training Collar.
Note the ring to which the leash is attached. (Bruce Plotkin)

TRANQUILIZERS See *box*, DRUGS AND DOG TRAINING,
p. 104.

TRAVEL See AIRPLANE TRAVEL; CAR PROBLEMS: CAR TRAVEL;
VISITING WITH A DOG.

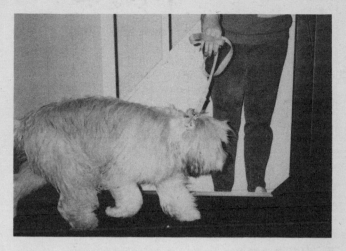

Spanky, a wheaten terrier, using a Treadmill. Notice his owner is standing by holding his leash for safety while he works out. (Bashkim Dibra)

TREADMILL EXERCISE

If it's difficult for you to give your high-energy dog enough regular outdoor Exercise, a treadmill can be a wonderful help.

To teach a dog to walk on a treadmill, put it on the machine. Stand next to the dog on its right so the animal is in the traditional Heeling position. (If you have not taught your dog to heel in Obedience Training, it should be on your left, feet in line with yours.) Start the treadmill on slow and, holding the leash in your right hand, slap your left thigh to encourage the dog to walk. As soon as the dog is walking nicely at your side, increase the treadmill's speed gradually. Soon the dog will have to trot to keep even with you. Most dogs get into the rhythm right away and thoroughly enjoy their brisk "walks."

Slow the machine gradually when it's time to stop and have the dog stay in place until the tread is completely stationary. For safety's sake, always hold the leash while a dog is on a moving treadmill and never leave a dog alone.

See also EXERCISE, DOGS' NEED FOR.

TREATS *See box,* FOOD REWARDS AS TRAINING TOOLS, p. 132; TABLE SCRAPS, FEEDING.

TUG-OF-WAR *(See also box,* AGGRESSIVE BEHAVIOR IN DOGS, p. 7; *box,* DOMINANT BEHAVIOR, p. 98; PLAY PROBLEMS: TOO-ROUGH PLAY.)

Problem: When Max was growing up, his family had a boxer. Max's father always played tug-of-war with the dog, saying it was necessary for the animal's muscular development and would "toughen him up." The dog always seemed to enjoy the game immensely, but as he matured he became quite aggressive and the family eventually had to get rid of him. Now Max has a boxer puppy of his own and wonders whether it's a good idea to play tug-of-war with her or not.

DIAGNOSIS

Tug-of-war is a behavior cubs and puppies engage in with each other. Each animal grabs one end of a stick or toy and pulls and pulls, trying to get it away from the other. It's usually accompanied by growling. This type of play is practice for serious adult battles. It's actually a war game that brings out aggression in any puppy or dog.

When a person plays tug-of-war with a puppy or dog, he too is playing a war game, competing with his pet for an object. Tug-of-war forces a puppy to become a rough competitive player, whether it wants to or not. If the puppy is a naturally aggressive breed, tug-of-war encourages it and gives it an excuse to be aggressive with you. This behavior often escalates until a dog becomes aggressive with all humans.

TREATMENT

- The single most important rule about tug-of-war is this: If there are children in your world, your own children or neighbors' youngsters who might wander into your yard, don't teach your dog to play tug-of-war, no matter what it's basic temperament is. A dog that's learned to play this game may easily decide to grab and tug on a child's clothing or a toy and become aggressive when the child resists and tries to pull away.
- If no children live anywhere nearby and you're intent on playing tug-of-war with your pet, use your judgment. Don't allow your dog to become too intent or aggressive. If it begins to growl seriously, put its ears back, or raise its hackles, tell it "No" and stop the play immediately. You must retain your leadership role at all times, especially if your dog is at all aggressive, or the game will soon convince it it can bully you.
- Be careful your dog doesn't decide everything you pick up is a potential tugging object—otherwise you'll end up with lots of torn clothes and towels. If a dog that regularly plays tug-of-war tries to grab something out of your hand, don't pull away and turn its actions into a competitive game. Drop the object, scold the dog, and immediately take the object away. Don't allow a dog that grabs your belongings to have the pleasure of keeping them or you'll never train it to stop grabbing things.

U

UNFRIENDLINESS See ALOOFNESS.

UNRULINESS See ABNORMAL ACTIVITY LEVELS: HYPER-ACTIVITY; BALL-PLAYING FETISH; BARKING PROBLEMS: EXCESSIVE BARKING; PLAY PROBLEMS.

URINARY INCONTINENCE See URINE LEAKING/DRIBBLING.

URINARY PROBLEMS

EXCESSIVE URINATION

Problem: Bill can't believe the size of the puddles his dalmatian is suddenly producing. It seems she squats for minutes several times when they go out and interrupts his sleep to be let out a couple of times during the night. She also seems to need to drink water all of the time, emptying her bowl time and again.

DIAGNOSIS
Although excessive urination is a physical, not behavioral, problem, it can result in annoying behavior, such as a dog's having accidents in the house and needing to go out all the time.

When a dog produces excessively large amounts of urine it's almost always accompanied by increased thirst and water-drinking. It can also be due to the failure of a dog's body to conserve water.

Kidney failure, infections, and systemic diseases such as diabetes and hyperthyroidism are among the conditions that can cause excessive urination in a dog.

TREATMENT

- A dog that is urinating excessively should be seen immediately by a veterinarian for diagnosis and treatment.
- Do not withhold or ration water when a dog exhibits excessive urination.
- If a dog that is urinating excessively has difficulty holding its urine and makes mistakes in the house, don't scold or punish it. A formerly well-trained dog will be upset enough when it's forced to make a mistake.
- While your dog is being medically treated for excessive urination, it will ease both your problems if you can provide it with an Indoor Comfort Station or a dog door so it has easy access to the outdoors.

EXCITEMENT URINATION See URINE LEAKING/DRIBBLING.

FREQUENT URINATION *(See also box,* SCENT MARKING, p. 256; *box,* TERRITORIAL BEHAVIOR, p. 289; URINE MARKING.)

Problem: The Fredericks' nine-year-old otter hound, Cedric, seems to need to urinate all the time. When they take him for a walk he raises his leg on every single upright object, dribbles a little bit of urine, and then comes home and asks to go out in the yard, where he urinates again and again. This goes on continuously all day and throughout the night. He never seems to finish!

DIAGNOSIS

When a dog asks to go out constantly and then produces only a tiny amount of urine each time, it may be considered a bid for attention by its annoyed owner. If the dog is a male, the owner may also think the frequent urination is excessive territorial Urine Marking behavior. But careful observation may determine that it differs. A dog suffering from a medical condition resulting in frequent urination will produce only a tiny amount of urine each time, and its urine may contain some blood.

This type of frequent urination is caused by a bladder infection, or an obstruction of the urinary tract caused by stones or a tumor. Both male and female dogs can suffer from these conditions.

TREATMENT

- A dog that's urinating more frequently than usual should be seen by a veterinarian immediately. If the problem is due to an infection it can usually be quickly cleared up with medication; other problems can take longer.
- Never withhold or ration water if a dog is urinating frequently until you determine the cause of the problem.
- If a dog has mistakes in the house because of its need to urinate unusually often, don't scold the dog.
- As suggested in the discussion of Excessive Urination, page 306, a dog that feels the need to urinate frequently will feel less stressed if you can provide it with an Indoor Comfort Station or easy access to the outdoors until it gets better.

URINE LEAKING/DRIBBLING

LEAKING/DRIBBLING IN A YOUNG DOG (See also box, SUBMISSIVE BEHAVIOR, p. 276.)

Problem: Angela can't understand what's wrong with her nine-month-old golden retriever, Jimmy. He's been completely house-trained for several months and stays alone all day without an accident of any sort. But every night when her husband, Mark, comes home from work, walks in the door, and shouts "Hello!" Jimmy runs excitedly to greet him, wagging furiously, rolls over onto his back as if to be petted, and then dribbles a pool of urine onto the floor.

DIAGNOSIS

Urine dribbling, or leaking, is commonly seen in wolf interaction. When a wolf that is not dominant in the pack is approached by a more dominant animal it doesn't want to challenge, it will always display Submissive Behavior. Rolling over on its back, it may lick the dominant wolf's face and dribble some urine to emphasize its helplessness.

Sometimes a young dog that is completely house-trained at all other times displays this same type of behavior with an owner, whom it perceives as dominant over it, when the owner arrives home and approaches it. This is sometimes erroneously referred to as "excitement" urination because it occurs during excited greetings. Most young dogs outgrow this behavior as they mature.

TREATMENT

- Urine-dribbling or leaking of this sort is something a dog cannot control. It should never be treated as "bad" behavior. Punishment of submissive urination will serve only to make the dog more anxious and submissive and will exacerbate the problem.
- To help a dog overcome this problem, downplay your homecoming. Don't greet the dog excitedly or even pat it until it's had an opportunity to go outside and relieve itself. Save your greetings until it comes back inside.
- If you don't have a yard the dog can immediately go out in, put a leash right by the door. As you come in, make a loose loop out of the leash, put it around the dog's neck, and walk the dog around the apartment for a moment to calm it down. Then you can take the dog for a walk after you've caught your breath.

LEAKING IN AN OLDER DOG (See also OLDER DOG PROBLEMS.)

Problem: One day when Rosalie was sitting watching TV with her ten-year-old Yorkie, Tina, on her lap, she was startled to feel a warm wetness on her leg. When she looked she realized that Tina, still sound asleep, had leaked urine all over her. Now Rosalie's worried that Tina's really sick and she's afraid of what she'll find out when she takes her beloved pet to the veterinarian.

DIAGNOSIS

Older dogs often develop various urinary disorders. Urinary incontinence can occur when a dog's bladder is unable to retain a normal amount of urine and some leaks out.

A hormone imbalance may cause older spayed female dogs to leak urine when they're sound asleep and relaxed. Large dogs sometimes suffer from urinary incontinence when their hind limbs begin to weaken and they lose muscle tone.

Incontinence in younger dogs may be due to a congenital defect of the urinary tract or spinal disease. In cases such as these, urine leaking most often occurs when a dog barks or coughs.

TREATMENT

- A dog that leaks urine because of a physical problem has no control over its actions and should never be punished or scolded.
- Never withhold water from a dog with a urinary disorder. This will cause dehydration and may exacerbate other diseases or disorders.
- A hormone imbalance can be treated with hormone-replacement medication, and often one course of medicine clears the problem up indefinitely.
- When urinary incontinence is due to other physical causes, your veterinarian will be able to advise you how to proceed.

URINE MARKING *(See also box,* MALE DOGS' BEHAVIORAL CHARACTERISTICS, *p.* 198; *box,* SCENT MARKING, *p.* 256; *box,* TERRITORIAL BEHAVIOR, *p.* 289.*)*

Problem: After her divorce, Liz rented a small, nicely furnished apartment until she could decide where she wanted to live. She moved in with her wirehaired terrier, Alex, who seemed to accept the new living arrangements calmly. Several weeks later, Liz happened to move a chair in the living room and noticed a small stain on the carpet. Looking around carefully, she discovered similar stains next to the legs of all the furniture in the apartment and the horrid truth dawned on her. Alex had raised his leg and urinated a small amount on all the furniture in the apartment! She set to work cleaning up as well as she could, and wondered what to do to prevent Alex from "rechristening" everything as soon as she went out again.

DIAGNOSIS

Urine marking is an important aspect of Territorial Behavior, indulged in by both wolves and dogs. An intact (uncastrated) male dog will urine-mark his territory instinctively. A well-trained dog may not feel the need to mark indoors in familiar surroundings, but as soon as he's moved to new living quarters, his need to delineate his turf will naturally surface again. Highly territorial female dogs may also urine-mark.

A dog of either sex may urine-mark if it feels its territory threatened in some way. The arrival into the home of a new pet, a baby, or even an adult may initiate this behavior.

TREATMENT

- If the dog is a male, the first step to take is to have him castrated, no matter what his age. The male hormone testosterone is partially responsible for Territorial Behavior. It will take a while for all of the testosterone to leave a dog's body, but once it does, urine-marking behavior should lessen. *(See box,* CASTRATION OF MALE DOGS—FACTS & MYTHS, p. 57.)

- In the meantime, to reprogram a dog to appropriate urinating behavior, prevent it from further marking. Confine it when you're not at home. A Crate is ideal, especially if the dog is accustomed to one. Alternatively, you can use a Gate to close the dog in a room with no furnishings, such as a kitchen or bathroom. Keep the dog by your side, on leash, when you're at home so it won't be able to wander into another room and mark.
- *With your veterinarian's approval,* you can ration your dog's water-drinking. Give the dog a drink about half an hour before it's time to walk it, several times a day.
- Even if your dog has outgrown the need for a strict Schedule, now is the time to return to one until the urine-marking problem is resolved. It's especially important to schedule regular walks to make sure the dog has ample opportunity to urinate outdoors. When it does, Praise it.
- The smell of urine, even its own, may stimulate a dog's urge to urinate. Thoroughly clean and deodorize any previously marked areas.

V

VACATION, TAKING A DOG ON *See* AIRPLANE TRAVEL; CAR PROBLEMS: CAR TRAVEL; EXPLORATORY BEHAVIOR; VISITING WITH A DOG.

VERBAL COMMANDS/CORRECTIONS *See box,* TALKING TO YOUR DOG, p. 282.

VETERINARIAN *See box,* VISITS TO THE VETERINARIAN, p. 317.

VICIOUSNESS *See* IDIOPATHIC AGGRESSION; LEARNED AGGRESSION; *box,* RAGE SYNDROME, p. 252.

VISION IN DOGS

In general, a dog's sense of vision is thought to be less well developed than other senses. But a dog's vision suits its needs well.

For example, although a dog can't see as well in bright daylight as a person can and has poor color vision, its retinas contain more light receptors than ours do, so it can see very well in low light. A dog's eyes also have a region around the retina called the tapetum. The tapetum reflects light back into the retina and further enhances a dog's night vision.

Along with all other animals except man, dogs have what's known as a third eyelid (nictitating membrane), which cleans and lubricates the eye surfaces and protects them from accidental injury in rough terrain such as underbrush.

Dogs' large eye pupils provide them with a wide visual field. This excellent peripheral vision is what enables them to react quickly to movement and triggers their instinctive Chase and Flight Behaviors. It also makes a dog highly responsive to its owner's hand motions and body language. This means you can effectively communicate with your dog by utilizing its keen peripheral vision.

VISITING WITH A DOG (See also CAR PROBLEMS: CAR TRAVEL; EXPLORATORY BEHAVIOR.)

Problem: Phil is going to visit his sister for a week and wants to take his Shih Tzu, Missy, with him to avoid the trouble and expense of boarding the dog. His sister says she doesn't mind, but she's never had a dog and Phil wonders if taking Missy with him will cause problems.

DIAGNOSIS

Many dog owners take their pets with them when they visit family and friends. It can work out well or badly depending on both dog and owner.

When a dog goes with its owner to visit in someone else's home, it's quite different from a stay in a hotel or motel. Not only are the rules of the house likely to be quite different from those at home, but the presence of unknown people and even other pets is apt to put a dog on edge. A dog in a new place will always want to explore the entire area, both inside and out, which may cause a problem, too. To add to the dog's anxiety, its owner may be nervous and anxious too, possibly overconcerned about his pet's behavior.

TREATMENT

- Before you take your dog with you to stay in someone else's home, be absolutely certain it will really be all right with your host or hostess. If you detect any hesitancy, reconsider and try to make other arrangements for your pet. People who have never had a dog, or who don't know dogs well, may have very different ideas from yours about how a pet should behave. Your life, and your dog's, will be made miserable by an overfussy worrier.

- If there are resident pets your dog hasn't met in the household, find out ahead of time if they normally have the run of the house. If they do, it's probably better to leave your dog at home; otherwise it may have to be closed up for the entire visit. It's unusual for a resident pet, no matter how good-natured, to welcome an unknown dog with equanimity.

- Bring everything your dog will need to feel secure. In addition to obvious things such as food and a favorite toy, bring food and water bowls, a Crate, bed, or blanket for the dog to sleep on, and several new Chew Toys or other toys to give the dog during your stay.

- Unless your dog is very well obedience-trained, keep it by your side on a leash all the time it's indoors. This will avoid all types of accidents and will allow you, your hostess, and your dog to relax.

■ Don't allow your dog to do anything that might be against house rules. Even if you always let it sit next to you on the couch, ask permission before you allow it to get up on your hostess's furniture.

■ If your dog's been trained to use an Indoor Comfort Station, this will come in very handy in new surroundings.

■ Never go out and leave your dog alone in a strange house. It may never have suffered from Separation Anxiety before, but chances are it will if you "abandon" it in someone else's house. If you must leave it alone, close it in a Crate, or in a small room where there's nothing it can destroy in its anxiety. Leave something of yours with it to reassure it you'll be back.

VISITORS, BEHAVIOR WITH See FACE-RUBBING; HERDING BEHAVIOR PROBLEMS; JEALOUSY: JEALOUSY OF AN ADULT PERSON; JUMPING PROBLEMS: JUMPING ON PEOPLE IN THE HOME IN GREETING; ONE-MAN DOGS; SNIFFING PEOPLE AND OTHER DOGS IN GREETING; TERRITORIAL AGGRESSION.

VISITS TO THE VETERINARIAN

It can be both annoying and embarrassing if your dog acts wild, fearful, or aggressive when you take it to the veterinarian's office. More than this, a badly behaved dog may require severe restraint or even anesthetic to have routine procedures performed. These options can be costly, are possibly dangerous to the dog, and are guaranteed to make the animal more difficult to treat the next time.

Your very first trip to a veterinarian with your puppy can influence your pet's subsequent feeling about all doctors. Even if you're a bit nervous and apprehensive, try not to convey this to your puppy. Don't overreact or baby your puppy if it cries or becomes upset when it's being routinely examined or getting a shot. Stay cheerful and matter-of-fact and your puppy will get the message there's nothing to be afraid of.

As your puppy grows up, accustom it to handling with regular massage, brushing, and other grooming procedures. A puppy that's frequently touched all over won't be concerned when a veterinarian examines it or has to treat any part of its body.

At the same time, a puppy that's well socialized will trust people and enjoy interacting with them and won't ever be aggressive with strangers out of fear (*see* FEAR-INDUCED AGGRESSION). If you live near the veterinarian's office, pop in with the puppy from time to time between appointments, just to say hello. The puppy can have a treat or a pat and get to know and trust the people who work there. This is especially helpful for a naturally nervous puppy.

Finally, a dog that's been obedience-trained will learn to stand quietly on command and allow itself to be examined.

See box, OBEDIENCE TRAINING, p. 218; *box,* SOCIALIZATION, THE KEY TO A WELL-ADJUSTED DOG, p. 271.

VOCALIZING BEHAVIOR

In the wild, individual wolves often vocalize to communicate with other pack members. Their excellent hearing enables them to judge distance and direction so each animal can learn where every other pack member is.

Dogs also indulge in vocalizing behavior, especially when they feel lonely or abandoned. A dog that is left alone may howl or bark to call its owners, or pack. When vocalizing becomes excessive it can be a serious behavior problem.

Many dogs learn to use whining noises to get their owners to pay attention to them. This form of vocalization can also turn into an annoying unwanted behavior, one that owners may want to control.

See also BARKING PROBLEMS: EXCESSIVE BARKING; HOW TO INTERPRET YOUR DOG'S BODY LANGUAGE, FACIAL EXPRESSIONS, AND VOCALIZATIONS, p. xi; HOWLING; WHINING; YAPPING/YIPPING BEHAVIOR.

VOMITING *(See also* CAR PROBLEMS: CAR SICKNESS; DRINKING PROBLEMS.)

Problem: Bruce doesn't know what to do about his pug's bothersome habit of getting herself so excited she throws up. Every time she goes out for a walk and sees another dog, she pulls on the leash so hard she vomits up foam. Even in the house when they play ball, she begins to huff and huff and then spits up on the rug.

DIAGNOSIS

Dogs seem to be able to vomit at will if they eat something indigestible or drink water too fast. Many dogs regularly spit up, producing only a small foamy bit of matter. This is often because of overexcitement or nervousness in a strange situation. Dogs with short, pushed-in noses frequently suffer from this problem.

Vomiting a large volume of food, however, is always a sign a dog is sick, whether from a systemic or infectious disease, intestinal parasites, or eating rotten food or something poisonous.

TREATMENT

- If a dog vomits a lot of matter and the vomiting persists or is accompanied by other signs of illness such as loss of appetite, drooling, Diarrhea, or obvious discomfort, it's important to see a veterinarian for treatment.
- Try to prevent your dog from eating bits of plants, a lot of grass, or whatever else makes it spit up.
- When a dog continuously spits up small amounts of foam, try to determine the cause of its overexcitement.
- Don't allow a dog to reach the point of hysteria when you're playing a game with it. As soon as the dog shows signs of overexcitement, stop the game and put the toy away. Have the dog sit quietly near you and pat it to calm it down.
- If a dog becomes frenzied at the sight of other dogs when you're walking outdoors, do the same thing. As soon as you see an approaching dog, have your dog sit next to you and pat and talk to it reassuringly until the other dog passes. Many dogs outgrow the tendency to become overexcited at the sight of other dogs.

VOICE, USING YOUR See box, TALKING TO YOUR DOG, p. 282.

W

WALKING ON A LEASH See LEASH PROBLEMS; PULLING ON A LEASH.

WATCHDOGS See BARKING PROBLEMS: TEACHING A DOG TO BARK ON SIGNAL; LEARNED AGGRESSION.

WATER BALLOONS AS TRAINING TOOLS

A water-filled balloon tossed at a dog works in much the same way a Noisemaker or Throw Chain does to capture a dog's attention.

There are two ways to use a water balloon. When the balloon is tossed on the ground near the dog, the impact will break it and splash water on the dog, startling it so it stops what it's doing and looks to you for further instructions. For more serious infractions, when you want to stop a dog in its tracks, toss a water-filled balloon directly at the dog's body or face so it thoroughly shocks the animal and drenches it with water on contact.

The nice thing about a water-filled balloon is that it's soft, so there's no danger of hurting a dog if you make a direct hit when you toss the balloon from a moving car or bicycle, or from a distance outdoors.

See CHASING PROBLEMS.

WATER DRINKING See DRINKING PROBLEMS.

WETTING: See CRATE PROBLEMS: CRATE SOILING; HOUSE-TRAINING PROBLEMS; URINATION PROBLEMS; URINE LEAKING/DRIBBLING; URINE MARKING.

WHINING (See also AFFECTION, EXCESSIVE/DEMANDING; BARKING PROBLEMS: EXCESSIVE BARKING; HOWLING; box, VOCALIZING BEHAVIOR, p. 318; YAPPING/YIPPING BEHAVIOR.)

Problem: Her little terrier is driving Sharon up a wall with his constant whining for attention. Every time she sits down to read or watch TV, her dog comes and sits in front of her and whines. He whines and whines until she either lets him out, picks him up, or tosses him a biscuit. Then once she settles down again, he starts in with his grating, high-pitched whining. It's enough to make her scream in frustration!

DIAGNOSIS

Although wolf cubs whine and squeak to communicate, adult wolves almost never whine unless they're hurt or become very excited. They never whine to get attention from other adult animals.

It's natural for a young puppy to whine, or cry, when it's left alone for the first time (*see* SEPARATION ANXIETY). But many puppies learn that whining will quickly capture their owners' attention and bring them back. When owners continuously overreact to a puppy's whines and lavish attention on it, the animal never outgrows its whining behavior. It's found out that whining is a surefire way to get what it wants.

Some adult dogs naturally whine when they're excited or anxious, but continual whining on the part of any dog is a form of spoiled behavior.

TREATMENT

- When a lonely puppy whines, you must be careful not to reinforce its behavior. If you immediately rush back into the room as soon as a puppy whines, you'll convey the message that whining will produce company. Even a scolding is more welcome to a lonely puppy than being left alone. As long as you're sure everything's all right, ignore a puppy's whining and it will usually diminish in a day or two.
- If an adult dog whines for attention, its behavior must be modified so it learns that whining will result in an unpleasant reaction from you.
- The minute a dog begins to whine, say "No!" To reinforce your command, clap your hands sharply or throw a Noisemaker on the floor in front of the dog.
- Never reward a dog for whining. Although it may be easier to cave in and stop the whining by giving the dog attention, remember that is what created the problem in the first place. When the dog remains quiet, then give it a biscuit, a pat, or other reward. *(See box,* FOOD REWARDS AS TRAINING TOOLS, p. 132; *box,* PRAISE TO MODIFY A DOG'S BEHAVIOR, p. 244.)
- If a dog whines in a strange situation—when it's riding in a carrying case on a plane, for instance—reassurance in the form of a word or pat will usually make it less anxious. When a dog whines out of excitement if it sees another dog from the window, for instance, there's no need to do anything. The whining will stop when the cause for excitement is out of sight.

WORK, TAKING A DOG WITH YOU *(See also box,* SOCIALIZATION, THE KEY TO A WELL-ADJUSTED DOG, p. 271.)

Problem: Anna has to drive on back roads to get to her job in town, and it's often dark when she leaves work and has to walk some distance to her car. When she told her husband her lonely commute was making her increasingly nervous, he suggested she take their shepherd mix, Olga, to work with her. Anna's delighted at the idea but wonders how her boss and coworkers will react to Olga's presence in the office.

DIAGNOSIS

For many years, well-trained Seeing Eye dogs have been accepted into the workplace, and now hearing dogs and other dogs in helping capacities are found at work with their owners.

Now more and more ordinary people are taking dogs to work with them. There are several reasons for this. All family members may work long or irregular hours that make it difficult to leave a dog home; or there may be an ongoing behavior problem that occurs when a dog is left alone at home, such as excessive barking *(see* BARKING PROBLEMS: EXCESSIVE BARKING, PROBLEM 2); or, last but not least, an owner may need personal security either at work or en route to and from the job.

In many work situations, a well-socialized, well-behaved dog not only is acceptable but may even be welcomed. Of course, you'll have to determine ahead of time how your boss and coworkers feel about this.

TREATMENT

To ensure your dog is acceptable in the workplace, take these steps.

- Most important, be sure your dog is well trained. If it hasn't had Obedience Training, you should train it yourself to meet these minimum standards of acceptable behavior:

Basic House-Training
No Barking at people or noises during work hours
No Jumping on people or grabbing their things
No Chasing after people
No Chewing anything other than appropriate toys
Understands Go to Your Place
Understands Down/Stay

- Exercise the dog well immediately before you go inside.
- Be sure the dog is clean and well-groomed. Clip its nails so they're not long or rough. Brush and comb it every morning before work. (*See* BRUSHING PROBLEMS; NAIL-CLIPPING PROBLEMS/TECHNIQUES.)
- Stress can cause a dog to shed excessively, so bring a brush or comb and some fabric softener mixed with water in a plastic spray bottle to calm flying fur.
- Have the following additional supplies on hand in the workplace: a bowl for water; a roll of paper towels for spills or accidents; plastic bags for the same purpose; some type of deodorizer in case of an accident; toys and/or Chew Toys; a blanket or bed if your dog ordinarily uses them. If your dog is used to a cage or Crate, bring it along, or purchase a second one to leave at work.
- You may want to give your dog a biscuit or other treat during the day, but avoid feeding it a whole meal—it's too messy. Save dinner until you get home. Do have fresh water available all the time.
- Keep the dog on a short leash, by your side, unless everyone in the workplace agrees it can be loose.
- Walk the dog whenever you have a break. At first, do this more often than you usually do. Nerves and excitement because of strange surroundings and people may make your dog need to urinate frequently.
- From time to time, reassure the dog and tell it how good it is when it behaves quietly throughout the day.
- If your dog seems unduly stressed, you may need to rethink your arrangements.

Y

YAPPING/YIPPING BEHAVIOR (See *also* BARKING PROBLEMS: EXCESSIVE BARKING; *box,* VOCALIZING BEHAVIOR, p. 318.)

Problem: Family and friends alike are sick to death of Dolores's Pomeranian because of his constant yapping. It seems he's never quiet except when he's asleep, and even then the slightest noise causes him to jump up yapping and yipping. It's getting so nobody wants Dolores and her dog around.

DIAGNOSIS

Yapping and yipping are forms of Vocalizing Behavior. Young wolf cubs often emit short barks or high-pitched yaps when they're trying to get attention from adult wolves. It's part of their language.

All dogs may yap occasionally, but toy dogs in particular yap a lot to get attention and because they're apt to be nervous and high-strung. Sometimes it seems they think they have to be especially noisy and aggressive because of their small size. When a small dog yaps and yips, its naturally high voice becomes shrill and is especially grating and irritating to human ears.

Indulgent owners often think this kind of vocalizing is part of a small dog's nature and allow their pets to get into the habit of continual yapping.

TREATMENT

- Just like excessive barking, yapping behavior is a sign of a spoiled, willful dog that's running its owner, and should be treated the same way. *See* BARKING PROBLEMS: EXCESSIVE BARKING.
- In addition, squeeze a dog's muzzle closed with your hand the minute it starts to yap, just as you would with a Nipping puppy. This is the same treatment a too-yappy wolf cub would get from its mother, only she'd use her mouth to hold its mouth closed.
- The instant your dog starts to yap when you're outdoors, give an immediate Leash Correction and say "No."
- If your small dog continues to yap after you've corrected it, try this. Pick the dog up and turn it upside down in your arms in a Submissive position. Stroke underneath its chin so the dog is forced to look at you and focus on your face. At this point all of the distractions that prompted the dog's yapping will fade into the background and the dog will stop its noise. Do this every time the dog begins to yap, especially outdoors, and it will soon get out of the habit of yapping continually.
- Try to keep your own voice low-pitched and firm when you correct your dog. If you "yap" at your pet in a high, excited voice, the dog may join in with you. Don't allow your dog to do this or to talk back to you under any circumstances.

YELLING AT A DOG (See also box, TALKING TO YOUR DOG, p. 282.)

Problem: Moe has a beagle that won't obey him. Whenever the dog is out in the yard and Moe wants it to come in, he stands on the back steps and yells "GET OVER HERE! GET OVER HERE!" again and again as he points at the ground with his finger. The dog pays no attention, but continues to look out at the street through the fence. The same thing happens in the house when Moe's sitting in the living room watching TV and the dog is out in the hall. "GET OVER HERE! GET OVER HERE!" Moe yells, pointing at the floor by the chair to no avail. The dog just lies where it is, calmly chewing on a bone. Moe wonders what's the matter with the dog.

DIAGNOSIS

Owners who continually yell at their dogs are usually trying to make up for the fact that their pets were never properly trained in the first place. They hope if they yell a lot the dog will eventually obey them.

Unfortunately, the opposite is usually true. When a dog hears nothing but continuous yelling it soon becomes completely desensitized to the sound of its owner's voice and doesn't listen or respond at all anymore.

There's a potentially dangerous side effect when a dog has learned to turn a "deaf ear" to its owner's yelling. If there's danger, an oncoming truck, for example, the dog won't listen to its owner when he yells at it.

TREATMENT

A dog that's become tuned out because of continuous yelling can be resensitized to listen to its owner.

- Take the dog to an obedience class so you can learn how to communicate with it without yelling and the dog in turn can learn to recognize what you want it to do and respond to you.
- If this isn't possible, use a leash to make corrections and teach the dog to come to you when you call. With a Training Collar on the dog, attach it to a long lead. Let the dog wander off in the yard or inside the house. Then call it to you in a normal voice, no yelling. Immediately snap the leash if the dog doesn't obey right away. Do this as often as necessary at first until the dog figures out it's better to come to you than to have its neck continually snapped. Don't pull on the dog or try to haul it to you; this won't teach it anything. Use a short snap-release, snap-release until the dog gets the message. Praise the dog when it does come to you. *(See also box, LEASH CORRECTIONS, p. 192.)*

- If your voice is normally loud and boisterous, try to substitute a low, serious tone for a yelling tone when you're calling your dog or telling it to do something. Practice using accents and inflections to convey your meanings instead of raising your voice, and Praise your dog often when it acts in acceptable ways so it will understand when you're pleased with it.

YOUNGSTERS AND DOGS See CHILDREN AND DOGS.

Z

ZIGZAG BEHAVIOR (See also PULLING ON A LEASH; box, SMELL, DOGS' KEENEST SENSE, p. 268.)

Problem: Victoria and her husband have a vizsla (Hungarian pointer/retriever) that's a prize-winning hunting dog. He's won a number of prizes for his excellence in the field. Now he's retired and his owners have moved to the city. Despite his wonderful training, Victoria can't get him to walk properly with her on leash no matter how hard she tries. Whenever she takes him out to the park he constantly pulls her from one side of the path to the other in a zigzagging fashion while he sniffs and sniffs the air frantically as if scenting. He runs into other people who are walking along on the path and has almost tripped her up a couple of times.

DIAGNOSIS*

The hunting ability of dogs is directly inherited from wolves, and dogs have traditionally been trained to take on various roles to help their owners hunt. Among hunting dogs are the breeds that are especially adept at locating prey by smell. All dogs have highly developed senses of smell, but some kinds of hunting dogs have been selectively bred over generations to possess exceptionally sensitive and discriminating olfactory glands.

Scientists know airborne scent travels in an outgoing vortex, or cone, that begins at the scented item and opens out into a large V. Each side, or leg, of the V contains air-borne scent. When a dog is attempting to locate something using his scent, it travels in a zigzag or crisscross manner, from one leg of the V to the other, sniffing and sniffing the air as it gets closer and closer to the tip of the cone where the item is.

A dog that's been bred and trained to follow an airborne scent will naturally travel in this zigzagging manner whenever it's outdoors where scents abound.

TREATMENT

- In order to walk comfortably with a dog that tends to zigzag all the time, go back to basic Obedience Training to reinforce the lessons in proper Heeling and leash walking.
- Keep an active hunting dog on a very short lead whenever you walk in public so you can give an immediate Leash Correction if necessary.
- If your hunting dog is retired from the field, don't deprive it completely of its inborn desire to follow an airborne scent. At least once a week, take it out to a field or park on a very long lead and let it indulge in zigzag behavior as much as it wants.